CUT THE COST COOKBOOK

CUT THE COST COOKBOOK

Sonia Allison

Collins *Glasgow and London*

William Collins Sons & Co Ltd
London · Glasgow · Sydney · Auckland
Toronto · Johannesburg

Cover Design: *Casseroles by courtesy of Pointerware,
Waggon Wheel design,* available in other designs.

Made and printed in Great Britain by
William Collins Sons & Co Ltd, Glasgow

Contents

	page
Good Food from Europe	7
Dieting on a Budget	63
Grow your Own	83
When Time is Money	95
Budget Celebrations	112
Living Alone	132
Low-cost Entertainment	136
Student Fare	152

Conversion Charts

Oven Temperatures

°C	°F	Gas No.	Oven Heat
110°C	225°F	$\frac{1}{4}$	very cool
130°C	250°F	$\frac{1}{2}$	very cool
140°C	275°F	1	cool
150°C	300°F	2	slow
170°C	325°F	3	moderately slow
180°C	350°F	4	moderate
190°C	375°F	5	moderately hot
200°C	400°F	6	hot
220°C	425°F	7	very hot
230°C	450°F	8	very hot

Ounces	Grammes
1	30
2	55
3	85
4	115
5	140
6	170
7	200
8	225
9	255
10	285
11	310
12	340
13	370
14	400
15	425
16	455

Pounds	Kilos
1	$\frac{1}{2}$
2	1
3	$1\frac{1}{2}$

Pints	Millilitres
$\frac{1}{4}$	142
$\frac{1}{3}$	189
$\frac{1}{2}$	284
1	568
2	1,136

This chart shows metric equivalents to the nearest 5 grammes

Good Food from Europe

Continental housewives have always been noted for their thrift, and for making the best possible use of basic and inexpensive ingredients, bargains procured from weekly markets, left-overs in their store cupboards and a hefty sprinkling of imagination. They cook with an element of flair, love and enthusiasm, thus providing their families with simple good food which tastes as appetizing as it looks. Luxury dishes are, in the main, kept for celebrations and special occasions and therefore in this European round-up, I have included only the sort of meals the average continental housewife would make from day to day—nothing elaborate or particularly fancy; just hearty family fare with the occasional speciality thrown in for good measure!

Belgium

BELGIAN LAYER CAKE

10–12 portions

8 ounces margarine, softened
3 ounces icing sugar, sifted
2 tablespoons salad oil
1 egg
1 teaspoon vanilla essence
1 pound plain flour
2 level teaspoons baking powder
$\frac{1}{2}$ level teaspoon salt
$\frac{1}{2}$–$\frac{3}{4}$ pound red jam
little extra icing sugar

Cream the margarine and sugar together until light and fluffy. Beat in the oil, egg and essence. Sift the flour with the baking powder and salt and, using a fork, gradually work it in. Draw together with the finger tips. Wrap in foil and chill for 1 hour. After 45 minutes preheat the oven to moderate, 325°F or Gas 3 (170°C). Cut the dough in half. Coarsely grate one half into an 8-inch loose-based cake tin ensuring that the base is completely covered. Spread the jam on top to within $\frac{1}{2}$ inch of the edges. Grate the rest of the dough on top. Bake in the centre of the oven for 1–1$\frac{1}{4}$ hours or until the cake is golden. When it is cold, remove it from the tin (but leave the cake standing on a metal base). Sift some icing sugar over the top. Cut into thinnish wedges when cold.

BABY LAYER CAKES

about 12–14

These are useful for entertaining and for children's parties. Make up mixture as in previous recipe. Grate half dough into paper cake cases standing in ungreased bun tins. Top with little jam or lemon curd. Grate rest of dough on top of each. Bake in centre of oven (same temperature as large cake) 25–30 minutes. Dust with sifted icing sugar.

CARBONADES FLAMANDES

serves 4

1 ounce margarine, dripping or cooking fat
2 large onions, chopped or grated
1–2 garlic cloves, chopped (optional)
1$\frac{1}{2}$–2 pounds beef shin or skirt, cubed
$\frac{1}{2}$ pint Guinness
salt and pepper to taste
1 dessertspoon brown sugar
2 tablespoons tomato ketchup
2 level tablespoons cornflour
3 tablespoons cold water

A very tasty beef stew made with beer. Economical too, because the cheapest cut of meat may be used.

Heat the margarine in a pan. Add the onions and garlic. Cover and cook over a low heat for 10–15 minutes or until pale gold. Add the beef. Fry a little more briskly until well browned. Add the Guinness, seasoning, sugar and ketchup. Bring to the boil. Cover and simmer slowly until the meat is tender; 2–2½ hours. Stir the stew occasionally. Mix the cornflour to a cream with the cold water. Stir into the stew. Bring to the boil, stirring. Simmer for 2 minutes or until thickened. Serve with boiled potatoes and green vegetables to taste.

To pressure cook *Pressure cook stew for 15 minutes at 15 pounds pressure. Afterwards thicken with cornflour as recommended in the method above.*

FLEMISH RED CABBAGE WITH APPLES

serves 4–6

1 medium red cabbage (about 2½ pounds)
½ pint water
2 large cooking apples, peeled, cored and sliced
1 large onion, chopped
4 tablespoons vinegar
1 level tablespoon brown sugar
2 level teaspoons salt

This is an appetizing vegetable dish which teams happily with pork, bacon and sausages. It is also worth trying with cold meats and poultry.

Shred the cabbage finely. Put it into a large saucepan together with all the remaining ingredients. Bring to the boil, and then lower the heat. Cover and simmer gently for 1½ hours, stirring frequently. Uncover. Continue to simmer gently until almost no liquid remains. Serve very hot.

Left-over cabbage *Put the cabbage into a pan with 1 or 2 tablespoons of water. Cover. Heat through slowly.*

CHICORY AND BACON IN CHEESE SAUCE

serves 4–6

4 large heads chicory
salted water
squeeze of lemon
4 slices boiled bacon or ham
1 ounce cornflour
½ pint milk, skimmed if liked
3 ounces strong Cheddar cheese, grated
salt and pepper to taste
toasted breadcrumbs

A very popular dish in Belgium. It is simple to make and substantial and may be served as a main course with plain boiled potatoes. Salad is an appropriate accompaniment.

Remove outer leaves of chicory and core at base of each (to prevent bitterness). Cook in boiling salted water and lemon juice 20–25 minutes. Drain. Reserve ¼ pint liquor. Wrap bacon round each chicory head. Arrange in greased heatproof dish. Mix cornflour to smooth cream with little cold milk. Pour into pan with rest of milk. Add chicory liquor. Cook, stirring, until sauce comes to boil and thickens. Simmer 1 minute. Add 2 ounces grated cheese. Stir until melted. Season. Pour over chicory in dish. Sprinkle with rest of cheese and crumbs. Brown under hot grill. Serve straight away.

WATERZOOI DE VOLAILLE

serves 6

1 boiling fowl (3–4 pounds)
cold water
salt and pepper to taste
2 onions, sliced
2 leeks, well-cleaned and coarsely chopped
2 celery stalks, chopped
½ small head white cabbage, shredded
1 level tablespoon cornflour
3 tablespoons undiluted evaporated milk
1 egg yolk

A kind of chicken stew, usually enriched with thick cream and eggs. Instead, I use cornflour and evaporated milk, making it much less costly but still good.

Joint bird. Remove surplus fat and discard. Put joints into large pan. Add water. Season. Bring to boil. Remove scum. Lower heat. Cover. Simmer 2–2½ hours or until bird is *just* tender. Add vegetables. Cook further 30 minutes. Strain, reserving ¾ pint liquor. (Keep remainder for soup or stews.) Transfer chicken and vegetables to warm dish. Keep hot. Mix corn-flour to cream with milk. Combine with reserved liquor. Pour into pan. Cook, stirring, until sauce comes to boil and thickens. Simmer 1 minute. Season. Beat in yolk. Pour over chicken and vegetables. Accompany with freshly boiled rice (3–4 ounces per person) and cooked carrots sprinkled with chopped parsley.

To pressure cook *Pressure cook for 30 minutes at 15 pounds pressure before adding the vegetables.*

POULETS SANS TETES
(BIRDS WITHOUT HEADS)

serves 4

**4 thin slices stewing beef
(about 3 by 5 inches)
2 medium onions
1 level tablespoon finely chopped parsley
4 streaky bacon rashers
flour
1 ounce dripping or margarine
¼ pint stock or water
2 medium carrots, sliced
1 small turnip, diced
salt and pepper to taste**

Beat beef until very thin (or ask butcher to do this). Chop 1 onion. Sprinkle over beef slices with parsley. Top each slice with bacon rasher. Sprinkle with pepper. Roll up. Tie securely with thick thread. Coat with flour. Melt dripping in pan. Add beef rolls. Fry until well browned and sealed. Slice remaining onion. Add to pan with rest of ingredients. Bring to boil, stirring. Lower heat. Cover. Simmer 1–2 hours or until beef is tender. Stir occasionally. Accompany with creamed potatoes and cooked vegetables.

To pressure cook *Cook for 20 minutes at 15 pounds pressure*

FISH WATERZOOI

serves 4

**1½ pounds cod or coley fillet, skinned
cold water
1 large onion, sliced
2 celery stalks, coarsely chopped
salt and pepper to taste
1 ounce *each,* margarine and flour
¼ pint undiluted evaporated milk
1 egg yolk
1 level tablespoon chopped parsley**

Cut fish into serving-sized pieces. Put into shallow pan and just cover with water. Add vegetables. Season. Bring to boil. At once reduce heat to low simmer. Poach fish 5–7 minutes. Transfer fish to warm serving dish. Reserve ¼ pint fish liquor. Melt margarine in saucepan. Stir in flour. Cook 2 minutes without browning. Gradually blend in fish liquor and milk. Cook, stirring, until sauce comes to boil and thickens. Season. Simmer 1 minute. Beat in egg yolk. Pour over fish. Sprinkle with parsley. Rye bread is the traditional accompaniment; if preferred, serve rice or boiled potatoes.

GOZETTE

serves 4–6

This is like an enormous apple turnover, worth making if there are plenty of garden windfalls about. Roll 1 large packet of frozen puff pastry (thawed first) into a fairly big, thin round. Cover 1 half of round with sliced apples (about 1–1½ pounds) to within 1 inch of edges. Sprinkle with handful of seedless raisins, about 2–4 ounces brown sugar and little cinnamon. Moisten edges with cold water. Fold in half, forming semi-circle. Press edges well together to seal then pinch up between finger and thumb. Put on to greased baking tray. Brush with milk. Sprinkle with caster sugar. Bake in centre of hot oven, 425°F or Gas 7 (220°C) 10 minutes. Reduce temperature to moderate, 350°F or Gas 4 (180°C). Bake further 20–30 minutes. Serve hot or cold.

TARTE AU RIZ

serves 8

This is a rice tart, widely made in Verviers and Liège. Here is a simplified version which is suitable for the tea-table or as an after-dinner sweet.

Place a 7- to 8-inch flan ring on a baking tray and line it with home-made or frozen, flaky or puff, pastry. Open can of rice pudding. Stir in 2 egg yolks, 1 teaspoon vanilla essence and 2 level teaspoons cornflour. Beat egg whites to stiff snow. Fold into rice. Pour into pastry case. Bake in centre of hot oven, 425°F or Gas 7 (220°C) about 30 minutes. Cool. Sprinkle top with caster sugar before serving.

BRUSSELS CRAMIQUE

makes 1 loaf

3 ounces caster sugar
5 tablespoons warm water
1 level tablespoon dried yeast granules
1 pound plain flour
1 level teaspoon salt
1 ounce margarine
2 ounces raisins
¼ pint and 4 tablespoons warm milk
1 egg yolk

A teabread-cum-cake made with yeast.

Dissolve 1 teaspoon sugar in the warm water. Sprinkle yeast on top. Leave in warm place 15–20 minutes or until mixture froths up. Sift flour and salt into bowl. Rub in margarine. Add rest of sugar and raisins. Work to dough with yeast liquid, milk and yolk. Add little extra flour if mixture is on wet side. Knead about 10 minutes or until smooth and elastic. Cover with greased polythene. Leave in warm place to rise; dough should double in size and spring back when pressed lightly with floured finger. Turn out on to floured surface. Knead lightly until smooth. Transfer to well-greased 1 pound loaf tin. Cover with greased polythene. Leave to rise again until dough reaches top of tin. Bake in centre of hot oven, 425°F or Gas 7 (220°C) about 45 minutes or until Cramique has shrunk slightly away from sides of tin, and top is

golden brown. Turn out and cool on wire rack. Serve sliced and buttered.

WAFFLES
(GAUFRES DE BRUXELLES)

4 ounces self-raising flour
pinch salt
1 ounce caster sugar
1 egg, separated
1 ounce margarine, melted
¼ pint milk (skimmed or diluted evaporated if liked)
½ teaspoon vanilla essence

These one finds nearly all over Belgium and because a little waffle mixture goes a long way, they are a practical proposition for those with waffle irons.

Sift flour, salt and sugar into bowl. Add yolk and margarine. Gradually work in milk and essence. Beat until smooth. Whisk white to firm snow. Gradually fold batter mixture into it. (Consistency should be like thick cream.) Heat lightly oiled waffle iron. Pour in enough batter to cover surface; do not overfill or mixture will run out of sides. Close iron. Cook 2–3 minutes, turning iron once if non-electric. Remove waffle, which should be crisp and golden. If it sticks, cook minute or so longer. Repeat with rest of batter mixture. Serve freshly made, topped with butter or margarine and golden syrup or honey.

Waffles with cream or ice cream *For a special treat, top waffles with whipped cream or scoops of vanilla ice cream. If liked, trickle bought chocolate sauce over top.*

ECONOMICAL WHIPPED CREAM

This is similar to the whipped cream so popular on the Continent. Combine equal quantities of double and single cream. Beat until softly stiff. Use immediately as it tends to melt fairly quickly.

Italy

POTATO SALAD WITH TUNA

serves 4

2 pounds cooked potatoes
5 tablespoons French dressing (bought
or home-made)
1 can (7 ounce) tuna
1 medium onion, grated
salad cream
salt and pepper to taste
1 small green pepper or 1 level tablespoon chopped parsley

Tuna is extremely popular throughout Italy and when combined with potatoes, as in this recipe, makes a tasty and filling summer main course which is both quick and easy to prepare.

Dice potatoes. Toss with dressing. Drain tuna. Flake fish. Add to potatoes with onion. Add sufficient salad cream to moisten, tossing all ingredients well together. Season. Arrange on 4 individual plates. Garnish with rings of green pepper or parsley.

POTATO SOUP

serves 4

2 medium onions, chopped
2 tablespoons margarine or dripping
6 medium potatoes
1 small ham bone
2 pints water
salt and pepper to taste
3 tablespoons evaporated milk
grated Cheddar cheese

Another filling and warming soup which can be turned into a complete meal by the addition of grated cheese.

Fry onions gently in margarine until pale gold. Grate potatoes. Add to pan with all remaining ingredients except milk and cheese. Bring to boil. Lower heat. Cover. Simmer slowly for 30 minutes. Stir in milk. Serve each portion thickly topped with grated cheese.

HOT CHEESE SQUARES

These are inexpensive appetizers which can also make a rather unusual and fairly cheap hors d'oeuvre. Allow one fairly thick slice of bread for each person. Remove the crusts and then cut each slice into four squares. Fry the bread in hot oil until crisp and golden on both sides. (If liked use bacon or other dripping instead of oil.) Drain the fried bread on paper towels. Top each square with a slice of cheese; Bel Paèse is the traditional one to use but Cheddar will do. Brown under a hot grill. The cheese squares can be served as they are or topped with anchovy fillets.

BRODO MISTO

serves 4

A simple and cheap soup which can be made easily with stock cubes. Dissolve 1 chicken and 1 beef stock cube in $1\frac{1}{2}$ pints water. Bring to boil. Add 2–3 ounces baby pasta or vermicelli. Simmer about 5 more minutes. Serve piping hot, sprinkled with grated cheese or chopped parsley.

ZUPPA PAVESE

serves 4

This is a useful supper snack.

Make $1\frac{1}{2}$ pints chicken or beef stock using stock cubes and water. Slowly bring to boil. Meanwhile, fry 4 slices bread in margarine or bacon dripping until golden on both sides. Remove to 4 warm soup plates. Lightly poach 4 eggs. Place one on top of each bread slice. Fill plates with boiling stock. Sprinkle with grated cheese. Serve very hot.

MINESTRONE

serves 6

1 large ham bone or 2 meaty bacon
knuckles
2 large onions, chopped
3 medium carrots, sliced
1 small parsnip, diced
1 medium head white cabbage, shredded
4 ounces dried haricot beans, soaked
overnight and drained
1 medium-sized can (about 1 pound)
tomatoes
3 pints water
salt and pepper to taste
3–4 ounces elbow macaroni
grated cheese for serving

Put bone or knuckles into large pan. Add all remaining ingredients except macaroni and cheese. Bring to boil. Lower heat. Cover. Simmer about 2 hours or until beans are tender, adding little extra water if soup seems to be thickening up too much. Add macaroni. Cover and cook further 15 minutes. Serve each portion topped heavily with grated cheese.

Bacon Knuckles *These often tend to be over-salty. To reduce this, put into pan. Cover with cold water. Bring to boil. Drain. Repeat once more. After Minestrone is cooked, remove bacon from bones, chop up and return to soup.*

Minestrone with Meat *Between 8–10 ounces diced stewing beef may be added to soup in addition to ham bone.*

Minestrone with Rice *Use Italian or American long grain rice for macaroni. Use same quantity.*

STRACCIATELLA

serves 4

1½ pints chicken or beef stock
(made with cubes and water)
2 eggs
3 level dessertspoons semolina
3 level tablespoons grated stale cheese
salt and pepper to taste

An egg soup, widely appreciated in Rome.

Bring stock to boil. Beat eggs with all remaining ingredients. Add few tablespoons boiling stock. Mix well. Return to rest of stock in pan. Bring to boil, whisking. As egg cooks, it will separate into thin strands, giving the soup its characteristic appearance. Accompany with crusty rolls and butter or margarine.

SPAGHETTI BOLOGNESE

serves 4 to 5

Sauce

2 tablespoons salad oil
2 large onions, finely chopped
1 large garlic clove, finely chopped
8 ounces raw minced beef
4 level tablespoons tomato concentrate
(can or tube)
1 level tablespoon cornflour
1 pint water
1 bay leaf
1 level teaspoon mixed herbs
1–2 level teaspoons salt
pepper to taste
about 3–4 ounces (raw weight)
spaghetti per person
grated cheese for serving

Heat oil in pan. Add onion and garlic. Fry gently until pale gold; about 10 minutes. Add beef. Fry little more briskly, breaking it up with fork all the time, until well browned. Add all remaining ingredients except spaghetti and cheese. Bring to boil, stirring. Lower heat. Cover. Simmer 1 hour over low heat. Stir frequently. Serve over freshly cooked spaghetti. Sprinkle each serving with cheese.

To cook spaghetti *To cook spaghetti—or any other large pasta—as they do in Italy, watch cooking time carefully because the pasta should be al dente; firm and still chewy, not sticky and over-soft. Cook in plenty of boiling, salted water for 12–15 minutes; rarely longer.*

To cook small pasta *Cook as directed above, but allow only 5–7 minutes.*

To prevent pasta from sticking *Add 1 or 2 teaspoons oil to the water.*

SPAGHETTI ALLA CARBONARA

serves 4

1 pound spaghetti, freshly cooked
3–4 eggs
3–4 tablespoons evaporated milk
4 ounces Cheddar cheese, finely grated
salt and pepper to taste

Drain spaghetti well. Put into large warm bowl. Beat eggs with remaining ingredients. Add to spaghetti. Toss thoroughly, using two large forks. (Heat coming from spaghetti will partially cook and set eggs.) Serve straight away. Accompany with tomato ketchup if liked.

MACARONI WITH CHICKEN LIVERS

serves 4

Inexpensive packs of frozen chicken livers are frequently available at supermarkets and when served atop macaroni, make a cheap and tasty meal.

Thaw 1 pound chicken livers. Slowly fry 1 chopped onion in little dripping for about 10 minutes or until golden. Add livers. Fry gently 15 minutes or until cooked through and browned. Turn frequently. Add squeeze of lemon, $\frac{1}{4}$ pint water and seasoning to taste. Cook further 5 minutes. Arrange 4 portions freshly cooked macaroni (about 3–4 ounces raw weight per person) on to 4 warm plates. Top with liver mixture. Serve straight away.

LASAGNE

serves 4

6 ounces lasagne (leaves of white pasta)
1 ounce margarine
1 ounce flour
$\frac{1}{2}$ pint milk (skimmed or diluted
evaporated if liked)
4 ounces Cheddar cheese, grated
salt, pepper and mustard to taste
Bolognese sauce (page 12)
tomato ketchup

Preheat oven to moderate, 350°F or Gas 4 (180°C). Cook Lasagne in plenty of boiling salted water 10–15 minutes. To make cheese sauce, melt margarine in pan. Stir in flour. Cook 2 minutes without browning. Gradually blend in milk. Cook, stirring, until sauce comes to boil and thickens. Stir in 3 ounces cheese. Leave over low heat until melted. Season. Drain Lasagne thoroughly. Grease fairly deep heatproof dish. Cover base with layer of Bolognese sauce. Add layer of cheese sauce. Top with layer of Lasagne. Repeat, finishing with layer of cheese sauce. Trickle tomato ketchup over top. Sprinkle with rest of cheese. Reheat in centre of oven 25–30 minutes.

Lasagne Verdi *Make exactly as above, but use green Lasagne (which is coloured and flavoured with spinach) instead of the white.*

RAVIOLI

serves 4–6

Dough

8 ounces plain flour
1 level teaspoon salt
1 egg, beaten
1 dessertspoon salad oil
2 tablespoons hot water

Filling

8 ounces raw minced beef
1 small onion, grated
salt and pepper to taste
large pinch ground nutmeg
1 tablespoon warm water

Making one's own Ravioli obviously takes much longer than buying it ready prepared, but it is reasonably easy to cope with, works out a lot cheaper and is well worth the effort if spare time is available.

To make dough, sift flour and salt into bowl. Make central well. Drop in egg, oil and water. Work to dough with finger tips. Transfer to well-floured surface. Knead 20–25 minutes or until no longer sticky. Cover with damp cloth. Leave on one side while making filling.

13

To make filling, combine all ingredients well together. Divide dough into 2 pieces. Spread patterned tablecloth (old one will do admirably) on work surface. Dust heavily with flour. Roll out 1 portion of dough thinly. Stretch gently with finger tips until pattern of cloth shows through. Avoid tears and breaks. Repeat with second portion of dough, making it slightly larger than first. Place smaller piece of dough on floured surface. Brush lightly all over with water. Top with small heaps of filling, leaving space around each. Cover loosely with second piece of dough. With finger tips, press 2 layers of dough together in between heaps of meat. Stamp out Ravioli with biscuit cutter, cutting round dough and avoiding filling. Drop into large saucepan of boiling salted water. Cook until Ravioli float to top; 5–7 minutes. Lift out of pan with draining spoon. Toss with butter or margarine. Sprinkle with grated cheese.

Ravioli with Tomato Sauce *Cook as above and combine with home-made or bought tomato sauce.*

PLAIN RISOTTO

serves 4

1 ounce margarine
1 dessertspoon salad oil
1 medium onion, chopped
12 ounces Italian or round grain pudding rice
2 pints water or chicken stock (use stock cube)
salt and pepper
1 extra ounce butter or margarine
4 ounces Cheddar cheese, grated

Heat margarine and oil in saucepan. Add onion. Cover pan. Cook slowly until soft and still pale. Add rice. Cook 3 minutes, stirring all the time. Gradually blend in water or stock. Season. Bring to boil. Lower heat. Cover. Simmer about 30 minutes when rice should have absorbed most of the liquid. Stir in butter or margarine. Put equal amounts on to 4 warm plates. Sprinkle with cheese. Serve straight away.

Risotto with Meat *After rice has been cooking 15 minutes, add 6–8 ounces coarsely chopped cold, cooked meat (remains of joint for example). Continue to simmer for further 15 minutes. Serve each portion sprinkled with cheese.*

Risotto with Poultry *After rice has been cooking 15 minutes, add 6–8 ounces coarsely chopped cold, cooked poultry. Continue to simmer for remaining 15 minutes. Serve each portion sprinkled with cheese.*

Risotto with Meat or Poultry and Vegetables *To 'stretch' Risotto, add meat or poultry as suggested above. After the Risotto has been cooking for 25 minutes stir in a mixture of cold, cooked vegetables such as peas, beans, sweet corn, diced carrots and small cauliflower florets, etc. Serve each portion sprinkled with cheese.*

Risotto with Eggs *Just before serving, stir into the Risotto 4–6 coarsely chopped hard-boiled eggs. Serve each portion sprinkled with cheese.*

Pizzas

There are innumerable Pizzas and innumerable ways of making them. Here are a few recipes.

TRADITIONAL PIZZA

serves 4–5

Base

$\frac{1}{2}$ level teaspoon sugar
$\frac{1}{4}$ pint lukewarm water
1 level teaspoon dried yeast granules
8 ounces plain flour
1 level teaspoon salt
$\frac{1}{2}$ ounce margarine

Topping

2 tablespoons salad oil
1 small onion, finely chopped
1 garlic clove, chopped
5 level tablespoons tomato concentrate
(can or tube)
1 level teaspoon *each,* dried basil and sugar
3 tablespoons water
4 ounces Cheddar cheese, grated
3 large tomatoes, skinned and sliced
12 canned anchovy fillets (optional)
12 black or green olives (optional)

To make dough base, dissolve sugar in warm water. Sprinkle yeast on top. Leave in warm place about 20 minutes or until mixture froths up. Sift flour and salt into bowl. Rub in margarine. Mix to dough with yeast liquid, adding little extra flour if very sticky. Turn on to floured surface. Knead about 10 minutes or until smooth, elastic and no longer tacky. Cover with greased polythene. Leave in warm place until dough doubles in size and springs back when pressed lightly with floured finger. Uncover. Knead lightly on floured surface until smooth. Roll out into large round, oblong or square, no thicker than $\frac{1}{4}$-inch. Transfer to greased baking tray.

To make topping, heat oil in pan. Add onion. Fry gently until pale gold. Stir in garlic, tomato concentrate, basil, sugar and water. Spread over dough to within $\frac{1}{2}$ inch of edges. Sprinkle with cheese. Garnish with tomato slices, anchovies and olives. Meanwhile, preheat oven to very hot, 450°F or Gas 8 (230°C). Leave Pizza to stand in warm place 15 minutes. Bake in centre of oven 25–30 minutes. Cut into 4 or 5 portions. Serve while still hot.

To vary *Flakes of canned tuna or salmon, or even slivers of salami or luncheon meat, may be used instead of anchovies.*

SCONE-BASED PIZZA

serves 4

Instead of yeast dough, make base with scone mixture. Sift 8 ounces self-raising flour, 1 level teaspoon baking powder and 1 level teaspoon salt into bowl. Rub in 1 or 2 ounces margarine. Mix to soft dough with $\frac{1}{4}$ pint cold milk. Knead lightly on floured surface. Roll out into $\frac{1}{4}$-inch thick round. Stand on greased baking tray. Cover with same topping as given in previous recipe. Bake just above centre of very hot oven, 450°F or Gas 8 (230°C) 25–30 minutes. Cut into wedges. Serve hot.

QUICKLY-MADE INDIVIDUAL PIZZAS

serves 4

Fry 4 large slices white bread in bacon or beef dripping until crisp and golden on *one side only.* Drain. Spread unfried sides thinly with tomato concentrate mixed with a little sugar. Sprinkle with garlic salt and mixed herbs. Sprinkle heavily with grated Cheddar cheese. Garnish with slices of tomato, also anchovy fillets and olives if liked. Brown quickly under hot grill. Serve straight away.

CHICKEN CACCIATORA

serves 4

4 medium-sized joints roasting chicken
flour
2 ounces margarine or dripping
1 large onion, chopped
2 garlic cloves, chopped
1 medium can (about 1 pound)
Italian tomatoes
2 level tablespoons tomato concentrate
(can or tube)
1 level teaspoon sugar
$\frac{1}{4}$ pint water
salt and pepper to taste
4 ounces sliced mushrooms
(traditional but optional)

Coat chicken with flour. Heat margarine in pan. Add chicken. Fry until crisp and golden all over. Remove to plate. Add onion and garlic to remaining margarine in pan. Fry gently until pale gold. Add all remaining ingredients except mushrooms. Bring to boil. Replace chicken. Simmer 30 minutes. Add mushrooms. Simmer further 15 minutes or until chicken is tender. Serve with freshly boiled rice or pasta.

CHICKEN MARENGO

This is similar to the above, except that 1 teacup of finely chopped parsley is usually added with the mushrooms. For those who like black olives, a dozen or so stoned ones may be added with all the other ingredients.

GNOCCHI

serves 4–5

1 pint milk (skimmed if liked)
5 ounces coarse semolina
2 level teaspoons salt
pepper to taste
2 ounces margarine
4 ounces strong stale Cheddar cheese, finely grated
large pinch ground nutmeg
1 large egg, beaten
1 extra ounce margarine

This is one of the simplest Italian dishes to make, yet is also one of the most satisfying, nourishing, inexpensive and tasty.

Well grease fairly large dish or shallow tin (Swiss roll tin is ideal). Put milk and semolina into pan. Add salt, pepper and margarine. Bring to boil, stirring. Simmer till mixture is very thick (5–7 minutes). Remove from heat. Beat in 3 ounces cheese, nutmeg and egg. Spread into dish or tin. Leave in cold place until firm. Cut into squares with wetted knife. Well grease shallow, heatproof dish. Fill with layers of Gnocchi squares. Sprinkle with rest of cheese. Dot with flakes of margarine. Reheat and brown towards top of hot oven, 425°F or Gas 7 (220°C) 15 minutes. Serve with canned tomatoes, which have been heated through, and green vegetables.

To vary *If you happen to be near an Italian shop, try using Polenta instead of semolina.*

Gnocchi Florentine *Line base of heatproof dish with layer of canned spinach purée before putting in the Gnocchi.*

L'OSSO BUCO

serves 4

4 pounds shin of veal
flour
4 tablespoons salad oil
1 large onion, coarsely grated
1 medium carrot, coarsely grated
1 medium can (about 1 pound)
Italian tomatoes
1 level tablespoon tomato concentrate (can or tube)
¼ pint dry cider or chicken stock
¼ pint water
Salt and pepper to taste
2 level tablespoons finely chopped parsley
1 garlic clove, very finely chopped
1 level teaspoon finely grated lemon peel

A Milanese dish made with the least expensive cut of veal—the shin.

Ask butcher to saw veal into 3-inch pieces. Coat each lightly with flour. Heat oil in large pan. Add veal. Fry until well-sealed. Remove to plate. Add onion and carrot to remaining oil in pan. Fry slowly until pale gold. Blend in tomatoes, tomato concentrate, cider or stock, and water. Season. Bring to boil, stirring. Replace veal. Reduce heat. Cover. Simmer about 1½ hours or until veal is tender. Transfer to warm dish. Sprinkle with parsley, garlic and lemon peel. Serve with Risotto (page 14) or plain boiled rice.

ZABAIONE

serves 6

4 large eggs, separated
4 level tablespoons caster sugar
1 large wine glass sweet sherry
(or use Marsala if you happen to have it)

I am including this adaptation of one of Italy's most popular sweets because eggs—never very expensive—are the main ingredient and a glass of sweet sherry, especially round about Christmas time, can usually be spared.

Put egg yolks and sugar into basin standing over saucepan of hot water. Whisk until warm, much paler in colour and very thick. Stir in sherry. In separate bowl, beat whites to stiff snow. Gently fold in yolk mixture. When smooth and evenly combined, transfer to 6 glasses. Serve straight away. Accompany with sweet, crisp biscuits.

WHOLE CARAMELIZED ORANGES

serves 4

4 large oranges
cold water
8 ounces granulated sugar
½ pint warm water
1 teaspoon orange essence

This equally famous dessert is a refreshing end to any meal; try during the winter months when oranges are at their cheapest and best.

Peel oranges. Carefully cut away white pith from peel of 2 oranges, discard pith and cut rest of peel into thin shreds. Put into pan with a little cold water. Boil 15 minutes. Drain. Put sugar and warm water into saucepan. Dissolve, stirring, over low heat. Bring to boil. Boil briskly until syrupy and fairly thick. Leave to cool slightly. Add essence. Put oranges, one at a time, into pan. Turn over and over until completely coated with syrup. Remove to serving dish. Add cooked peel shreds to remaining syrup in pan. Simmer until they look transparent, and syrup itself turns golden. Remove from heat. Pile equal amounts of peel on top of oranges. Coat with syrup from pan. Chill thoroughly before serving. Accompany with knives and forks for easy eating.

Germany

PEA AND BACON SOUP

serves 6–8

8 ounces streaky bacon rashers, cut into strips
3½ pints cold water
8 ounces split peas, soaked overnight and drained
1 large onion, chopped
pepper to taste
2 medium carrots, thinly sliced
2 celery stalks, chopped
1 large potato, coarsely grated
½ level teaspoon marjoram
chopped parsley

Put bacon and water into saucepan. Bring to boil. Remove scum from surface. Add peas, onion and pepper to taste. (Bacon should provide enough salt.) Cover. Simmer 2 hours. Add rest of ingredients (except parsley). Cover. Boil gently further 30 minutes. Adjust seasoning to taste. Serve each portion heavily topped with chopped parsley.

BERLIN POTATO SOUP

serves 6–8

1 or 2 meaty bacon knuckles
3½ pints cold water
1 large carrot
1 small parsnip
2 pounds potatoes
2 bay leaves
pepper
ground nutmeg
chopped parsley

Put knuckles into large pan. Cover with cold water. Bring to boil. Drain. Repeat. (This helps to remove excessive saltiness.) Return knuckles to pan with 3½ pints water. Meanwhile dice carrot, parsnip and potatoes. Add to pan with bay leaves and pepper. Bring to boil, stirring. Lower heat. Cover. Simmer 45 minutes. Remove bay leaves and bones. If there is a lot of meat left on knuckles, cut it up and reserve. Rub soup and liquid through sieve or blend until smooth in liquidizer goblet. Return to pan with cut-up bacon. Heat through. Adjust seasoning to taste. Add light sprinkling nutmeg. Serve piping hot. Top with parsley.

MARINADED FRIED HERRINGS

serves about 6

3 pounds fresh herrings, split, cleaned
and boned
salt and pepper
flour
fat or dripping for frying
2 large onions, cut into thin rings
½ pint water
¼ pint malt vinegar
2 bay leaves
1 level tablespoon mustard seeds
1 peppercorn
salt to taste

Wash and dry herrings. Sprinkle with salt and pepper. Coat with flour. Fry on both sides in hot fat until crisp and golden; about 7 minutes. Remove from pan. Drain on paper towels. Transfer to shallow serving dish. Cover with onion rings. Bring all remaining ingredients to boil. Boil 10 minutes. Leave until cold. Pour over herrings. Cover. Refrigerate 1–2 days. Serve with wholemeal or rye bread and butter. The usual drink? Strong beer!

BLACK FOREST BACON PANCAKE

serves 3–4

4 ounces plain flour
large pinch salt
6 tablespoons milk
4 eggs, beaten
2 level tablespoons chopped parsley
or chives
4 ounces lean bacon, chopped
small piece green bacon fat

Sift flour and salt into bowl. Gradually beat to smooth and creamy batter with milk and eggs. Leave to stand 10 minutes. Stir in parsley or chives. Add bacon. Wipe inside of large omelet pan (about 10 inches in diameter) or heavy-based frying pan with green bacon fat. Heat until hot. Pour in egg mixture. Cook over medium heat until underside is golden. Carefully turn over. Cook until golden. Cut into wedges and serve straight away from pan. Accompany with salad or green vegetables to taste.

Note If turning the pancake presents complications, stand frying pan a few inches below preheated hot grill and cook until top is golden brown.

BAVARIAN OX HEART

serves 4–6

2 pounds ox heart, well-washed
water
2 cloves
1 large onion
2 bay leaves
1 medium leek, well-washed and sliced
2 medium celery stalks, broken
2 medium carrots, sliced
salt and pepper to taste
1½ ounces margarine or dripping
1½ ounces cornflour
2 level teaspoons brown sugar
1 to 3 tablespoons malt vinegar
½ level teaspoon marjoram
2 tablespoons canned cream

Put heart into pan. Cover with cold water. Bring to boil. Remove scum. Press cloves into peeled onion. Add to pan with bay leaves and prepared vegetables. Season. Simmer slowly 1½ hours or until heart is tender. Lift out of pan. Cut into slices. Strain liquor and reserve ¾ pint. Melt margarine in clean pan. Stir in cornflour. Cook slowly 3 minutes or until mixture begins to turn golden. Gradually blend in heart liquor. Bring to boil, stirring. Add sugar, vinegar to taste and marjoram. Replace heart. Heat through 10 minutes. Stir in cream. Adjust seasoning. Serve with freshly boiled noodles. Accompany with salad.

MARINADED PORK CASSEROLE

serves 4–6

2 pounds lean stewing pork
cider
1 bay leaf
2 peppercorns
3 cloves
1 garlic clove, sliced (optional)
½ level teaspoon dried thyme
salt and pepper to taste
2 pounds potatoes
2 large onions
½–1 ounce margarine

Cube pork. Put into glass or enamel dish. Cover with cider. Add bay leaf, peppercorns, cloves, garlic and thyme. Turn meat over and over in marinade. Cover. Refrigerate about 8 hours, turning meat at least twice. Strain marinade. Bring to boil in pan. Season to taste. Peel and thinly slice potatoes and onions. Fill well-greased casserole dish with alternate layers of pork, potatoes and onions, beginning and ending with potatoes. Pour marinade into dish. Top with flakes of margarine. Cover. Cook in centre of moderate oven, 325°F or Gas 3 (170°C) for 2 hours. Uncover during last 30 minutes to brown potatoes.

SAUSAGES IN BEER

serves 4

1 to 1½ pounds large pork sausages
water
flour
1 ounce lard or dripping
1 level tablespoon flour
½ pint beer
salt and pepper to taste

Put sausages into large frying pan. Half-fill with water. *Slowly* bring to boil. Reduce heat. Cover. Simmer 5 minutes. Drain thoroughly. Wipe dry with paper towels. Coat with flour. Wash and dry frying pan. Return to heat. Add lard. Heat until hot. Add sausages. Fry over medium heat until crisp and golden brown all over. Remove to warm plate. Stir flour into remaining fat in pan. Cook gently 2 minutes. Gradually blend in beer. Bring to boil, stirring. Simmer 2 minutes. Season. Pour over sausages. Serve with boiled potatoes and cabbage.

KOENIGSBERG MEAT BALLS

serves 4

Sauce

1 ounce margarine
2 level dessertspoons capers
2 level dessertspoons mild vinegar
2 level tablespoons cornflour
1¼ pints beef stock (use cube or
beef extract and water)
1 teaspoon Worcester sauce
large pinch sugar
salt and pepper to taste

Meat Balls

2 large slices white bread
warm water
1 pound raw minced beef
1 large onion, grated
1 small egg, beaten
½ level teaspoon grated lemon peel
1 level teaspoon continental mustard
salt and pepper to taste
chopped parsley to garnish

Originally from Koenigsberg, this dish consists of mildly flavoured meat balls in a piquant caper sauce. Different from all other meat ball recipes and quite delicious. Best accompanied with rice.

To make sauce, put margarine, capers and vinegar into pan. Heat until hot. Stir in cornflour. Cook 2 minutes. Blend in stock. Cook, stirring, until sauce comes to boil and thickens. Add rest of sauce ingredients. Leave over low heat. To make meat balls, soak bread 5 minutes in water. Squeeze dry. Put into bowl. Add all remaining ingredients except parsley. Mix well. Shape into 12 balls. Add to caper sauce. Cook gently 15–20 minutes. Transfer to warm dish. Sprinkle heavily with parsley.

Koenigsberg Meat Balls with Peas *If liked, add 4–5 tablespoons cooked peas 10 minutes after adding meat balls.*

PORK AND CARROT STEW WITH POTATO DUMPLINGS

serves 4

1½ pounds carrots
½ pound turnips
3 level tablespoons dripping
2 medium onions, chopped
1 pound stewing pork, cubed
hot water
salt and pepper

Dumplings

1 pound freshly boiled potatoes
2 eggs, beaten
6 ounces cornflour
pinch ground nutmeg
salt and pepper to taste
chopped parsley to garnish

Thinly slice carrots and turnips. Heat dripping in pan. Add onion. Fry gently until pale gold. Add pork. Fry little more briskly until well sealed and golden. Add carrots and turnips and enough hot water to cover. Season. Slowly bring to boil. Lower heat. Cover. Simmer 1 hour. Prepare dumplings. Mash potatoes while still hot. Add other ingredients except parsley. Leave until cold. Shape into small dumplings with wet hands. Two-thirds fill large saucepan with hot water. Add salt to taste. Bring to boil. Add dumplings. Lower heat. Cover. Simmer about 15 minutes or until dumplings float to top. Transfer pork stew to large warm dish. Lift dumplings out of water with a draining spoon. Arrange on top of stew. Sprinkle with parsley. Serve straight away.

HEAVEN AND EARTH

serves 4

½ pound cooking apples
(garden windfalls are ideal)
water
1 level dessertspoon granulated sugar
1 pound freshly boiled potatoes
½ ounce margarine
little warm milk
salt, pepper and ground nutmeg to season
1 large onion, sliced
1 ounce margarine or dripping
8 fairly thick slices luncheon meat

An unusual combination of ingredients from the Rhine area, making an interesting and reasonably priced main course.

Peel, core and slice apples. Cook with merest trace of water until soft and pulpy. Beat until smooth with sugar. Mash potatoes finely. Add margarine and enough milk to give creamy mash. Beat well. Season. Combine with hot apple. Transfer to warm dish. Keep hot. Separate onion into rings. Fry in hot margarine until golden. Move to one side of pan. Add meat slices. Fry on both sides until crisp. Arrange onions and meat on top of apple/potato mixture. Serve straight away.

For speed *Use packet of instant mash (4–5 servings) made up as directed on packet. Season with salt, pepper and nutmeg.*

HAMBURGER RUNDSTUECK

A very simple snack dish which makes excellent use of left-over roast meat and gravy. Allow one crusty round roll per person. Halve roll. Cover both halves with slices of roast meat. Pour one tablespoon of piping hot gravy over each half. Serve straight away. Very good if topped with freshly milled black pepper.

HAMBURGIAN LABSKAUS

serves 4

1 pound corned beef
2 large onions, chopped
1½ ounces dripping
2 pounds freshly boiled potatoes
hot milk
salt and pepper to taste
4 eggs

Chop corned beef. Fry onions gently in the dripping until pale gold. Add beef. Fry 10 minutes, turning frequently. Mash potatoes finely. Cream well with little hot milk. Gradually stir in meat and onion mixture. Heat through slowly until very hot. Meanwhile fry eggs. Put meat and potato mixture on to 4 warm plates. Top each with a fried egg. Accompany with gherkins and pickled beetroot.

STUFFED POTATO DUMPLINGS

serves 6

2 pounds potatoes
1 egg, lightly beaten
salt
plain flour

Filling

1 medium onion, chopped
½ ounce margarine
8 ounces raw minced beef
2 level tablespoons finely chopped parsley
5 level tablespoons fresh
white breadcrumbs
salt and pepper to taste
2 extra ounces margarine

This makes a hearty cold-weather dish.

Peel potatoes. Wash. Cook 1 pound *only* in boiling salted water until soft. Grate remainder. Wipe dry in tea towel. Mash cooked potatoes. Combine with grated raw ones. Stir in egg, salt and sufficient flour to form firm dough. Leave to rest 30 minutes. Prepare filling. Slowly fry onion in margarine until soft but not brown. Stir in mince and parsley. Fry briskly 3 minutes, breaking up meat with fork all the time. Add 1 tablespoon breadcrumbs. Mix thoroughly. Season. Take about 4 tablespoons potato dough. Roll out flat on floured surface. Put 1 tablespoon filling in centre. Work dough round filling, pinching edges well together, to form round dumpling. Repeat, using rest of dough and filling. Drop, a few at a time, into large saucepan of gently boiling salted water. Cook until dumplings float to top; about 15 minutes. Carefully lift out of water with draining spoon. Put into warm bowl. Melt extra margarine in small pan. Add rest of crumbs. Fry gently until golden, turning. Spoon over dumplings. Serve with salad.

CURLY KALE WITH BACON AND BARLEY

serves 4–6

1 pound lean boiling bacon
(or use 2 meaty knuckles)
4 pounds curly kale
½ breakfast cup pearl barley, washed
pepper to taste

One of those German family recipes where no one seems to know exactly how much of anything to use! However, this adaptation works well for me and it is worth a try even though the preparation is on the long side.

Cover bacon—or knuckles—with cold water. Bring to boil. Drain. Repeat. (This removes excess saltiness.) Wash kale thoroughly in kitchen sink filled with cold salted water. Remove all tough stalks. Chop or tear up leaves coarsely. Put, a handful at a time, into large saucepan. Cook down over medium heat. (Water clinging to kale after washing should be adequate.) Add more kale. Repeat until all kale has been added to pan and has cooked down considerably. Add barley and pepper. Stir well. Add bacon. Cover pan. Simmer very slowly for 1½–2 hours, stirring occasionally. Remove bacon. Cut meat into pieces. Mix with kale. Serve very hot with fried potatoes.

To prepare in advance *The flavour of this particular dish is much better if prepared one day before needed and then reheated before serving. If it appears to be on dry side, add few tablespoons water.*

WESTPHALIAN SAUSAGE AND POTATO BRAISE

serves 4

2 pounds potatoes
8 large pork sausages
hot water
flour
1 ounce dripping
1 level teaspoon marjoram
salt and pepper to taste
¼ pint undiluted evaporated milk
2 level tablespoons finely chopped parsley

Peel potatoes. Parboil. Drain. Thinly slice. Put sausages into flameproof casserole. Cover with hot water. Bring slowly to boil. Drain. Wipe sausages dry. Coat with flour. Heat dripping in casserole. Add sausages. Fry until brown all over. Arrange layers of potato slices on top, sprinkling marjoram, salt and pepper between layers. Pour milk into dish. Cover. Cook in centre of moderate oven, 350°F or Gas 4 (180°C) 40 minutes. Sprinkle with parsley. Serve from dish.

WESTPHALIAN BEAN SOUP

serves 6

4 ounces dried haricot beans,
soaked overnight and drained
1 pint water
salt
3 medium carrots, sliced
2 pints beef stock (use cubes)
½ level teaspoon marjoram
salt and pepper to taste
½ ounce margarine
2 level tablespoons finely chopped parsley

Cook beans in water, with salt added, until soft. Reserve about 2 tablespoons whole beans. Rub remainder through sieve; alternatively, blend until smooth in liquidizer goblet with some of the cooking water. Put all remaining ingredients, except margarine and parsley, into pan. Bring to boil. Lower heat. Cover. Simmer 30 minutes. Add bean purée. Adjust seasoning to taste. Stir in margarine and parsley. Pour into warm bowls. Add few whole beans to each.

BEAN AND BACON STEW POT

serves 4

1 pound broad beans,
(weighed after podding)
8 ounces fresh peas,
(weighed after podding)
8 ounces carrots, sliced
2 level tablespoons finely chopped parsley
1 pound potatoes, thickly sliced
2 medium onions, finely chopped
1 leek (white part only), finely chopped
8 ounces streaky bacon, chopped
2 ounces margarine or dripping
salt and pepper
¼ pint hot water
extra chopped parsley for garnish

Combine first 5 ingredients in bowl. In flame-proof casserole, slowly fry onions, leek and bacon in half the margarine for about 10 minutes. Add the combined vegetables. Season. Add water. Dot top with flakes of remaining

margarine. Cover. Cook over very low heat 40 minutes. Sprinkle with parsley. Serve from casserole.

Oven-cooked Bean and Bacon Stew Pot *If preferred, put all ingredients into casserole dish. Cover. Cook in centre of moderate oven, 350°F or Gas 4 (180°C) for 1 hour. Sprinkle with parsley before serving.*

Using dried beans *When broad beans are out of season, 6–8 ounces dried haricot beans, soaked overnight and drained, may be used instead. To speed up cooking time, simmer the dried beans in boiling salted water for 30 minutes, before combining with rest of ingredients.*

SUMMER CASSEROLE

Serves 4–5

8 ounces haricot beans, soaked
overnight in 3 pints water
1½ pounds mildly salted belly of pork
1 pound runner beans,
topped and tailed, side strings removed
and diagonally sliced
8 ounces carrots, thinly sliced
1 pound new potatoes, scraped and
thinly sliced
pepper to taste
8 ounces cooking apples
2 medium onions, chopped
1 ounce dripping
2 level tablespoons finely chopped parsley

Put beans and water in which they were soaking in large pan. Add pork. Bring to boil. Lower heat. Cover. Simmer until both are tender—1–1½ hours. Add runner beans, carrots and potatoes. Season with pepper. (Salt from pork should be adequate.) Cover. Cook gently 30 minutes. Peel and core apples. Slice thinly. Add to saucepan. Cook further 10 minutes. Meanwhile, fry onions gently in dripping until pale gold. Stir into the saucepan. Remove the pork from the saucepan and slice it. Arrange vegetables and liquor from pan in a serving dish. Stand the meat slices on top. Sprinkle with parsley. Serve straight away.

Home baking takes the biscuit

FOR the lucky people who don't have to count calories and can indulge in some home baking once in a while, JEAN BALFOUR suggests easy cake and biscuit mixtures.

WITH the inevitable increase in the price of cakes and biscuits in the shops it becomes ever more obvious that home baking is worth while. It may involve a little more planning than when buying, but it need not be hard work. With cake mixers, non-stick tins, and time-saving methods galore, many of the tiresome tasks have been taken out of home baking.

And the freezer owners have the added advantage of being able to bake a good batch, freeze some, or all of it.

Like methods, tastes have also changed. Rich, elaborate cakes are now only wanted for special occasions, and the present-day trend is towards simple, plain-style cakes, buns, and biscuits which suit both budgets AND figures!

So my baking suggestions this week are trimmed to everyday requirements — the cake mixture that can be partly used at once and the remainder set aside for freezing if liked. the biscuits that can be adapted and decorated, and all of them easily prepared at one baking session.

Before beginning, plan the procedure. Make the oven do its full stint of work when it is on and bake two or three items while you are in the mood. Although few cakes can be cooked in conjunction — you can't obviously pop in scuits while a sponge or at it cake is cooking —

you can follow one up after the other in quick succession so that heat is not wasted.

It is generally advisable to make the longest cooking cake first and while this is in the oven prepare buns, biscuits or scones.

Check all your ingredients before starting. Have eggs at room temperature (out of the fridge for at least thirty minutes) before using them, otherwise they will tend to curdle when added to creamed ingredients. Butter should be slightly softened, but creaming margarines and fats need no preliminary attention.

See that flavouring, raising agents, etc. are at hand and get the required cake tins prepared. Set the oven at the heat needed.

Finally, make a note to take the telephone off the hook at the crucial moment of baking — when putting in or taking out a cake. If a call is im-

portant caller will try again, but in the space of a few minutes a cake can be spoiled!

This is a three-in-one cake to bake, eat or freeze as liked. It is a slight variation of the traditional Victoria sandwich mixture and is prepared like this.

SANDWICH CAKES

You need: 6oz. margarine, 6oz. castor sugar, 7oz. self-raising flour, ½ level teaspoon baking powder, 3 large eggs, 1 tablespoon milk.

Line the base of two (7in.) round sandwich tins and one (7in.) square shallow tin with greased greaseproof paper and grease the sides of the tins. Set the oven at 4 370 deg. Fahr, and place on a shelf in the middle of the oven.

Cream the margarine with the sugar either in a mixer or by hand until soft, light in colour and texture. Sift the flour with the baking powder. Beat the eggs into the

creamed mixture, one at a time, adding a dessertspoonful of the flour with the second and third egg. Fold in the remainder of the flour with a metal spoon, adding the milk with it to make a soft spongy consistency.

Divide between the three prepared tins, putting a spoonful more in the square tin than the round ones. Smooth the top of the cakes with a knife, spreading the mixture right to the edges. Put the three cakes on the same middle shelf of the heated oven (they should all fit into one shelf of an average oven) and bake at the given heatf or 25 to 30 minutes. If necessary and when nearly ready, move the positions slightly so that the three cakes brown evenly.

When ready — they should be risen and just firm to the touch when pressed with the forefinger — remove from the oven, leave to cool in the tins for a few minutes, then turn out and cool on wire

trays. Strip off the paper before the cakes are cold.

The two round sandwich cakes can be stored or put in the freezer. To freeze, wrap in polythene or foil, label and use within four months. Thaw at room temperature before filling with butter icing, jam or cream. Sandwich together.

I like to use the square cake this way. I cut it across into halves, put coffee butter icing on one half and sandwich this with the other. A dusting of icing sugar or another layer of coffee icing on top makes a nice finish and it proves a pretty oblong cake that cuts up pleasantly and is god for a coffee morning or tea. Sometimes I add chopped walnuts to the icing.

You can flavour the whole cake mixture with vanilla or orange — the grated rind of a large orange for the three-egg mixture. On the other hand, if you are quick you can add the grated rind of ½ orange to the mixture that goes into the square tin, adding it lightly at the last minute. This can then be turned into an orange cake with orange butter icing.

BASIC BISCUIT MIXTURE

You need—4oz. butter or margarine, 2oz. castor sugar, 1 medium-sized egg, 8oz. self-raising flour, a few drops vanilla essence.

Set the oven at 4 or 375 deg. Fahr. Use non-

stick biscuit pans if you have them, otherwise lightly grease one or two shallow trays. Biscuits require space during baking because they spread but the mixture will not come to any harm if a little is left over and a second batch made.

Cream the fat and sugar together until light and fluffy, using a mixer for speed, or beating with a spoon if preferred. Beat in the egg, a little at a time. Fold in the flour (sifted) and the vanilla essence. Mix to a fairly firm dough. If the dough is too soft to handle, or difficult, cover and refrigerate for half hour before rolling out.

Then roll out on a lightly floured surface after giving it a gentle knead to remove any cracks. It should be ⅛ to ¼ inch thick when rolled out. Cut into shapes with star, moon, round, and fluted biscuit cutters, place on the prepared tins and bake towards the top of the heated oven for about 15 minutes, or until firm and a light golden colour. Cool in the tins for a few minutes, then transfer to wire trays and leave till quite cold.

This biscuit mixture will provide about three dozen biscuits of different shapes and sizes. Some attractive plastic cutters are now in the shops and for a small outlay are a good buy.

other cold warrior, had been toppled from his position as the number-two man in Clandestine Services and the agency had packed him off to London as station chief.

"I want to install my own team," the director said, trying not to lose his temper.

"And what if I don't understand?" Mother asked.

He was one of the few men in the agency who dared to speak to the director that way. He drew his courage from the same well which had so long sustained J. Edgar Hoover: his files. Mother, like Hoover, enjoyed the considerable leverage which devolves upon a man who is empowered to follow, to peek, and to tap. It was his job to make sure that the company was not penetrated by the other side. In performing his duties, Mother tried to think like a KGB officer: whom in the CIA would he most like to recruit? His answer to this question was a list of 50 people in the agency whom he kept under surveillance. He also ran spot checks on the other 17,500 company employees. His files were bloated with other people's secrets. Mother, like Hoover, simply had too much on agency personnel to be an easy man to "retire."

"If you won't accept a transfer," the director said, "I may have to ask for your resignation."

"And what if I refuse to resign?" Mother asked. "What would you do to me then? Would you do to me what you did to that Vietnamese girl? I hope not, because the record-ings of her screams make

secretary of state.

"They are giving me quite a reputation as a swinger," the secretary said. "But I don't mind. Now when I go to a dinner party and I'm boring, the others at the table think it's their fault."

The line had become one of the secretary's favourites.

The secretary of state and the director of the Central Intelligence Agency were lunching in the secretary's private dining-room in the State Department. The conversation, like the meal, began with light openers but inevitably progressed toward the meat of the matter, as the director had known it would.

"Have you taken care of that personnel problem we discussed," the secretary asked.

"I talked to him," the director said, "but he's being difficult."

"He is a difficult man," the secretary said, "and that makes my job difficult. Sometimes I think he's a bigger barrier to peace in the Middle East than the terrorists."

The secretary enjoyed being secretive too much to explain such a statement. Therefore, he left unstated his suspicion that Mother, through his agents, had allied himself with Right-wing forces in Israel, especially within the military. Time after time, the secretary had been on the verge of persuading the Israeli political leaders to give up territory in return for promises of peace; then the political leaders would confer with the military leaders and the secretary was always having his picture taken.

when Allen Dulles was the director, he called my friend in to his office and asked: "Why did you say Bedell Smith (a former director) doesn't like my brother Dulles(?"

(John Foster) "My friend said, "I remembered where it was that he had had that conversation. It was while he was in bed with his wife. Saxonton had bugged his bedroom."

"Yes," that's how it works." "If you complain, he tells

JAMES SCHLESINGER . . . followed the bureaucratic precedent.

you, 'If you didn't want to give up your right to smoke cigarettes, you shouldn't have taken a job in an explosives factory.'"

"Of course," the secretary smiled, "I understand why Saxonton is so greatly feared. But now you must make a decision. Whom do you fear more, him or me?"

When the lunch was over the director went to his car and the secretary went into the State Department's press room to hold a news conference. His eye was caught by Washington's only female television sound technician. She looked like the women with whom the secretary was always hav-ing his picture taken.

apology for his car. It was too small, needed a tune-up, could use a wash.

"If I had wanted a limousine," the director said, "I could have arranged for one."

The two men crammed themselves into a small, canary-yellow 240-Z. Hill took a deep breath and turned the key. The car wouldn't start at first. It never would. He choked it and kept on try-ing. Finally he resus-citated the engine. Hill apologized again.

The director wanted Hill to drive him out to "the farm," which is to the army. As they drove through the Virginia woods, Hill found himself recalling his own training at the enclave. He remembered the courses where he had received instruction on "agent-handling," "flaps and seals," and "locks and picks." But his most vivid memory was of the night of the border-crossing.

His class set off in teams of two in the middle of the night to cross a Communist border — complete with barbed wire, watchtowers, searchlights, and roving Commie guards — which stretches for two miles through the Virginia woodlands. Hill and his partner, came upon a deep ditch which was filled with oil and other repugnant slime. Slipping down into this muck was easy enough, but climbing up the other side was almost impossible. Every time they tried to crawl out, they slid back into the mire. They felt like bugs trying to crawl out of a

agency, so he had made his career on the dark side. The dark side penetrated the "enemy" with spies such as rigging elections, mounting coups, and just plain murder. The light side, his side, monitored radio transmissions, studied satellite photographs, and read the enemy's scientific journals. Advancement was faster on the light side, which appealed to Hill, but he knew he almost certainly had no chance of becom-ing the top man. Directors always came from the dark side — a monopoly which the light side deeply resented.

That was the principal schism within the com-pany: the light side against the dark. But there were other divisions, too. The dark side was split into spies and political opera-tors. The spies just wanted to find out what other governments were up to; the operators wanted to control other govern-ments or else overthrow them. Richard Helms, who had run the agency in the sixties, had come out of the clean side of the dark

wet. The "East German security officers" who interrogated Hill scared him to death.

Hill felt more or less the same way as he chauf-feured the director deeper into the forest. Every time he started to say some-thing, he suddenly had the feeling that he was about to set off another trip wire. So he sat silently and waited for the director to initiate some kind of con-versation.

Hill's experiences at the farm had helped persuade him that he did not belong on the dark side of the agency, so he had made his for a bad cold. Until now. Now he thought he saw a way to make that report his lever.

"It has come to my attention," the director told Hill, "that John Saxonton was behind many of the questionable activi-ties performed by our agency in this country. It has also come to my atten-

deputy director of opera-tions, inherited not only Schlesinger's job but his report on wrongdoing as well.

Unlike Schlesinger, Col-by had worked his way up in the company, and so he had more of a vested interest in covering up the company's past mistakes. However, since he had spent most of his career out of the country, he saw to it that the report focused on d omestic transgressions. Still, the new director tended to regard the report with the affection usually reserved

ALLEN DULLES . . . former CIA director.

tion that several of these activities may have over-stepped our charter. I realise that it is difficult to assign blame to one of our own, but in this case, lit the climate in which w now operate, I do no believe we can afford

APPLE CAKE

serves 8–10

Pastry

12 ounces plain flour
2 level teaspoons baking powder
1 level teaspoon salt
3 ounces *each,* **margarine and cooking fat**
or lard
4 ounces caster sugar
1 egg, beaten
1 tablespoon milk
1 teaspoon vanilla essence

Filling

3 pounds cooking apples
3 ounces caster sugar
1 level teaspoon cinnamon

Topping

Cold milk
Sifted icing sugar

This cake-cum-pudding tastes super and is easy to make and heavenly with vanilla ice cream, custard or simply by itself.

Sift flour, baking powder and salt into bowl. Rub in fat finely. Add sugar. Toss ingredients lightly together. Mix to fairly stiff paste with egg, milk and essence. Knead gently until smooth. Foil wrap and then refrigerate for 1 hour. To prepare the filling peel and core the apples, slicing thinly. (Browning of fruit doesn't matter.) Preheat oven to moderately hot, 375°F or Gas 5 (190°C). Divide pastry equally into thirds. Roll out one-third. Use to cover base of 8-inch loose-bottomed cake tin, or spring pan form (the type with a clip-on side). Roll out next third of pastry into strip same depth as tin and long enough to go round it. Press against inside of tin. Pinch edges of pastry, where they meet at base, well together. Prick pastry lightly with fork. Line base and sides with foil to prevent pastry from rising as it cooks. Bake in oven centre 15 minutes. Remove foil. Fill with layers of apples, sugar and cinnamon, beginning and ending with apples. Reduce oven temperature to moderate, 350°F or Gas 4 (180°C). Roll out rest of pastry. Use to cover cake. Brush with milk. Bake in centre of oven 35–45 minutes. Leave about 30 minutes before removing from tin (but let

cake remain on metal base). Sprinkle heavily with sifted icing sugar. Serve warm or cold.

Apple Cake with Raisins *Make exactly as previous recipe but add 2 or 3 tablespoons seedless raisins with the apples.*

Using rum in the cake *Germans are very partial to apple and rum combinations. Therefore if you have any dark rum to spare, sprinkle the apples with 1 or 2 tablespoons.*

SAUERBRATEN

serves 4

1 pint water
½ pint malt vinegar
1 medium carrot and onion, sliced
2 medium celery stalks, broken
handful of parsley
2 bay leaves
3 cloves
2 level teaspoons salt
1½ pounds boned brisket or silverside
1 ounce dripping
2 level tablespoons cornflour
salt and pepper
1 level teaspoon brown sugar
3–4 tablespoons undiluted
evaporated milk

A world-famous dish in which beef is marinaded in the cool for 2 days.

Put first 8 ingredients into pan. Bring to boil. Simmer 10 minutes. Transfer to large glass or enamel bowl. Immerse meat in marinade. Cover securely. Refrigerate 2 days. Drain meat thoroughly. Fry in hot dripping until brown all over. Add half strained marinade. Bring to boil. Lower heat. Simmer very gently 1½–2 hours or until meat is tender. Lift out of pan. Carve into slices. Put on to warm platter. Keep hot. Strain rest of cold marinade. Blend smoothly with cornflour. Pour into clean pan. Bring to boil. Season. Add sugar. Stir in milk. Pour sauce over slices of meat. Serve with noodles.

To pressure cook *Cook meat in half the marinade at 15 pounds pressure for 30 minutes.*

SAUERKRAUT WITH SAUSAGES

serves 4–6

2 ounces bacon dripping
2 medium onions, chopped
4 ounces fatty bacon pieces, chopped
2 pounds sauerkraut, canned usually;
sometimes bottled
2 fairly large cooking apples,
peeled and grated
1 level tablespoon sugar
1 pint water or stock
salt and pepper to taste

So beloved by most Germans, Sauerkraut is undoubtedly a wholesome meal for hearty appetites, especially if served with plenty of boiled or creamed potatoes and mugs of strong beer!

Heat dripping in large pan. Add onions. Fry gently until soft and just beginning to change colour. Add bacon. Fry 5 minutes. Add undrained sauerkraut and all remaining ingredients. Bring to boil, stirring. Lower heat. Cover. Simmer gently 1 hour, stirring occasionally. Leave overnight. Cover, reheat 30 minutes. Uncover. Simmer until most of the liquid has evaporated. Serve with freshly fried pork sausages or cooked Frankfurters.

Wine in sauerkraut *If there happens to be a little spare white wine left over after a party or special occasion, add it to the sauerkraut while it is cooking, in addition to water or stock. It adds tremendously to the flavour. Sweet cider may also be used.*

If sauerkraut is too acidy *Add extra sugar to taste.*

For economy *Bacon may be omitted altogether, although a few bacon rinds—removed at end of cooking time—should be included for flavour.*

ROTE GREUTZE

This is a blissfully refreshing dessert, extremely popular all over Germany during the height of summer when soft fruits are at their cheapest and ripest. In its simplest form, Rote Greutze is a mixture of soft fruits (raspberries, strawberries and gooseberries for example) stewed with water and sugar to taste (not too much sugar because the Greutze should be a bit sharp), and thickened to a soft blancmange-like consistency with arrowroot, cornflour or potato flour. The usual proportion of thickener is about $\frac{1}{2}$ ounce to every pint of stewed fruit. Before being added and boiled up with the fruit, it should first be mixed to a smooth cream with a little cold water. The Greutze is frequently flavoured with lemon peel, lemon juice, vanilla and/or cinnamon and thoroughly chilled. Bowls of Greutze are then topped with cold milk—never cream—and eaten either as a dessert or for a light snack meal with brown bread and butter.

Rote Greutze with stone fruit *If using plums, greengages or damsons, it is customary to remove the stones before thickening the Greutze. The same applies to cherries.*

Rote Greutze with red- or blackcurrants *Mixture should be passed through a fine sieve before being thickened.*

France

FRENCH ONION SOUP

serves 6

2 ounces margarine
1$\frac{1}{2}$ pounds onions
2 level tablespoons flour

2 pints beef stock (use cubes)
salt and pepper to taste
6 slices French bread
3 ounces Cheddar cheese, grated

Heat margarine in pan. Add onions. Cover. Fry gently about 15 minutes or until soft and golden brown. Stir in flour. Cook 2 minutes.

Gradually blend in stock. Cook, stirring, until soup comes to boil. Cover. Simmer 20 minutes. Stir occasionally. Before serving, toast bread on one side only. Cover untoasted sides heavily with cheese. Brown under hot grill. Stand in 6 warm soup plates, toasted cheese sides uppermost. Fill with piping hot soup. Serve straight away.

Vegetarian Onion Soup   *Use water instead of stock.*

ECONOMICAL VICHYSSOISE

serves 6

2 ounces margarine
2 large onions, chopped
1 pound old potatoes,
weighed after peeling
1 pint chicken stock (use cubes)
¼ pint milk (skimmed if liked)
salt and pepper to taste
1 small can cream
about 2 tablespoons chopped chives
or green part of leek

This is a delightfully sophisticated and ice-cold, summer soup made, basically, from potatoes.

Heat margarine in saucepan. Add onions. Cover. Cook *very gently* until onions are soft but still white. Thickly slice potatoes. Add to pan with stock and milk. Season. Bring to boil. Lower heat. Cook until potatoes are soft. Rub mixture through sieve. Add cream. Beat until completely smooth. Adjust seasoning. Chill. Stir well before serving. Transfer to 6 bowls. Sprinkle top of each with chives or green part of chopped leek.
Note   If soup is on thick side, thin down with little extra cold milk.

Blender Vichyssoise   *If preferred, the soup may be blended until completely smooth in a liquidizer goblet.*

BREAD SOUP

Serves 4–5

1 ounce margarine
2 medium onions, chopped
1 garlic clove, chopped
1½ pints chicken stock (use cubes)
3 large slices white bread,
de-crusted and cubed
¼ pint milk, skimmed if liked
1 large egg
salt and pepper to taste
2 level tablespoons chopped parsley

Heat margarine in pan. Add onion and garlic. Cover. Fry gently until soft but not brown; about 10 minutes. Add stock and bread. Bring to boil, whisking all the time. Beat milk and egg well together. Remove soup from heat. Add egg mixture. Mix well. Season. Transfer to warm soup bowls. Sprinkle with parsley.

Vegetarian Bread Soup   *Water from vegetables such as cabbage, carrots, peas, beans, etc., may be used instead of chicken stock.*

FRENCH CABBAGE SOUP

serves 8

1 medium-sized head of cabbage
2 ounces margarine or dripping
2 large onions, chopped
1 large leek, slit, well-washed
and chopped
2 medium carrots, thinly sliced
1 small turnip, cut into strips
1 small parsnip, diced
4 ounces haricot beans, soaked overnight
2 large potatoes, diced
1 garlic clove, chopped
¼ level teaspoon dried thyme
salt and pepper to taste
3 pints water
4 large slices white bread, halved
extra margarine or dripping for frying

Shred cabbage finely. Heat margarine in large pan. Add onions, leek, carrots, turnip and parsnip. Stir well. Cover. Cook over low heat

15 minutes until vegetables are partially cooked but still white. Drain beans. Add to pan with all remaining ingredients except bread and margarine. Bring to boil. Lower heat. Cover. Simmer about 1 hour or until beans are tender. Fry bread in hot margarine until golden on both sides. Put into 8 warm soup plates. Fill with soup. Serve steaming hot.

CABBAGE SOUP WITH PORK

serves 8

Often the French cook a piece of salted belly of pork with their cabbage soup. This is sometimes sliced and served as a main course with vegetables following the soup, or left until cold and eaten with salad and crusty French bread. If adding salted pork to soup, *use no additional salt.* If you think pork is on salty side, put into pan, cover with cold water and bring to boil. Drain. Repeat. (This reduces excessive saltiness.) Add to soup.

BOEUF EN DAUBE

serves 4

2 pounds beef shin
4 ounces unsmoked bacon
2 large carrots
2 large onions
2 garlic cloves
2 ounces margarine or dripping
2 level tablespoons tomato concentrate
(can or tube)
2 level tablespoons finely chopped parsley
1 bay leaf
½ level teaspoon mixed herbs
¾ pint dry cider
2 level tablespoons cornflour
5 tablespoons cold water

Cube beef. Chop bacon. Slice carrots and onions. Chop or crush garlic. Heat margarine in pan. Add vegetables and garlic. Cover. Cook gently for 10–15 minutes or until pale gold. Add meat and bacon. Fry more briskly until well browned. Add all remaining ingredients except cornflour and water. Bring to boil. Lower heat. Cover. Simmer 2–2½ hours or until meat is tender. Mix cornflour to smooth cream with water. Stir into meat mixture. Cook until

thickened, stirring. Serve with boiled potatoes and green vegetables to taste.

To pressure cook   *Cook for 15 minutes at 15 pounds pressure. Thicken with cornflour.*

NAVARIN OF LAMB

serves 4–6

2–2½ pounds boned shoulder of lamb
(weight after boning)
flour
1 ounce dripping
8 small onions
1 garlic clove, crushed
1 pint hot water
2 level tablespoons tomato concentrate
(can or tube)
2 pounds new potatoes
1 level tablespoon chopped parsley
½ level teaspoon thyme
1 small bay leaf
salt and pepper to taste

Preheat oven to moderate, 350°F or Gas 4 (180°C). Cut meat into cubes. Remove as much surplus fat as possible and discard. Coat lamb cubes with flour. Heat dripping in large flameproof casserole. Add lamb. Fry briskly until lightly browned. Add onions and garlic. Fry further 5 minutes. Combine water with tomato concentrate. Pour slowly into pan. Surround meat with potatoes. Sprinkle with parsley and thyme. Add bay leaf. Season. Cover. Cook in centre of oven 1–1¼ hours or until meat is tender. Before serving, skim off any fat that has risen to top.

COD PATE PROVENCALE

serves 4–6

2 pounds smoked fillet of cod
6 tablespoons salad oil
¼ pint milk
1–2 garlic cloves, crushed
freshly milled black pepper
juice of 1 small lemon
2 hard-boiled eggs, cut into wedges

26

Put fish into shallow pan. Cover with cold water. Bring to boil. Drain. Repeat. (This removes excess saltiness from fish.) Skin fish. Return fish to clean pan. Mash finely. Stand over low heat. Gradually blend in oil and milk. Beat until mixture is thick, paste-like and very hot. Add garlic, pepper and lemon juice. Pile into warm dish. Garnish with egg wedges. Accompany with freshly made toast.

To store Ratatouille *Put into large bowl. Cover closely when cold. Keep in refrigerator up to 1 week.*

To freeze Ratatouille *Put into containers, leaving 1-inch headroom at top of each for expansion. Cover, and seal with freezer tape, label and date. Store up to 6 months in domestic deep freeze. Thaw before using.*

RATATOUILLE

serves 8

2 large onions, chopped
2 garlic cloves, chopped
2 ounces margarine or 3 tablespoons salad oil
2 large aubergines (eggplant)
1 pound marrow, peeled
1 large green pepper
1 medium can (1 pound) tomatoes
1 level teaspoon salt
1 teacup finely chopped parsley for garnish

I find Ratatouille extremely useful. It not only makes a good vegetable accompaniment to almost any meat, egg or poultry dish, but is equally good in its own right, served on a bed of freshly cooked fluffy rice and topped thickly with grated Cheddar cheese. At the height of summer, when the vegetables are readily available and reasonably low-priced, I tend to make double, or even treble, the quantity of ingredients and keep some in reserve.

Fry onions and garlic in margarine or oil over low heat for 15 minutes. Keep pan covered. Wash and slice unpeeled aubergines. Cut marrow into cubes. De-seed green pepper and cut flesh into strips. Add to onions and garlic with tomatoes and salt. Cover. Simmer 1 hour or until vegetables are tender. Uncover. Continue to cook until some of the liquid has evaporated and Ratatouille is fairly thick.

To pressure cook Ratatouille *Pressure cook for 15 minutes at 15 pounds pressure. Afterwards cook for a little while, uncovered, until Ratatouille has thickened and some of the liquid evaporated.*

TRIPE—CAEN STYLE

serves 6

3 pounds dressed tripe
2 pig's trotters, chopped through
4 medium leeks, trimmed, slit and well washed
6 cloves
6 medium onions
2 large carrots, sliced
1 small bay leaf
$\frac{1}{2}$ teacup parsley sprigs
1 level teaspoon thyme
1 pint dry cider
salt and pepper to taste

Preheat oven to cool, 275°F or Gas 1 (140°C). Cut well-washed tripe into 3-inch squares. Put into large, heavy casserole. Add trotters and leeks. Press cloves into onions. Add to casserole with carrots and all remaining ingredients. Cover securely. Put into centre of oven and cook 6–7 hours. Refrigerate overnight. Remove layer of fat from surface. Transfer contents of casserole to saucepan. Bring slowly to boil. Boil gently 15 minutes. Remove bones and bay leaf before serving. Accompany with boiled potatoes.

To pressure cook *Put all ingredients into pressure cooker. Pressure cook $1\frac{1}{4}$ hours at 15 pounds pressure.*

SALAD NICOISE

serves 6

1 garlic clove
1 medium-sized lettuce
French dressing
1 pound cooked potatoes, diced
6 large tomatoes, skinned and sliced
1 medium can (about 1 pound)
sliced green beans, drained
2 cans (each about 7 ounces) tuna or
3 cans mackerel fillets, drained
1 dozen black olives
1 small can anchovies, drained
2 level tablespoons capers
2 hard-boiled eggs, sliced

This is an enjoyable, all-in-one, main course.

Rub large salad bowl with cut clove of garlic. Wash lettuce. Shake leaves dry. Put into bowl. Moisten with dressing. Pile potatoes in centre. Add tomato slices, beans, and large pieces of tuna or mackerel. Coat well with dressing. Garnish attractively with last 4 ingredients. Serve with crusty bread and butter.

QUICHE LORRAINE

serves 6

Pastry

6 ounces plain flour
½ level teaspoon salt
3 ounces mixture margarine and
cooking fat
about 8–9 teaspoons cold water to mix

Filling

6 rashers streaky bacon,
coarsely chopped
½ pint creamy milk or
undiluted evaporated milk
1 whole egg and 3 yolks
salt and pepper to taste

Preheat oven to moderately hot, 400°F or Gas 6 (200°C). Sift flour and salt into bowl. Rub in fats finely. Mix to stiff dough with water. Knead lightly until smooth. Roll out on floured surface. Use to line 8-inch flan ring standing on lightly greased baking tray. To prepare filling fry bacon slowly until fat begins to run. Drain. Arrange over base of flan case. Beat milk, egg and yolks well together. Season. Gently pour into flan case. Place in centre of oven. Bake 15 minutes. Reduce temperature to moderate, 325°F or Gas 3 (170°C). Bake further 25–30 minutes or until Quiche is golden brown and puffy. Remove from oven. Cut into wedges. Serve while still hot.

Using and keeping spare egg whites *These can be used up in meringues, snows and fruit fools, etc., and may also be kept up to about 1 week in the refrigerator, provided they are in a well-covered container. To freeze egg whites, put into small container, cover and seal with special freezer tape. Leave in domestic deep freeze up to 9 months. Thaw completely before using.*

PIPERADE

serves 4

2 large onions, chopped
2 ounces margarine
1 large green pepper, de-seeded and
cut into strips
1 medium can (about 1 pound) tomatoes
½ level teaspoon mixed herbs
8 eggs
4 tablespoons milk
salt and pepper to taste
4 long streaky bacon rashers,
freshly grilled

Basically an egg dish, Piperade makes a tasty lunch or supper dish at comparatively little cost.

Fry onions gently in margarine until soft but still white. Keep pan covered and allow about 12–15 minutes. Add pepper strips. Fry further 5 minutes. Lift tomatoes out of can. (Reserve liquid for soups and stew.) Add to onions and green pepper with herbs. Cover. Simmer 15 minutes. Meanwhile, beat eggs and milk well together. Season. Add to vegetable mixture. Cook over low heat, stirring continuously, until mixture is lightly scrambled. Pile equal amounts on to 4 warm plates. Top each with bacon rasher.

Rice

For fluffy, separate and dry rice, the best to use is American long grain. Directions for cooking are usually on pack but if not, try this simple method. Bring 2 teacups water and 1 level teaspoon salt to brisk boil. Add 1 teacup rice. Stir once. Simmer 15–20 minutes or until grains are separate and have absorbed all the moisture. Fluff up with fork. Enough for four.

To store left-over rice *Put into container and cover securely. Store in cool larder up to 3 days; in refrigerator up to 1 week.*

To reheat rice *Put cooked rice into saucepan. Add 3–6 tablespoons water, depending on quantity. Cover. Leave over low heat about 5–7 minutes, shaking pan frequently. Grains will then be as fluffy as freshly cooked rice.*

ROAST CHICKEN NORMANDY

serves 4

**4 medium to large joints roasting chicken
salt and pepper
4 streaky bacon rashers
1½ level tablespoons cornflour
½ pint cider
5 tablespoons undiluted evaporated milk**

Preheat oven to hot, 425°F or Gas 7 (220°C). Stand chicken joints in greased roasting tin. Sprinkle with salt and pepper. Drape 1 bacon rasher over each joint. Put into centre of oven. Reduce temperature to moderate, 350°F or Gas 4 (180°C). Roast 45 minutes to 1 hour. Remove joints to serving dish and keep hot. Remove bacon. Pour off all but 2 tablespoons fat from roasting tin. Stand tin over medium heat. Stir in cornflour. Cook 2 minutes, stirring and scraping tin all the time. Gradually blend in cider. Cook, stirring, until sauce comes to boil

and thickens. Simmer 2 minutes. Add milk. Adjust seasoning to taste. Stir well. If sauce seems too thick, thin down with little water. Pour over chicken. Serve with boiled potatoes. Accompany with cooked vegetables or salad.

POULET AU RIZ

serves 6–8

**1 medium-sized boiling fowl
2 cloves
2 large onions
2 large carrots
½ small bay leaf
handful of parsley
2 pints water
2–3 level teaspoons salt
pepper to taste**

Sauce

**2 ounces margarine
2 ounces flour
4 tablespoons undiluted evaporated milk or single cream
juice of 1 medium lemon
about 8 ounces (raw weight) freshly cooked long grain rice
about 1 level tablespoon finely chopped parsley**

Put chicken into saucepan. Press cloves into onions. Add to pan with carrots, bay leaf, parsley and water. Season. Bring to boil. Remove scum. Lower heat. Cover. Simmer about 2–2½ hours or until bird is tender. Lift fowl out of pan. Keep hot. Strain stock, discarding vegetables. To make sauce, melt margarine in pan. Stir in flour. Cook 2 minutes without browning. Gradually blend in 1 pint chicken stock. (Reserve any remainder for soup and stews.) Cook, stirring, until sauce comes to boil and thickens. Cook 5 minutes. Add milk or cream and lemon juice. Adjust seasoning. Arrange hot rice in border round large, warm dish. Carve chicken and place in centre. Coat with sauce. Sprinkle with chopped parsley.

To pressure cook *Cook chicken for 30 minutes at 15 pounds pressure. Afterwards make sauce as directed above.*

CHICKEN FRICASSEE

serves 6

Cook boiling fowl as directed for Poulet au Riz (page 29). Make sauce with half chicken stock and half milk. Dice chicken. Heat through in sauce. Serve with freshly cooked rice or flat ribbon noodles. If liked, a dash of ground nutmeg may be added to sauce.

FRIED CHICKEN NORMANDY

serves 4

Heat 3 ounces dripping or margarine in large frying pan. Lightly dust 4 chicken joints with flour. Sprinkle with salt and pepper. Put into hot fat, skin-side up. Fry until golden. Turn. Fry until golden. Cover pan. Fry gently 30 minutes or until chicken is tender. Keep chicken hot. Make sauce as directed above.

For garlic flavour *Rub chicken joints all over with 1 or 2 cut cloves of garlic before roasting or frying.*

CHEESE SOUFFLE

serves 2

1 ounce margarine
1 ounce flour
¼ pint milk (skimmed if liked)
salt and pepper to taste
1 level teaspoon prepared mustard
3 whole eggs and 1 extra white
4 ounces dry Cheddar cheese, very finely grated

Very typically French, the soufflé is, with a bit of practice, easy to make, economical on ingredients and highly nutritious.

Preheat oven to moderately hot, 375°F or Gas 5 (190°C). Well grease 2-pint straight-sided soufflé dish. Melt margarine in pan. Stir in flour. Cook 2 minutes without browning. Gradually blend in milk. Cook, stirring continuously, until mixture thickens sufficiently to

30

form ball in centre of pan, leaving sides clean. Remove from heat. Leave 2 minutes. Beat in salt, pepper, mustard, egg yolks and cheese. In clean bowl, beat egg whites to stiff snow. Gently cut and fold into yolk mixture with metal spoon. When smooth and well blended, transfer to prepared dish. Put into centre of oven. Bake 40 minutes. Remove from oven. Serve immediately, as all soufflés fall rapidly. Accompany with grilled or fried tomatoes and a green vegetable. Alternatively, try a green salad tossed with French dressing.
Warning note Do not open oven door while soufflé is cooking or it will sink immediately and refuse to come up again!

Bacon or Ham Soufflé *Make exactly as Cheese Soufflé, substituting 4 ounces very finely chopped or minced bacon or ham for cheese.*

Chicken Soufflé *Make exactly as Cheese Soufflé, substituting 4 ounces very finely chopped or minced chicken for cheese. If liked, flavour with a dash of ground nutmeg.*

Fish Soufflé *Make exactly as Cheese Soufflé, substituting 4 ounces very finely mashed and drained canned salmon, tuna or mackerel fillets for cheese. If liked, flavour soufflé with a squeeze of lemon, 1 teaspoon Worcester sauce and ½ level teaspoon finely grated lemon peel.*

LIVER PATE MAISON

serves 12

1¼ pounds pig's or lamb's liver, sliced
1 ounce dripping
1 pound unsalted belly of pork, cubed
½ pound stewing steak, cubed
1–2 garlic cloves
¼ level teaspoon ground nutmeg
5 tablespoons dry red wine, dry cider or beef stock
2 level teaspoons salt
freshly milled black pepper

This is a lot cheaper to make than to buy, and any left-over pâté can be used as a sandwich filling or topping for open sandwiches.

Fry liver slowly in dripping until pale gold on both sides and half-cooked. Cut into smallish pieces. Pass twice through mincer with pork, steak and garlic. Stir in nutmeg. Add wine, cider or stock, salt and freshly milled pepper. Mix thoroughly. Transfer to 2-pound loaf tin or dish, lined with foil and lightly brushed with oil or melted fat. Cover with foil. Leave to stand 1 hour. Stand in roasting tin containing 2 inches or so warm water. Cook in centre of cool oven 300°F or Gas 2 (150°C) about $1\frac{1}{2}$–$1\frac{3}{4}$ hours; pâté is cooked when it shrinks slightly from sides of tin. Leave until cold before turning out of tin or dish and cutting.

Alternative method of cooking *Shape meat mixture into loaf. Stand on large piece of greased foil. Wrap fairly loosely into parcel, making sure all joins are tightly closed. Stand foil-wrapped loaf in roasting tin containing 1 inch warm water. Bake as above. Unwrap. Slice when cold.*

STUFFED LAMB SHOULDER

serves 6–8

1 medium-sized shoulder of lamb, boned
1 medium onion, finely chopped
1 garlic clove, finely chopped
1 pound pork sausagemeat
$\frac{1}{2}$–1 level teaspoon dried rosemary,
crushed between finger and thumb
1 egg, beaten
2 tablespoons water
salt and pepper to taste
3 extra tablespoons water or dry cider

An interesting way of stretching the weekend joint.

Preheat oven to moderately hot, 375°F or Gas 5 (190°C). Stand lamb on work surface. Mix all remaining ingredients, except extra water or cider, together thoroughly. Spread over lamb. Roll up loosely. Tie securely at 1-inch intervals with thick thread. Stand in roasting tin. Add 3 tablespoons water or dry cider. Roast in centre of oven $1\frac{1}{2}$–2 hours, depending on size of joint. Leave to stand 10 minutes before carving into slices. Accompany with gravy, made from pan juices, and vegetables to taste.

CASSOULET

serves 8–10

2 pounds haricot beans, soaked overnight
$1\frac{1}{2}$ pounds pork sausages
2 lamb breasts, boned and roasted
2 pounds spare rib of pork,
boned and roasted
8 ounces unsmoked bacon, with
rinds removed but reserved
4 cloves
2 large onions, left whole
2 garlic cloves, crushed
1 small bay leaf
handful of parsley, chopped
salt and pepper to taste
3 level tablespoons fresh white
breadcrumbs

This is an adaptation of a hearty Toulouse hot-pot dish which, because it takes a while to cook, is ideal to make at the same time as a rice pudding or rich fruit cake, thus saving fuel costs.

Drain beans. Cook in boiling salted water until tender but still firm. Drain, reserving 1 pint water. Cut sausages into chunks. Cut lamb into strips. Cube pork. Dice bacon. Snip rinds into small pieces with scissors. Well grease deep, heavy casserole. Fill with $\frac{1}{2}$ the drained beans and $\frac{1}{2}$ the bacon rinds. Add sausages, lamb, pork, bacon, cloves, onions, garlic, bay leaf and parsley. Season. Top with rest of beans and bacon rinds. Pour reserved bean water into casserole. Sprinkle top with crumbs. Cover with lid or foil. Cook one shelf below centre of cool oven, 300°F or Gas 2 (150°C) for about 3 hours, adding little extra water if the Cassoulet seems to be drying out. Uncover during last 30 minutes to brown crumbs slightly.

MOCK CASSOULET

serves 6–8
Tip a large can baked beans in tomato sauce into greased heatproof casserole. Add 1 pound cold, cooked pork sausages (cut into chunks), 6 rolled rashers streaky bacon and chopped-up remains of weekend joint. Add 2 crushed garlic cloves. Top with second can baked beans.

Sprinkle with 3 level tablespoons fresh white crumbs. Dot with flakes of margarine. Cook near top of moderately hot oven, 375°F or Gas 5 (190°C) for 45 minutes or until top layer of crumbs are well browned.

Mousses

To make a true Mousse is a complicated and expensive operation and hardly the sort of sweet one would include on an everyday family menu. However, these variations serve just as well and, although not as rich as traditional mousses, are still delicious to eat and always popular with children.

STRAWBERRY MOUSSE

serves 4

**1 strawberry flavour jelly
boiling water
1 small can evaporated milk, well-chilled
fresh or bottled lemon juice**

Make up jelly to $\frac{3}{4}$-pint with boiling water. Stir until completely dissolved. Leave in cool place until cold and *just beginning* to thicken and set. Whisk milk until frothy. Add lemon juice, a teaspoon at a time, until milk thickens to consistency of whipped cream. Gently fold in liquid jelly. When smooth and well-blended, transfer quickly (because at this stage mixture sets fast) to four sundae glasses. Before serving, decorate to taste with dessert topping, canned or whipped cream, fresh or canned fruit, nuts, etc.

STRAWBERRY FRUIT MOUSSE

serves 4

When fresh strawberries are about, try this version for a more authentic fruit flavour. Follow previous recipe but make up jelly to only $\frac{1}{2}$ pint with water. Dissolve. Stir in $\frac{1}{4}$ pint strawberry purée made by crushing strawberries

or blending until smooth in liquidizer goblet. Add juice of 1 orange. Proceed as previous recipe.

Raspberry Fruit Mousse *Make exactly as above, substituting raspberries for strawberries.*

Extra-light Mousse *One or two spare egg whites, whisked to stiff snow and folded into Mousse mixture at very end, makes it lighter and more foamy. It also goes further and will serve four to five people.*

Citrus Mousse *Make exactly as Strawberry Mousse, substituting 1 orange, lemon or lime jelly for the strawberry. If liked, add a little finely grated orange, grapefruit or lemon peel to the mixture. Serves 4.*

CHOCOLATE MOUSSE

serves 4

**4 ounces cooking or plain chocolate
$\frac{1}{2}$ ounce margarine
$\frac{1}{2}$ teaspoon vanilla essence
4 large eggs, separated**

Very rich, a little goes a long way and therefore this is a fairly economical sweet to make as a special treat.

Break up chocolate. Put, with margarine, into basin standing over pan of hot water. Leave until melted, stirring once or twice. Beat in vanilla and yolks. Whisk egg whites to stiff snow. Fold into chocolate mixture. When smooth and evenly combined, transfer to 4 'wine' glasses. Chill overnight. Serve just as they are or decorate with small mounds of whipped cream and chopped nuts.

Mocha Mousse *Follow above recipe, but dissolve 3–5 (depending on taste) level teaspoons instant coffee granules with the chocolate and margarine.*

Rum Mousse *Follow above recipe, substituting rum essence for vanilla.*

APRICOT TARTLETS

makes 12

Shortcrust pastry made with 6 ounces flour

Custard Filling

**2 ounces caster sugar
1 ounce flour
2 egg yolks
½ pint milk (skimmed if liked)
1 teaspoon vanilla essence**

Fruit Filling

1 medium can (about 1 pound) apricot halves

Glaze

**4 tablespoons syrup from can of apricots
2 level teaspoons *each,* arrowroot and caster sugar**

Roll out pastry fairly thinly. Use to line 12 fairly deep bun tins. Prick lightly all over. Line with pieces of foil to prevent pastry from rising as it cooks. Bake in centre of hot oven, 425°F or Gas 7 (220°C) 10 minutes. Remove foil. Return cases to oven until golden; about 5 minutes. Meanwhile, prepare filling. Put sugar and flour into bowl. Gradually blend in yolks, 4 tablespoons milk and essence. Bring rest of milk to boil. Stir into blended mixture. Return to saucepan. Cook, stirring continuously, until mixture comes to boil and thickens. Simmer 2 minutes. Cool to lukewarm. Divide equally between tartlet cases. Leave until cold. Top with apricot halves (well-drained), cut sides down. To make glaze, stir 2 tablespoons apricot syrup into arrowroot and sugar. When smooth, add rest of syrup. Pour into pan. Cook, stirring, until mixture thickens and clears. Leave until lukewarm before brushing over fruit.

Pineapple Tartlets *Make as Apricot Tartlets, substituting canned pineapple chunks for apricots.*

Mandarin and Cherry Tartlets *Make as Apricot Tartlets, substituting canned mandarins for apricots. Top each tartlet with ½ glacé cherry.*

Cherry Tartlets *Make as Apricot Tartlets, substituting canned or stewed stoned cherries (very well drained) for apricots.*

Strawberry or Raspberry Tartlets *Make as Apricot Tartlets, substituting 8–12 ounces halved fresh strawberries or same quantity whole fresh raspberries for apricots. Glaze by brushing with melted plum jam or redcurrent jelly.*

For speed *Use 1 small packet frozen short crust pastry instead of home-made pastry.*

As alternative *Omit glaze and use up egg whites by topping tartlets with meringue. Beat 2 whites to stiff snow. Add 1½ ounces caster sugar. Continue beating until mixture is very stiff and shiny. Pile equal amounts over tartlets. Flash bake in hot oven, 425°F or Gas 7 (220°C) 2–3 minutes or until pale gold. Serve as soon as possible, otherwise meringue might fall.*

RIZ A L'IMPERATRICE

serves 6–8

**1 medium can (about 1 pound) milk pudding (rice)
1 medium can (about 1 pound) custard
1½ envelopes gelatine
4 tablespoons cold water
4 tablespoons boiling water
4 level tablespoons apricot jam
1 teaspoon vanilla essence
2 ounces glacé cherries, chopped**

Like many classic dessert dishes in France, Riz à l'Impératrice demands time, expertise and a vast selection of ingredients. My adaptation tastes and looks attractive and is much more easily prepared than the original.

Combine milk pudding and custard well together. Soften gelatine in cold water for 5 minutes. Add boiling water. Pour into pan. Stir over low heat until dissolved. Add apricot jam. Mix thoroughly. Stir into rice/custard mixture with vanilla. When cold and just on setting point, stir in cherries. Transfer to 2–2½-pint fancy mould or basin, first rinsed with cold water. Chill until set. Turn out on to plate. Very good served with apricot or mandarin syrup.

ECONOMICAL CREPES SUZETTE

serves 4

4 ounces plain or self-raising flour
pinch salt
1 large egg
½ pint milk (skimmed if liked)
1 dessertspoon salad oil
2 ounces butter or table margarine
2 ounces caster sugar
Juice and finely grated peel of
1 large orange
Juice and finely grated peel of
1 large lemon
3 tablespoons sweet sherry, white
wine or undiluted orange squash

Sift flour and salt into bowl. Mix to thick, smooth and creamy batter with egg and half the milk. Beat briskly 5 minutes. Gently stir in rest of milk and oil. Cover. Refrigerate no longer than 1 hour. Well grease heavy-based large frying pan. Heat until hot. Pour in enough batter to cover base of pan thinly. Fry until underside is golden. Turn. Fry second side until golden. Repeat, using rest of batter (approximately eight pancakes). Melt butter or margarine in same pan. Add all the remaining ingredients. Keep over low heat. Fold each pancake into envelope shape. Bring ingredients in pan to gentle boil. Add pancakes, four at a time. Simmer in sauce 5 minutes, turning once. Repeat with rest of pancakes. Serve hot.

For luxury touch *Flame 1 tablespoon brandy or dark rum and stir into sauce just before serving.*

CREME CARAMEL

serves 4

2 ounces granulated sugar
3 tablespoons water
1 dessertspoon boiling water
½ pint milk
3 standard eggs and 1 yolk
1 ounce caster sugar

Preheat oven to moderate, 325°F or Gas 3 (170°C). Well grease a 6-inch round cake tin. Put granulated sugar and water into heavy-based pan. Dissolve over low heat, stirring. Bring to boil. Boil fairly briskly until syrup turns deep gold. Remove from heat. Stir in boiling water. Carefully pour into cake tin, covering base completely. Bring milk just up to boil. Remove from heat. Beat eggs and yolk well together. Whisk in milk and sugar. Strain into tin. Stand in roasting tin containing about 1 inch cold water. Place in centre of oven. Cook until set: about 1 hour or until knife inserted into centre comes out clean. Refrigerate when cold. Turn out of tin when thoroughly chilled.

Vanilla Crème Caramel *Add ½ to 1 teaspoon vanilla essence to egg mixture before pouring into tin.*

Orange or Lemon Crème Caramel *Add ½ level teaspoon finely grated orange or lemon peel to egg mixture before pouring into tin.*

Individual Crème Caramel *Line base of four individual well-greased tins (such as metal dariole moulds or castle pudding tins) with caramel. Fill with equal amounts of custard mixture. Stand in small roasting tin containing 1 inch water. Cook in centre of oven 30–40 minutes or until set. Turn out of moulds when thoroughly chilled.*

Meringues

Home-made meringues are infinitely nicer to eat than most of the bought ones and make little demands upon costly ingredients. Quite obviously, they are best sandwiched together with whipped cream, but flavoured butter creams (made with good quality table margarine instead of butter) or even dessert topping, make economical and pleasant substitutes.

The effect of humidity on meringues *A humid atmosphere has a detrimental effect on meringue-making, and when the weather is warm and moist, it seems to be impossible to produce satisfactory meringues.*

CREAM-FILLED MERINGUES

makes 8

**2 egg whites
pinch cream of tartar or
squeeze of lemon
5 ounces caster sugar
1 level dessertspoon cornflour**

Preheat oven to very cool, 225°F or Gas $\frac{1}{4}$ (110°C). Brush two flat baking trays with oil. Line each with double thickness greaseproof paper. *Do not brush paper with oil.* Put egg whites into clean, dry bowl. Add cream of tartar or lemon juice. Beat with whisk until very stiff. Gradually beat in 3 ounces sugar. Continue beating until meringue is very shiny, heavy and stands in firm peaks. Gently fold in rest of sugar and cornflour. Pipe or spoon approximately 16 rounds or ovals on to prepared trays. Leave a little room between each because they spread slightly. Bake in centre of oven for $1\frac{1}{2}$ hours. Gently peel each meringue away from paper with fingers. Turn upside down on trays. Return to oven for further 30–45 minutes or until meringues are dry and crisp. When completely cold, sandwich together with about $\frac{1}{4}$-pint double cream whipped.

To make cream go further *Beat $\frac{1}{4}$-pint double cream with 1 tablespoon each, milk and caster sugar.*

Beating cream *Cream should be very cold and whipped slowly and carefully with additions specified. Over-beating quickly turns cream into butter.*

Cream known as Whipping Cream *This is more economical and cheaper than double cream and whips very adequately to softish consistency. But it is not readily available in all areas. However, to produce home-made whipping cream, combine equal quantities of single and double cream and whip until softly stiff.*

Using canned cream as filling *Most canned creams do not thicken on beating but do firm-up if chilled. Put can of cream into refrigerator. Leave 12 hours. Open can. Carefully pour away liquid. Add little vanilla essence to cream, stirring it in gently with fork.*

To store meringues *If unfilled, well-dried-out meringues will keep for several months in airtight tin. When filled, they should be eaten within a few hours.*

Spare egg yolks
Invariably, if one makes meringues, one inherits egg yolks and the question of what to do with them arises. Below are some suggestions.

In potatoes *Beat them into creamed potatoes, allowing 1–2 yolks for every pound potatoes. You now have Duchesse Potatoes. These may be served as they are (and often prove a very good way of getting egg yolk into faddy children) or may be piped or spooned on to lightly greased baking tray and browned in moderately hot oven, 400°F or Gas 6 (200°C).*

As a glaze *Beat them lightly with a dash of water and brush over tops of pastry-covered pies or tarts before baking. This produces an appetizing golden glaze.*

Welsh Rarebit *Beat them into a rarebit mixture before spreading on toast. This not only increases nutritive value, but also improves the colour.*

Mayonnaise *Use them up by making home-made mayonnaise.*

Mock Hollandaise Sauce *Turn $\frac{1}{2}$ pint of ordinary white sauce into a Mock Hollandaise by beating in 2 yolks, juice of 1 small lemon and dash of nutmeg.*

Yolk Scramble *Blend yolks with equal amount of milk. Put into pan. Season well. Add healthy knob margarine. Scramble lightly. Pile on to slice of toast. A snack for one.*

To freeze egg yolks (sweet) *Beat every 2 yolks with 1 dessertspoon caster sugar. Pack into container. Cover, seal and label. Freeze up to 9 months. Thaw in carton before using.*

To freeze egg yolks (savoury) *Beat every 2 yolks with $\frac{1}{3}$ level teaspoon salt. Pack into container. Cover, seal and label. Freeze up to 9 months. Thaw in carton before using.*

MERINGUE BASKETS

These are useful to have on hand—tucked away in an air-tight tin—for unexpected guests.

Make up meringue mixture given on page 35 in recipe for Cream-Filled Meringues. Spoon 8 heaps—well apart—on to two large prepared baking trays. Shape into rounds. Using back of teaspoon, hollow out centres (but leave base of at least ¼ inch in thickness). Build up sides to form 'baskets'. Bake 1¾–2 hours. Cool slightly. Peel carefully away from paper. Turn upside down on trays. Return to oven further 45 minutes, or until baskets are well dried out and crisp. When completely cold, fill with one of these: ice cream; well-drained, canned, fruit salad topped with canned custard; dessert topping and fresh, canned or frozen berry fruits; dessert topping with well-drained canned peach slices or apricots; whipped or canned cream and grated chocolate or chopped nuts.

BUTTER CREAM

Ideally, this should be made with pure butter and sugar. But there are compromises. Half butter and half margarine may be used; so may all margarine, provided it is of table quality and contains a percentage of butter as well. What should never be used is lard or cooking fat, since the flavour is unacceptable. To make basic butter cream, beat 4 ounces softened margarine (or mixture of butter and margarine) until light. Gradually beat in 8 ounces sifted icing sugar, vanilla essence to taste and 1 or 2 teaspoons milk. Continue to beat until mixture is smooth, very light and fluffy and about twice its original volume. At this stage it will be very soft, but it firms up if it is refrigerated for a short while before it is used.

Quantities of butter cream for meringues and cakes *Half basic recipe should be sufficient for 14–16 meringue halves and also for filling 7-inch sandwich cake. Full quantity of butter cream should be made if top and sides of 7-inch cake are to be covered as well.*

Coloured Butter Creams *Tint butter creams pale orange, yellow, pink or green by beating in, at very end, appropriate food colourings.*

Flavoured Butter Creams *Butter creams may be flavoured with orange or lemon by beating in—at very end—1 level teaspoon finely grated orange or lemon peel or few drops orange or lemon essence. If liked, tint as above.*

Rum Butter Cream *Make basic butter cream as directed, substituting rum essence for vanilla.*

Almond Butter Cream *Make basic butter cream as directed, substituting almond essence for vanilla. Tint pale green.*

Coffee Butter Cream *Dissolve 1 level tablespoon instant coffee granules in 1–2 tablespoons hot milk. Cool. Beat into butter cream at very end. Omit vanilla essence.*

Chocolate Butter Cream *Make up basic butter cream as directed but omit milk. Instead, substitute 1 level tablespoon cocoa powder blended until smooth with 3 tablespoons boiling water. Cool completely before adding.*

Mocha Butter Cream *Make as Chocolate Butter Cream, adding 1 level tablespoon instant coffee granules to cocoa powder and boiling water. Omit vanilla.*

Switzerland

BASIC MUSELI

Allow 3–4 tablespoons per person

**4 ounces rolled oats
4 ounces seedless raisins**

**4 ounces chopped nuts
(unsalted peanuts or hazel nuts)
2 ounces soft brown sugar**

This now very popular and healthy breakfast food is expensive to buy in packets so for addicts, of which there appear to be many, this home-made recipe should be welcome. It is nutritious, satisfying, and makes a good start to a busy day.

Combine all ingredients. Store in airtight tin. The night before, soak required amount of Museli in either skimmed milk, diluted evaporated milk, fresh milk or milk and water mixed. Cover. Refrigerate. To serve, put into bowls and pass extra milk separately.

Museli with Wheat Germ *If liked, add 2 heaped tablespoons wheat germ to basic recipe above.*

Fruit Museli *After Museli has been refrigerated overnight, and immediately before serving, add fresh fruit to taste, choosing from selection of sliced bananas, chopped up apples and/or pears, seedless grapes, sliced strawberries, raspberries, chopped dates, etc.*

Fruit Juice Museli *Instead of serving refrigerated Museli with milk, pass fresh or canned orange or grapefruit juice.*

Yogurt Museli *Instead of milk, serve refrigerated Museli with natural yogurt and pass extra sugar.*

CHEESE FONDUE

Serves about 10

1 large crusty French loaf
2 level tablespoons cornflour
4 tablespoons cold water
1 garlic clove
1½ pounds strong Cheddar cheese
½ pound Lancashire cheese
1 pint dry cider

Genuine Swiss Fondue is made with ingredients such as Gruyère and Emmenthal cheese, Swiss or German wine and kirsch: all, alas, costly. My fondue works out considerably cheaper and though it has a slightly different flavour from the original, it is good and satisfying to eat all the same, especially on blustery winter days. One Swiss tradition could still be observed though—any man who drops his bread into the fondue must pay his rightful forfeit—a kiss for the cook!

Cut loaf into bite-size cubes. Put into bowl. Mix cornflour to smooth cream with water. Rub inside of large, heavy flameproof casserole with cut clove of garlic. Grate Cheddar cheese coarsely. Crumble Lancashire cheese. Mix both cheeses together. Pour cider into casserole. Leave over medium heat until bubbles slowly rise to surface (do not allow to boil). Add cheese, a handful at a time. Stir until melted. Repeat until all cheese has been added. Still stirring, bring to boil. Add cornflour cream. Mix well. Cook until mixture thickens. Simmer 2 minutes. Put plate warmer or spirit stove on table. Stand dish of fondue on top to keep hot. To eat, spear cubes of bread on to fork. Swirl round in cheese mixture and eat. Accompany with hot lemon tea or black coffee—no alcohol or cold minerals.

If fondue becomes too thick *Thin down with a little hot cider.*

If no spirit stove or plate warmer is available *Place three or four table mats on table (to prevent heat marks) and stand casserole of fondue on top. Alternatively, leave casserole over lowest possible heat on cooker and let everyone eat in kitchen.*

FONDUE BOURGUIGNONNE

An electrically heated skillet or deep metal pan (standing on plate warmer) is half-filled with good quality oil or clarified butter and put on the table. This is heated until hot. People then spear cubes of rump steak with long forks and cook them, to their own taste, in the hot oil or butter. The meat is then dipped into any one of up to about six or eight sauces and eaten.

Rump steak and elaborate sauces are hardly economical so I have adapted the original recipe into the more budget-minded Meat Ball Fondue with pleasing results; or so I am told!

MEAT BALL FONDUE

serves 6–8

Replace rump steak with 1½ pounds lean raw minced beef with 1 beaten egg, 1 small grated onion, 6 level tablespoons fresh white bread-crumbs and salt and pepper to taste. With damp hands, form into balls the size of large walnuts. Arrange, in a single layer, on a large plate. Take to the table. Supply long forks, and casserole or skillet of hot oil. Guests use their forks to spear a meat ball at a time and cook it to their own personal liking.

As an alternative   For those without Fondue Bourguignonne sets, electric skillets and spirit stoves, it is easier to precook meat balls and serve them hot with sauce dips. Simply put meat balls into a well-greased roasting tin. Cook near top of moderately hot oven, 400°F or Gas 6 (200°C) about 20–25 minutes. Pile on to warm platter. Take to table. Supply forks for spearing and sauces for dunking.

Pork Ball Fondue   Follow recipe for Meat Ball Fondue but substitute pork sausage meat for minced beef. If liked, add ½–1 level teaspoon dried sage to sausage mixture.

Mixed Meat Ball Fondue   Follow recipe for Meat Ball Fondue, but use half raw minced veal and half raw minced beef.

FONDUE SAUCES

Choose from the selection given below. Prepare in advance. Put into serving dishes. Cover. Refrigerate until needed.

Curry Yogurt   Beat 1 carton natural yogurt (approx. ¼ pint) with 3–4 level teaspoons curry powder, 2 teaspoons lemon juice or mild vinegar, 1 slightly rounded teaspoon icing sugar, ½ level teaspoon onion or garlic, salt and pepper to taste.

Piquant   Mix ¼ pint salad cream or mayonnaise with 1 tablespoon each, finely chopped gherkins and capers.

Spring Green   Mix 1 carton soured cream (approx. ¼ pint) with 2 level tablespoons scissor-snipped chives, 2 level tablespoons finely chopped parsley and ½ bunch finely chopped watercress.

Mustard   Mix 1 carton soured cream (approx. ¼ pint) with 1–2 teaspoons prepared English mustard, 1 level teaspoon icing sugar and 1 small finely grated onion. Thin down with little milk. Season to taste with salt and pepper.

Horseradish Paprika   Beat 1 carton (approx. ¼ pint) natural yogurt with 4 tablespoons horseradish sauce. Stir in 1 or 2 level teaspoons bright red paprika. Season to taste with salt, pepper and sugar.

Egg   Combine ¼ pint salad cream or mayonnaise with 3 hard-boiled eggs, either very finely chopped, grated or forced through fine sieve. Season to taste with pepper, salt, dash Worcester sauce and shake Tabasco or pinch cayenne pepper.

Tomato   Mix ¼ pint bottled tomato ketchup with 1 or 2 teaspoons finely grated onion, 2 teaspoons Worcester sauce, dash malt vinegar and 2 level tablespoons finely chopped parsley.

Tangy   Beat 1 carton (approx. ¼ pint) soured cream with salt and freshly milled black pepper to taste. Stir in ½ bunch finely chopped radishes, ½ bunch finely chopped spring onions and 2 finely chopped celery stalks. Add dash paprika, celery salt and cayenne pepper.

MAYONNAISE

2 egg yolks
½ level teaspoon dry, or
1 level teaspoon prepared, mustard
½ level teaspoon salt
good shake pepper
good pinch sugar
dash Worcester sauce
½ pint salad oil
2–4 tablespoons mild vinegar
1 tablespoon boiling water

Because home-made mayonnaise is used so extensively in European cooking, this seems as good a place as any to introduce it. Self-made is more economical than bought varieties of the 'real thing' and I think the flavour superior. Traditionalists always favour olive oil but as it is so costly over here, I use groundnut oil or a mixture of groundnut and corn. *All ingredients should be at room temperature.*

Put all ingredients, except oil, vinegar and water, into bowl. Beat thoroughly to blend. Still beating continuously, add oil *drop by drop.* When mixture starts to become heavy and thick, add 2 teaspoons vinegar. Continue to beat in oil drop by drop. When two-thirds oil has been incorporated, add 2 more teaspoons vinegar. Finally add rest of oil in slow, steady stream, beating continuously all the time. Stir in rest of vinegar and water (latter prevents separation). Transfer to container. Cover. Store in cool larder or least cold part of refrigerator up to about 2 weeks.

For milder flavour *Use lemon juice instead of vinegar or half vinegar and half lemon juice.*

For thinner mayonnaise *If a thinner mayonnaise is preferred, thin down with little extra vinegar, lemon juice or hot water.*

Curdled Mayonnaise *This sometimes happens if oil is added too quickly and/or is too cold. Simply put another egg yolk into basin. Very gradually beat curdled mayonnaise into it, starting with a drop at a time and beating continuously. As mayonnaise thickens, add curdled mixture a bit more quickly until all has been incorporated.*

Weather conditions affect mayonnaise *When skies are overcast and a summer storm threatens, mayonnaise will just not work, however carefully it is made.*

MAYONNAISE IN BLENDER

1 large egg
½ level teaspoon dry, or 1 level
teaspoon prepared, mustard
½ level teaspoon salt
Pinch cayenne pepper
½ level teaspoon sugar
shake white pepper
½ pint groundnut oil
4 tablespoons mild vinegar
(or mixture groundnut and corn)
1 tablespoon boiling water

An easy one for those with blenders. The texture is slightly more aerated than standard mayonnaise because both the egg yolk and white are used but otherwise it is excellent and blissfully quick to make.

Put first six ingredients, and 4 tablespoons oil, into blender goblet. Blend for a few seconds or until smooth. Remove lid—or cap in lid—and with blender at medium speed, add half remaining oil in slow, steady stream followed by half vinegar. Cover. Blend until thick. Uncover. Add rest of oil and vinegar. (2 tablespoons mild vinegar and 2 tablespoons lemon juice may be used.) Cover. Blend until smooth. Stop machine. Stir water into mayonnaise. Transfer to bowl. Cover. Store in cool larder or least cold part of refrigerator up to 2 weeks.

CHEESE TART

serves 4

6 ounces short crust pastry
(made with 6 ounces flour)
6 ounces strong Cheddar cheese, grated
¼ pint and 4 tablespoons milk
2 eggs and 1 yolk
salt and pepper to taste

Somewhat reminiscent of the French Quiche Lorraine, this tart contains no bacon but a fair proportion of cheese. Ideal, in fact, for vegetarians.

Preheat oven to hot, 425°F or Gas 7 (220°C). Roll out pastry on floured surface. Use to line 8-inch flan ring standing on lightly greased baking tray. Cover base with all but 1 ounce cheese. Beat milk, eggs and yolk well together. Season. Pour into flan case. Sprinkle rest of cheese on top. Put into oven. Immediately reduce temperature to moderate, 350°F or Gas 4 (180°C). Bake about 25–30 minutes or until pastry and filling are both golden. Remove flan ring. Cut tart into 4 wedges. Serve hot with salad.

For speed *Use 1 small packet frozen short crust pastry (thawed first) instead of homemade.*

ROESTI

serves 6

3 pounds potatoes, well-washed
1 large onion
4 tablespoons dripping
salt and pepper to taste

A well-known Swiss potato speciality, delicious with eggs and bacon.

Boil potatoes in skins. Drain. When cool enough to handle, remove skins. Grate potatoes coarsely. Finely chop onion. In large frying pan, heat dripping until hot. Add onion. Fry until golden. Add potatoes, Mix well. Sprinkle generously with salt and pepper to taste. Leave, uncovered, over low heat until golden brown crust forms on base of potato 'pancake'. Turn out on to warm plate. Cut into wedges. Serve straight away.

Austria

GOULASH SOUP

serves 5–6

1 large onion
1 tablespoon dried red and green
pepper flakes
hot water
2 rashers streaky bacon, chopped
1 ounce dripping
8 ounces beef shin, cut into small cubes
1 level tablespoon cornflour
1 level tablespoon paprika
2 level tablespoons tomato
concentrate (can or tube)
1 level teaspoon sugar
½ level teaspoon caraway seeds
2 pints water
salt and pepper to taste

Chop onion. Cover pepper flakes with hot water. Leave 10 minutes. Drain. Fry bacon in dripping 3 minutes. Add onion and pepper flakes. Fry gently 7 minutes or until pale gold. Add beef. Fry little more briskly until well-sealed and brown. Stir in all remaining ingredients in order listed. Bring to boil, stirring. Reduce heat. Cover. Simmer gently 1½ hours or until meat is tender. Stir occasionally. Serve piping hot.

Goulash Soup with Yogurt *If liked, top each serving with 1 tablespoon natural yogurt.*

Goulash Soup with Sausages *If preferred, omit meat altogether and add 6 Frankfurter sausages about 7 minutes before soup is*
ready. As there is no need to wait for meat to tenderize, simmer soup only 45 minutes.

Goulash Soup with Vegetables *Make Goulash Soup as directed. Add 2 to 3 boiled potatoes and 1 tablespoon cooked peas to each serving.*

CLEAR SOUP WITH SEMOLINA DUMPLINGS

serves 4

1 ounce margarine or dripping
1 egg, lightly beaten
2½ ounces coarse semolina
½ level teaspoon salt
light sprinkling pepper
1½ pints freshly made chicken or
beef stock (use cubes)
chopped parsley or chives

Cream margarine or dripping. Gradually beat in egg. Work in semolina. Add salt and pepper. Cover. Leave to stand 1 hour. Bring stock to boil. Using teaspoon dipped in water, scoop out pieces of dumpling mixture and drop gently into soup. Simmer 15 minutes. Ladle into warm soup bowls. Sprinkle with parsley or chives.

Vegetarian note *Use water instead of stock and include 3 level teaspoons yeast extract, and 1 level teaspoon onion salt instead of the ½ teaspoon salt listed in ingredients.*

WIENER SCHNITZEL

serves 4

4 pieces spare rib of pork, without bone
salt and pepper
flour
1 egg
2 teaspoons water
breadcrumbs
fat for deep frying

Perhaps one of the best-known dishes from Austria is the Schnitzel; veal, flattened until paper thin, coated with egg and crumbs and fried. This would be all too easy if veal fillet were only cheaper. But it isn't, so instead I use pork and challenge anyone to tell the difference !

Ask the butcher to beat each piece of spare rib until very thin—as he would veal. If he proves unwilling, this can be done at home by placing each piece of pork between 2 sheets of grease-proof paper and beating with rolling pin until flattened and very thin. Trim off surplus fat (which may be rendered down and used as dripping). Snip edges of each piece of pork with scissors to prevent them curling as they fry. Sprinkle with salt and pepper, then lightly coat all over with flour. Beat the egg and water together, dip each piece of pork in the mixture and then toss in crumbs. Leave 15 minutes for coating to harden. Heat fat until hot but not smoking. Add pork, 2 pieces at a time, so that they have room to float. Lower heat slightly. Fry 7–10 minutes. Drain well on paper towels. Accompany with lemon wedges.

Wiener Schnitzel Holstein *Make exactly as previous recipe but before serving, top each piece of pork with freshly fried egg.*

Wiener Schnitzel with Cheese *If liked, coat meat with egg and equal quantities of crumbs and dry cheese, very finely grated.*

Breadcrumbs for coating *When you next have a moderate oven going for a couple of hours or so, cover large baking tray with slices of stale white bread; crusts and all! Let them dry out and turn pale in colour. When completely cold, crush into fine crumbs with rolling pin. Alternatively, break bread up into small pieces and put, a few at a time, into blender goblet. Run machine until crumbs are fine. These crumbs are ideal for coating all kinds of food, and are superior to those glaring yellow ones to be found in packets.*

Breadcrumbs for stuffings *De-crust a small, day-old loaf and grate the bread. Alternatively, cube bread, put into blender goblet and run machine until crumbs are fine enough.*

STUFFED GREEN PEPPERS

serves 4

4 large green peppers
boiling water
1 ounce lard
1 large onion, chopped
4 rashers streaky bacon, chopped
8 ounces raw minced beef
4 ounces long grain rice
½ pint water
salt and pepper to taste
¼ pint tomato juice (can or bottle)

During the summer months, when imported green peppers are at their cheapest, this is a good dish to try, for it is both filling and appetizing.

Cut tops off peppers and reserve. Remove inside fibres and seeds. Cover peppers and reserved tops with boiling water. Leave 5 minutes. Strain. Leave peppers upside down to drain on paper towels. Heat lard in pan. Add onion and bacon. Cover. Fry about 10 minutes or until pale gold. Add beef. Fry little more briskly until well browned, breaking it up with a fork all the time. Add rice and water. Season. Bring to boil. Lower heat. Cover. Simmer 10 minutes. Remove from heat. Pack into peppers. Arrange, side by side, in a fairly deep heatproof dish. Add pepper tops. Pour tomato juice gently over peppers into dish. Cover with lid or foil. Cook in centre of moderate oven, 350°F or Gas 4 (180°C) 35–40 minutes or until peppers are soft.

To vary *Use beef stock or dry cider instead of tomato juice.*

CHICKEN PAPRIKA
(GOULASH)

serves 6

2 ounces lard or dripping
2 large onions, chopped
1 garlic clove, chopped
1 medium green pepper,
de-seeded and chopped
1 medium boiling fowl, cut into
serving size pieces
flour
1 medium can (about 1 pound) tomatoes
1 level tablespoon tomato concentrate
(can or tube)
1 level tablespoon paprika
1 level teaspoon sugar
½ pint water
2 level teaspoons salt
pepper to taste
½ level teaspoon caraway seeds
(optional)

I like this one because boiling fowl, cheaper than any other, can be used to advantage.

Heat lard in large pan. Add onions, garlic and green pepper. Cover. Fry gently 10–12 minutes or until pale gold. Coat fowl with flour. Add to pan. Fry briskly until browned all over. Remove from pan. Add all remaining ingredients to pan. Bring to boil. Lower heat. Replace chicken. Cover. Simmer gently 2–2½ hours or until chicken is tender. Stir frequently and add little extra water if sauce seems to be thickening up too much. Accompany with freshly boiled potatoes or noodles.

For luxury touch *Stir in 1 carton (¼ pint) natural yogurt or soured cream, just before serving.*

To pressure cook *After replacing chicken in sauce, pressure cook for 30 minutes at 15 pounds pressure.*

Meat Paprika (or Goulash) *Make exactly as Chicken Paprika, substituting 1½–2 pounds beef shin, pie veal or stewing pork for fowl. (A mixture of meats makes for an interesting combination.) Simmer between 1½–2 hours, depending on meat used.*

Meat Ball Paprika (or Goulash) *Well season 1½ pounds lean minced beef. Roll into small balls. Coat with flour. Fry as for chicken. Remove from pan. Simmer Paprika Sauce (covered) about 30–40 minutes. Replace Meat Balls. Cover. Simmer further 20–25 minutes.*

POTATO PAPRIKA

serves 6

2 pounds potatoes
1 ounce lard or dripping
1 large onion, chopped
6 streaky bacon rashers, chopped
1 level tablespoon paprika
2 level teaspoons salt
¼–½ level teaspoon caraway seeds
cold water

This teams happily with all types of sausages. *Note* Winter potatoes give the most satisfactory results. New or spring and summer potatoes are not particularly suitable for this recipe.

Peel potatoes. Wash. Cut into fairly big dice. Melt lard in large pan. Add onion and bacon. Fry gently until pale gold. Stir in paprika, salt and caraway seeds. Add potatoes. Just cover with water. Bring slowly to boil. Lower heat. Cover. Simmer 20 minutes or until potatoes are just tender.

AUSTRIAN SWEET-SOUR LIVER

serves 4

1 ounce lard or dripping
1 medium onion, chopped
1 pound pig's or lamb's liver, sliced
salt and pepper
1 level desertspoon flour
¼ pint boiling water
4 tablespoons natural yogurt
1 tablespoon vinegar
2 level teaspoons sugar

Heat lard in frying pan. Add onion. Cover. Fry gently about 10 minutes or until pale gold.

Meanwhile, season liver well with salt and pepper. Coat with flour. Add to pan. Fry on both sides until crisp and golden. Remove liver to plate. Stir flour into pan juices. Gradually blend in water. Bring to boil, stirring. Add remaining ingredients. Stir well. Adjust seasoning to taste. Replace liver. Mix thoroughly with sauce. Cover. Reheat gently about 10–15 minutes. Serve with boiled potatoes or noodles and green vegetables to taste.

APPLE STRUDEL

serves 8–10

Pastry

8 ounces plain flour
¼ level teaspoon salt
2 tablespoons salad oil
¼ pint lukewarm water

Filling

2 ounces table margarine, melted
(use butter for special occasions)
2 level tablespoons fresh white
breadcrumbs
1 large stale macaroon, crushed
2 pounds cooking apples, peeled and
very thinly sliced
2 ounces raisins
2 level teaspoons cinnamon
3 level tablespoons vanilla sugar (caster)
1 extra ounce margarine (or butter)
icing sugar for sprinkling over top

Easy when you know how and well worth the effort involved, for home-made Apple Strudel has a totally different flavour from shop bought, is considerably cheaper and is a practical way of using up garden cookers.

To make pastry, sift flour and salt into bowl. Make well in centre. Pour in oil and water. Mix to soft dough with finger tips. Knead good 20 minutes or until dough is smooth and pliable and no longer sticks to fingers. If, after this time, dough remains tacky, work in little more flour. Return dough to bowl. Cover with cloth. Leave to rest for 30 minutes. Cover large part of work surface with boldly patterned tablecloth (old one will do). Flour fairly heavily. Put dough in middle. Roll in all directions until *very thin*, keeping rolling pin well

floured. When pattern of cloth shows through, gently pull dough outwards (it should react and stretch like chewing gum!) and continue pulling until large and paper-thin; ignore irregular shape but avoid tears. Brush all over with melted margarine. Sprinkle with crumbs and macaroon. Cover with apples to within 1 inch of edges. Sprinkle with raisins, cinnamon and vanilla sugar. Fold ½-inch edges of pastry over filling. Roll up like Swiss roll, moving cloth forwards as you do so. Roll Strudel carefully on to well-greased baking tray. Top with thin flakes of margarine. Bake in centre of moderately hot oven, 375°F or Gas 5 (190°C) about 45 minutes or until pale gold. Remove from oven. Dust heavily with sifted icing sugar. Serve while still warm. Very good just as it is but may also be topped with single cream, whipped double cream, dessert topping, undiluted evaporated milk or scoops of vanilla ice cream.

CHEESE AND CHERRY STRUDEL

serves 8–10

Instead of apples, beat 1 pound curd cheese (available from most delicatessen counters) with 3 ounces vanilla sugar (caster), 1 whole egg, large pinch of salt and enough milk to give creamy but not wet consistency. Spread over with pastry to within ½ inch of edges. Drain 1 medium can cherries (Morello cherries are best but not always available). Remove stones. Arrange fruit on top of cheese filling. Roll up. Top with flakes of margarine. Bake as Apple Strudel.

To vary *Dot cheese mixture with blobs of black cherry jam instead of using canned cherries.*

Cheese and Apricot Strudel *Add 1 teaspoon (or more to taste) almond essence to cheese mixture above. Top with blobs of fruity apricot jam.*

VANILLA SUGAR

In northern Europe most cooks use vanilla sugar; it has a far more realistic flavour than bottled essence. If you want to flavour cakes, desserts, etc., with vanilla, just fill an air-tight storage jar with caster sugar and put in a vanilla pod. Leave to stand about 1 week before using, to give the vanilla time to penetrate sugar. As sugar gets used up, replace with more sugar. Keep this up until the pod loses its aroma ; about 6–8 months. The same may also be done with sifted icing sugar.

CINNAMON SUGAR

Another useful addition in the store cupboard. Either make as Vanilla Sugar, putting a cinnamon stick into sugar, or combine every pound caster sugar with 2–4 level teaspoons ground cinnamon. This is very useful for flavouring stewed apples and pears and for sprinkling over pastry-topped fruit pies and milk puddings.

SALZBURGER 'FRITTERS'

serves 4

**2 heaped tablespoons icing sugar
(or vanilla icing sugar)
3 large eggs
½ teaspoon vanilla essence
(omit if using vanilla sugar)
1 level teaspoon cornflour
1 ounce best quality margarine
(preferably with percentage of butter)**

These are a cross between fritters and a soufflé omelet and should be attempted only when money is more precious than time ! However, they make an unusual and fun dessert, especially if family, guests and what have you are eating in the kitchen.

Preheat oven to very hot, 450°F or Gas 8 (230°C). Sift icing sugar. Separate eggs. Beat yolks with 1 dessertspoon sugar, essence (if used) and cornflour. Beat egg whites to stiff snow. Gently fold egg yolk mixture into them. Melt margarine in large, heavy pan. When hot but not smoking, add heaped tablespoon of egg mixture—well apart, building them up, rather than allowing them to flatten in pan. Cook ½ minute or until fritters have set underneath. Quickly transfer pan to oven and leave about 2–3 minutes or until tops are lightly

44

browned. Remove carefully from pan. Arrange on warm dish. Sprinkle with rest of sugar. Serve immediately.
Warning note Make sure handle of pan is heat-resistant, or it may melt somewhat and become misshapen while in the oven.

VIENNA BREAD

makes 4 loaves

**2 level teaspoons sugar
½ pint tepid milk (110°F)
¼ pint tepid water
3 level dessertspoons dried yeast granules
1½ pounds plain flour
2 level teaspoons salt
1 ounce table margarine**

Dissolve 1 teaspoon sugar in milk and water. Sprinkle yeast on top. Leave in warm place until mixture froths up (about 20 minutes). Sift flour, salt and remaining sugar into bowl. Rub in margarine. Work to dough with yeast liquid. Turn out on to floured surface. Knead 10–15 minutes or until smooth and elastic and no longer sticky. Add little extra flour if dough, after kneading, remains tacky. Return dough to clean and lightly greased bowl. Cover with greased polythene. Leave to rise at room temperature until dough doubles in size and springs back when pressed lightly with floured finger. Turn on to floured surface. Knead lightly until smooth. Divide into 4 equal-sized pieces. Roll each into oval shape, about 10 inches long. Roll each piece up from long side to form tight roll. Transfer to greased baking tray with join underneath. Cover with greased polythene. Leave at room temperature until loaves double in size. Make three or four diagonal cuts on each. Bake in centre of preheated very hot oven, 450°F or Gas 8 (230°C) in which one large or two small tins of water have been placed to create steamy atmosphere. Bake 15 minutes. Open oven door to allow steam to escape. Remove tins of water. Bake loaves further 15–20 minutes or until crusty and golden. Cool on wire rack.

Poppy Seed Bread *Just before baking, brush loaves lightly with beaten egg or milk and sprinkle with poppy seeds.*

Vienna Rolls *Divide Vienna Bread dough into 20 equal-sized pieces. Roll into ovals. Roll up tightly. Put on to two or three greased baking trays, with joins underneath. Cover with greased polythene. When double in size, make three diagonal cuts on each. Bake as given for bread, allowing 10 minutes with steam and 8–10 minutes without. Cool on wire rack.*

If using fresh yeast *Allow 1½ ounces and add to milk and water. Stir until dissolved. Sift 2 teaspoons sugar with flour, etc., instead of one.*

To speed up first rising *Stand bowl of dough in sink filled with hand-hot water.*

If using dough hook attachment of mixer *Put yeast liquid into bowl. Rub margarine into sifted dry ingredients. Add to yeast liquid. Mix for 1 minute at lowest speed to form dough. Increase speed slightly. Continue to knead further 2–3 minutes.*

Holland

THICK DUTCH PEA SOUP

serves about 8

1 pound split peas
6 pints water
1 pound boiling bacon
1 bacon knuckle
cold water
2 celery stalks, chopped
2 large leeks, trimmed, split,
washed and chopped
2 medium carrots, sliced
3 large potatoes, peeled and diced
salt and pepper to taste
chopped parsley

An immensely popular soup meal, served all over Holland during the winter months.

Wash peas. Soak overnight in 3 pints water. Put into large saucepan. Bring to boil. Lower heat. Cover. Meanwhile, put bacon and knuckle into separate pan. Cover with cold water. Bring to boil. Drain. Repeat once more. (This reduces excessive saltiness.) Add bacon and knuckle to peas in pan with remaining 3 pints water, prepared vegetables and salt and pepper to taste. (Take care with salt; bacon may produce enough by itself.) Bring to boil. Reduce heat. Cover. Simmer 2½–3 hours or until peas are tender, adding little extra water if soup seems to be thickening up too much. Stir frequently. To serve, pour soup into large warm plates and sprinkle heavily with parsley. Slice bacon and serve separately with rye bread and mustard (continental variety).

To vary *Use unsalted, fresh belly of pork instead of bacon. Include bacon knuckle and boil it up twice as directed above to reduce saltiness.*

Sieved Pea Soup *Remove bacon or meat and bones from soup. Rub soup through sieve or liquidize, a little at a time, in blender goblet. If too thick, thin down with milk or stock. Reheat before serving.*

Warning *Do not pressure cook this soup for there is a possibility that the vent will become blocked. In any case, the amounts of ingredients are too much for family-sized pressure cooker.*

CLEAR SOUP WITH PORK BALLS

serves 4

1½ pint well-flavoured chicken stock
(home-made is best; cubes will pass)
8 ounces pork sausagemeat
½ level teaspoon dry mustard
2 level tablespoons fresh white
breadcrumbs
1 egg, beaten
pepper to taste

Leave stock simmering over low heat. Meanwhile, combine sausagemeat with rest of ingredients. Shape into small balls. Drop into soup. Simmer 20 minutes.

To vary *8 ounces raw minced pork (not remains of joint) may be used instead of sausagemeat.*

Clear Soup with Pork and Onion Balls   *If liked, add 1 small grated onion to meat ball mixture (either sausagemeat or raw pork).*

LAYERED FISH HOT-POT

serves 4

**1 pound potatoes, par-boiled
2 pounds fresh cod or
coley fillet, cooked
2 medium onions, sliced
2½ ounces margarine
1½ ounces flour
½ pint milk
½ pint fish, vegetable or chicken stock
salt and pepper to taste
1–2 level teaspoons continental mustard
1 ounce Gouda cheese, grated**

Slice potatoes fairly thinly. Flake fish (remove any skin and bones). Fry onions gently in 1 ounce margarine until pale gold. In separate pan, melt remaining margarine. Stir in flour. Cook 2 minutes without browning. Gradually blend in milk and stock. Cook, stirring, until sauce comes to boil and thickens. Simmer 2 minutes. Season. Stir in mustard. Fill fairly deep greased casserole dish with alternate layers of potatoes, fish, fried onions and sauce, beginning and ending with potatoes. Sprinkle with cheese. Reheat and brown towards top of moderately hot oven, 400°F or Gas 6 (200°C) 20–30 minutes.

YEASTED HAM PANCAKES

allow 1–2 per person

**¼ pint lukewarm water
1 level teaspoon sugar
2 level teaspoons dried yeast
8 ounces plain flour
½ level teaspoon salt
1 large egg, beaten
¾ pint lukewarm milk
lard for frying
6 ounces lean ham, chopped
gravy**

Put water into jug. Add sugar. Stir to dissolve. Mix in yeast. Leave in warm place until mixture froths up; about 20–30 minutes. Meanwhile, sift flour and salt into bowl. Make central well. Mix to thick, smooth, creamy batter with yeast liquid, egg and half the milk. Beat well. Cover. Leave to stand in warm place 30 minutes. Stir in rest of milk. Beat well. Cover. Leave to stand in warm place 45–60 minutes. Grease large, heavy-based frying pan with lard. Heat until hot but not smoking. Pour in sufficient batter to cover base of pan. Sprinkle with ham. Cook over medium heat until golden. Turn over and cook other side until golden. Fold in half in pan. Slide out on to warm plate. Repeat with rest of batter mixture. Serve topped with hot gravy.

To vary *Use chopped boiled bacon instead of ham.*

Sweet Pancakes *Make exactly as Yeasted Ham Pancakes but omit ham. When cooked, sprinkle with lemon juice and sugar. Fold up. Serve as hot as possible.*

DUTCH LUNCH SNACK

serves 4

**4 large slices white, brown or
caraway-seed bread
table margarine
slices of cold cooked meat
(remains of joint will do)
4 freshly fried eggs
salt and pepper
1 pickled cucumber, sliced**

Spread slices of bread with margarine. Cover completely with meat. Top each with fried egg. Sprinkle with salt and pepper. Garnish with cucumber slices.

To vary *Instead of cold roast meat, spread slices of bread with liver sausage, liver pâté or meat paste. Alternatively, top with slices of corned beef, luncheon meat or shop-bought silverside or brisket (already cooked).*

NASI GORENG

serves 4–6

1 large onion, coarsely grated
3 ounces margarine
12 ounces cold roast meat or
luncheon meat
12 ounces cooked long grain rice
(about 6 ounces raw)
12 ounces cold cooked vegetables
(diced roots, chopped greens, sweet
corn, green sliced beans, pieces of
cauliflower, etc.)
½–1 tablespoon Worcester sauce
1 tablespoon tomato ketchup
1 hard-boiled egg, sliced
2 tomatoes, skinned and sliced

There is a strong Indonesian influence in the cuisine of Holland and this recipe is a typical example.

Fry onion in 2 ounces margarine over low heat until pale gold; 7–10 minutes. Dice or coarsely chop meat. Add to onion. Fry 5 minutes, stirring. Add all remaining ingredients (including last ounce margarine) except eggs and tomatoes. Heat through until piping hot, stirring frequently with fork. Pile into warm dish. Garnish with egg and tomatoes.

To prevent sticking *Although few recipes for the above suggest this, I usually heat the mixture with 2–3 tablespoons stock or water. It fluffs the rice better and stops sticking.*

DUTCH SPICED STEAK

serves 4–6

2 ounces dripping
2 large onions, chopped
2 pounds stewing steak, in one piece
flour
1 large bay leaf
½ level teaspoon ground nutmeg
2 cloves
½ pint beef stock (use cubes)
salt and pepper to taste

Heat dripping in heavy stew pan. Add onions. Fry gently until golden; 7–10 minutes. Coat meat all over with flour. Add to pan. Fry fairly briskly until all sides are well-browned and sealed. Add all remaining ingredients. Bring slowly to boil. Lower heat. Cover. Simmer gently 2 hours or until meat is tender. Add little extra stock or water if liquor seems to be thickening up too much. Stir frequently. To serve, cut meat into slices. Coat with sauce. Accompany with vegetables to taste.

To vary *Use tomato juice or vegetable water instead of stock. Include ½–1 teaspoon continental mustard and/or Worcester sauce.*

SEMOLINA PUDDING WITH JAM SAUCE

serves 4

1 pint milk, skimmed if liked
2 ounces fine semolina
3 level tablespoons caster sugar
½ level teaspoon finely grated
lemon peel
1 egg, separated
knob margarine

Sauce

1 level dessertspoon cornflour
¼ pint water
4 level dessertspoons raspberry
jam or redcurrant jelly

Pour milk into pan. Add semolina, sugar and peel. Cook, stirring, until mixture comes to boil and thickens. Simmer 3–4 minutes. Remove from heat. Cool slightly. Beat in egg yolk and margarine. Beat egg white to stiff snow. Fold into semolina mixture. Spoon into four dishes. Chill. To make sauce, mix cornflour to smooth cream with water. Pour into pan. Add jam or jelly. Cook, stirring, until sauce thickens and clears. Pour hot sauce over cold puddings.

To vary *Omit lemon peel, and flavour either with vanilla sugar or vanilla essence. Also good is almond flavoured pudding with apricot jam sauce.*

DUTCH SHORTBREAD

about 1 dozen pieces

8 ounces table margarine, softened
8 ounces soft brown sugar
1 egg
8 ounces plain flour
1 level teaspoon cinnamon
½ level teaspoon salt

Preheat oven to moderate, 325°F or Gas 4

(180°C). Cream margarine and sugar until light and fluffy. Beat in egg. Gradually work in flour sifted with remaining ingredients. Press into ungreased Swiss roll tin. Bake in centre of oven until pale gold; 30–40 minutes. Remove from oven. Cut into twelve pieces while still warm. Remove from tin. Cool on wire rack. Store in air-tight tin when cold.

To vary *Use caster sugar instead of brown. Flavour with ½–1 level teaspoon finely grated lemon peel instead of cinnamon.*

Scandinavia

DANISH FRIKADELLER
(MEAT BALLS)

serves 6–8

1 pound raw minced beef
8 ounces raw minced pork
(or use pork sausagemeat)
1–1½ level teaspoons salt
1 medium onion, finely grated
½ level teaspoon ground allspice
4 ounces fresh white breadcrumbs
1 egg, beaten
¼ pint milk, skimmed if liked
pepper to taste
dripping for frying

Combine meats with all remaining ingredients except dripping. Mix thoroughly. With damp hands, shape into ovals about ¾ inch in thickness. Heat dripping about 1 inch deep in large, shallow pan. When hot but not smoking, add Frikadeller. Fry gently on both sides until cooked through and golden. Drain on paper towels. Serve hot with red cabbage (page 93), and Caramel Potatoes (see below).

CARAMEL POTATOES

serves about 6

1½ pounds small new potatoes, freshly cooked
1 teaspoon hot water

1 ounce caster sugar
2 ounces table margarine

Drain potatoes thoroughly. Leave until cold. Put water and sugar into heavy-based frying pan. Leave over low heat until sugar dissolves. Add margarine and leave until melted. Increase heat slightly and add potatoes. Fry gently, turning frequently, until golden-brown and lightly glazed.

If using 'old' potatoes *Par-boil first, cut into pieces the size of new potatoes and cook as above.*

Summer Frikadeller *Leave until completely cold and serve with mixed salad.*

FINNISH HOT-POT

serves 4–6

1 pound middle neck of lamb
8 ounces beef shin
8 ounces stewing pork
4 medium onions, sliced
1 large bay leaf
salt and pepper to taste
1–1½ pounds medium potatoes, peeled and quartered
water

48

Cut lamb into neat pieces. Remove and discard as much surplus fat as possible. Cut beef and pork into smallish cubes. Fill heavy casserole dish with alternate layers of meat and onions, tucking in crumbled bay leaf and sprinkling salt and pepper between layers. Add potatoes and just cover with water. Cover with lid or foil. Cook in centre of moderate oven, 350°F or Gas 4 (180°C), 1–1½ hours or until meat is tender. Uncover during last 30 minutes for top layer of potatoes and meat to brown. Serve with rye bread and green vegetables to taste.

NORWEGIAN FISH BALLS WITH PIQUANT SAUCE

serves 4–6

about 1 pound fish trimmings
2 large onions, quartered
1 medium carrot, coarsely sliced
1 celery stalk
2 pints water
2–3 level teaspoons salt
½ small bay leaf
2 cloves
2 pounds cod or coley fillet, skinned
1 medium onion
3 ounces fresh white breadcrumbs
1 large egg, beaten
salt and pepper to taste
2 ounces margarine
2 ounces flour
¼ pint milk
1–2 level teaspoons continental mustard
1 tablespoon tomato ketchup
2 teaspoons Worcester sauce
1 teaspoon vinegar
¼ level teaspoon mixed spice

To make fish stock, put trimmings into pan with quartered onions, carrot, celery, water, salt, bay leaf and cloves. Bring to boil. Lower heat. Cover. Simmer 1 hour. Strain. Mince fish fillet and onion (not too finely). Alternatively, chop fairly finely. Combine with crumbs, egg and salt and pepper to taste. Mix thoroughly. Shape into smallish balls with damp hands. Bring strained stock to boil. Add fish balls. Lower heat. Cover. Simmer gently 30 minutes. Lift out of stock with draining spoon. Put into serving dish. Keep hot. Strain stock, reserving ¾ pint. Melt margarine in clean pan. Stir in flour. Cook 2 minutes without browning. Gradually blend

in fish stock and milk. Cook, stirring, until sauce comes to boil and thickens. Add all remaining ingredients. Simmer 3 minutes, stirring continuously. Pour over fish balls. Serve with boiled potatoes and carrots.

Warning Do not attempt to make these fish balls with previously cooked or left-over fish because they will not hold together.

To vary *Instead of mustard, ketchup and Worcester sauce, the fish sauce itself may be flavoured with curry powder (between 2–5 level teaspoons only). Vinegar should be included.*

NORWEGIAN HASH

serves 6

1½ ounces margarine
1½ ounces flour
¾ pint beef stock
1 gravy cube
salt and pepper to taste
1 level tablespoon tomato concentrate
(can or tube)
1 pound cold cooked roast meat, poultry
or boiled bacon, coarsely chopped
8 ounces cooked peas
4 ounces left-over diced vegetables
(potatoes, carrots, swedes, celery,
sweet corn, etc)

Melt margarine in saucepan. Stir in flour. Cook 3–4 minutes or until just beginning to turn golden, stirring. Gradually blend in stock. Crumble in cube. Season. Bring to boil, stirring. Add tomato concentrate, meat, etc. Boil gently further 15 minutes. Add peas and vegetables. Reduce heat. Simmer gently 10 minutes or until piping hot. Serve with boiled potatoes or rice.

Mixed Meat Hash *Make as above but if preferred, use combination of meats such as 6 ounces cooked chicken, 6 ounces cooked lamb or beef and 4 ounces boiled bacon or ham.*

SWEDISH FRIKADELLER WITH SAUCE

serves 6–8

Make Danish Frikadeller (page 48). Keep hot. Stand pan—including pan juices in which Frikadeller were cooked—over medium heat. Stir in 1 level tablespoon flour. Cook until flour begins to deepen in colour. Gradually blend in ¼ pint stock. Cook, stirring, until mixture comes to boil and thickens. Simmer 2 minutes. Beat in 4 tablespoons undiluted evaporated milk, 1 tablespoon lemon juice and 2 level tablespoons chopped parsley. Season well. Pour over Frikadeller. Accompany with redcurrant jelly or cranberry sauce, boiled potatoes and gherkins.

DANISH HERRINGS WITH CURRY SAUCE

serves 4

4 large herrings, cleaned and boned
1 large egg
2 teaspoons water ⟩ beaten together
lightly toasted breadcrumbs for coating
dripping or oil for frying
1 ounce table margarine
1 ounce flour
2–4 level teaspoons curry powder
½ pint skimmed milk
large pinch sugar
salt and pepper to taste
squeeze of lemon juice
½ level teaspoon paprika
chopped parsley or chives

Wash and dry herrings. Coat with egg and water. Toss in crumbs. Fry in hot dripping or oil until crisp and golden on both sides, and also cooked through. Remove from pan. Drain on paper towels. Keep hot. To make sauce, melt margarine in pan. Stir in flour and curry powder. Cook 2 minutes without browning. Gradually blend in milk. Cook, stirring, until sauce comes to boil and thickens. Add all remaining ingredients except parsley or chives. Stir well. Heat through 2 minutes. Arrange herrings on four warm plates. Coat with sauce. Sprinkle with parsley or chives.

Other milks *If preferred, use fresh milk or diluted evaporated.*

To vary *For a soft, golden-brown coating, toss herrings in flour then dip in egg beaten with a little milk. Fry as directed.*

DANISH BACON MOUSSE

serves 4

8 ounces cooked bacon
aspic jelly powder to set 1¼ pints water
1¼ pints boiling water
2 large cooked carrots
3 medium gherkins
4 tablespoons mayonnaise or salad cream
1 tablespoon tomato ketchup

Cut bacon into tiny cubes. Dissolve aspic jelly in boiling water. Cool slightly. Pour a little jelly into 2½-pint fancy mould, first rinsed with cold water. Leave until half-set. Cut carrots and gherkins into rounds. Press about half carrots and gherkins, with few ham cubes, into half-set jelly in mould. (When turned out, pieces will show through jelly as decoration.) Cover with layer of liquid aspic. Chill until firm. Leave remaining aspic jelly in cold place until consistency of unbeaten egg whites. Whip lightly then beat in all remaining ingredients. Spoon gently into mould. Chill until firm and set. Unmould and serve as main course with summer salad.

To make it easier to turn out mould *Brush mould all over with corn oil instead of rinsing with cold water.*

OPEN SANDWICHES

Norway, Denmark and Sweden are especially known all over the world for their colourful and appetizing open sandwiches and below is a selection of some economical ideas for the famous Smorrebrod. Any bread—white, brown, Danish rye, etc.—may be used as a foundation, as can crackers, crispbreads and water biscuits. All bread and biscuits should be well-covered with table margarine, or butter for special occasions—particularly Danish which contributes its own special flavour. These act as insulation and prevent moisture from toppings seeping through to bread, etc., and making it soggy. Open sandwiches, with bread as base, should be served on plates and accompanied with cutlery; they are awkward to eat if held in the hand.

When catering *Allow 3–4 large open sandwiches per person if main meal; 1 or 2 if supper or lunch snack.*

Scarlet Pimpernel *Spread bread or biscuits with margarine. Cover with lettuce leaves. Top with grated Cheddar cheese. Decorate each with 2 tomato slices and teaspoon sweet pickle.*

Little Mermaid *Spread bread or biscuits with margarine. Cover with lettuce leaves. Top with pieces of pickled herrings (rollmops). Add dessertspoon of canned or home-made potato salad to centre of each. Sprinkle with mustard and cress and paprika.*

Sunburst *Spread bread or biscuits with margarine, followed by fish paste to taste. Top each with shredded lettuce or shredded white cabbage, which has been mixed with a small quantity of salad cream. Decorate with slices of hard-boiled egg and orange twists.*

Orange Twists *Slice unpeeled oranges fairly thinly. Make a slit in each slice from centre to outside edge and then shape into S-shaped twists.*

Swedish Special *Spread bread or biscuits with margarine followed by meat paste to taste. Top each with line of cold, lightly scrambled egg. Sprinkle with chopped chives and paprika. Add sprig of watercress to each.*

The Gay Hussars *Spread bread or biscuits with margarine. Cover with slices of luncheon meat. Add a tablespoon of chopped, pickled, beetroot to each. Top with a teaspoon of natural yogurt. Decorate with two trimmed spring onions.*

Country Cottage *Spread bread or biscuits with margarine. Cover first with lettuce leaves and then spread with cottage cheese. Add 2–3 canned peach slices and roll of grilled bacon to each.*

To make the bacon rolls *choose long streaky bacon rashers. Remove the rinds and discard them. Cut each rasher in half across the centre and roll it up like a Swiss roll. Thread these rolls on to one or two skewers. Grill until cooked, turning frequently.*

Garden of Eden *Spread bread or biscuits with margarine. Cover with slices of cold roast pork, bacon (boiled) or roast lamb. Top with slices unpeeled rosy apples, first dipped in lemon juice to prevent browning. Add dollop salad cream to each. Sprinkle lightly with curry powder.*

Country Style *Spread bread or biscuits with margarine. Cover with slices of liver sausage or spread with liver paste. Top with onion rings. Put dollop of cranberry sauce or redcurrant jelly on to centre of each. Garnish with sprig of watercress.*

Mediterranean *Spread bread or biscuits with margarine. Cover with alternate rows of sliced hard-boiled eggs and sliced tomatoes. Garnish each with 2 anchovy fillets and 1 black or green olive.*

Beefeater *Spread bread or biscuits with margarine followed by thin layer of horseradish sauce. Top with slices of cold roast beef or corned beef. Garnish each with mound of shredded lettuce or shredded white cabbage, first mixed with a little salad cream.*

Old Dutch *Spread bread or biscuits with margarine. Cover with slices of Gouda or Edam cheese. Grate 1 small beetroot, 1 hard-boiled egg and 1 small onion. Combine with salad cream. Put tablespoon on to centre of each sandwich. Top with slices of pickled cucumber.*

Sea Tang *Spread bread or biscuits with margarine. Cover with thin slices raw kipper fillet. This is delicious and tastes a bit like smoked salmon. Sprinkle with lemon juice and freshly milled black pepper. Garnish with onion rings or small spring onions and lettuce leaves.*

RODGROD MED FLODE

serves 6

8 ounces blackcurrants, stemmed
½ pint water
8 ounces redcurrants, stemmed
8 ounces berries
(strawberries, raspberries,
elderberries, etc.)
8 ounces caster sugar
arrowroot (available from chemists)

This is a type of Danish blancmange-cum-jelly, made with late summer fruits. Whipped cream is the traditional accompaniment but dessert topping or canned custard or cream make admirable substitutes.

Put blackcurrants and water into saucepan. Bring slowly to boil. Lower heat. Cover. Simmer gently 20 minutes or until currant skins are tender. Add remaining fruits. Cook until very soft. Add sugar. Stir until dissolved. Simmer further 10 minutes. Strain. Allow ½ ounce arrowroot to each pint juice. Blend to smooth cream with little cold water. Combine with strained juice. Cook, stirring, until mixture comes to boil and thickens. It should also look clear. Cool slightly. Pour into serving dish. Chill.

PEASANT GIRL WITH VEIL

serves 6

3 ounces margarine
8 ounces fresh breadcrumbs
3 ounces soft brown sugar
2 pounds cooking apples
little water
caster sugar
dessert topping or canned custard
drinking chocolate powder

A pleasant autumn sweet slightly resembling, as you will see, our own Apple Charlotte.

Melt margarine in large frying pan. Add crumbs and sugar. Cook over low heat until golden, stirring continuously with fork. Remove from

52

heat. Leave on one side. Peel, core and slice apples. Cook, with few tablespoons water, until soft and pulpy. Add sugar to taste. Beat until smooth. Leave until cold. Fill glass serving bowl (deep rather than wide) with alternate layers of apples and crumb mixture. Cover completely with dessert topping or custard. Sprinkle lightly with chocolate powder. Chill before serving.

Yeasted Spice Breads

Light-textured and spicy yeast cakes—known as Coffee Breads because they are served at mid-morning or mid-afternoon with coffee— are immensely popular in Scandinavia. Here is a selection of recipes, all using one basic and very economical dough mixture.

SPICY COFFEE BREAD

makes 1 loaf

1 level teaspoon sugar
¼ pint and 5 tablespoons lukewarm milk
1 level tablespoon dried yeast
2 ounces table margarine
1 pound plain flour, sifted
1 level teaspoon mixed spice
2 ounces soft brown sugar

Glaze

1 small egg
1 level teaspoon caster sugar
2 teaspoons water

Dissolve 1 teaspoon sugar in ¼ pint warm milk. Sprinkle yeast on top. Leave in warm place until mixture froths up; about 20–30 minutes. Melt margarine over low heat. Leave on one side to cool. Sift flour and spice into bowl. Add sugar. Mix to dough with yeast liquid, remaining milk and melted margarine. If very sticky, use little extra flour. Knead on floured surface until dough is smooth, elastic and no longer tacky; 15–20 minutes. Return to clean and oiled bowl. Cover with greased polythene.

Leave to rise in warm place (try warm linen cupboard, or a sink containing a few inches of hand-hot water), about 45 minutes or until dough doubles in size and springs back when pressed lightly with floured finger. Preheat oven to moderately hot, 400°F or Gas 6 (200°C). Turn risen dough on to floured surface. Knead lightly until smooth. Turn into well-greased 1-pound loaf tin. Cover with greased polythene. Leave to rise in warm place until dough reaches top of tin and is slightly domed. To glaze, beat egg with sugar and water. Gently brush over top of dough. Bake in centre of oven 40–50 minutes or until well-risen and golden. Turn out of tin. Cool on wire rack. Cut into slices when cold and either eat plain or accompany with butter or margarine and jam or honey.

If possible, make and eat on same day. If not, put loaf into plastic bag. Seal. Refrigerate until needed (no longer than 1 week). Two hours before serving, remove from refrigerator. Leave at room temperature about 1¾ hours. Afterwards warm through in hot oven, 425°F or Gas 7 (220°C) for 10–15 minutes.

Lukewarm *When working with yeast, the liquid must be of the correct temperature for dough to rise effectively. In this case lukewarm means a temperature of 110°F—i.e. when little finger is dipped into the milk, the milk should feel pleasantly warm; neither hot nor cold.*

Using fresh yeast *If this is readily available, use it instead of the dried. Omit teaspoon sugar in recipe. Heat milk and margarine together until lukewarm. Add 1 ounce fresh yeast. Stir until dissolved. Add to dry ingredients.*

First rising of dough—alternative times *This is useful to know, because rising times may be satisfactorily adjusted to suit your own day's plans. If leaving dough in kitchen, allow about 1½–2 hours. If a slow, overnight rise is preferred, put dough into greased plastic bag, close at top (leaving room for dough to expand) and leave up to 12 hours in refrigerator or cold larder. Allow dough to reach room temperature before kneading.*

Freezing uncooked dough *Sometimes it is convenient to make up more dough than is actually required and then deep freeze it for use later. After kneading thoroughly, divide dough*

up into 1-pound batches. Roll into large balls. Put into greased plastic bags. Seal tightly. Freeze straight away. Before use, unseal and open up bags to allow space for rising. Leave 5–6 hours at room temperature; overnight in refrigerator. When dough has risen to twice its original size, knead lightly. Shape and leave to rise for second time. Bake as directed in recipe. Freeze dough for up to 2 months.

Freezing baked coffee breads *Wrap in foil or polythene. Seal. Freeze for up to 1 month. To thaw, leave breads in their wrappers between 3–6 hours at kitchen temperature. If liked, they may be heated through quickly in a hot oven before serving.*

Fruity Plaits *Follow recipe for Spicy Coffee Bread but add 3–4 ounces mixed dried fruit with brown sugar. Divide dough in half. Divide each half into 3 pieces. Roll each piece into 20-inch long rope. Plait three together. Repeat with second portion of dough. Stand plaits on well-greased baking tray. Glaze with egg mixture. Bake in centre of oven (same temperature as Spicy Coffee Bread) for 30–40 minutes. Makes 2.*

Decorated Plaits *When cold, plaits may be covered with plain glacé icing and sprinkled with chopped glacé cherries or nuts.*

GLACE ICING

---

8 ounces icing sugar
water or lemon juice

Sift sugar into bowl. Mix to thickish icing with water or lemon juice, adding it teaspoon by teaspoon. Glacé icing very quickly becomes thin and over-runny if too much liquid is added.

Home-made Icing Sugar *Icing sugar is not always to hand and those with blenders can make it easily and quickly using either granulated or caster sugar. Just put required amount of sugar into blender goblets. Run machine until sugar is like fine powder. Use as required.*

CINNAMON RING BUNS

makes 16–18 buns

Make up dough as given in recipe for Spicy Coffee Bread (page 52). Roll out half-risen dough into 9-inch square, about ¼ inch thick. Brush with melted margarine. Sprinkle with two level tablespoons caster or soft brown sugar mixed with 1–2 level teaspoons cinnamon. Roll up like Swiss Roll. Cut into slices about ¾ inch thick. Stand on greased baking tray, leaving room between each. Repeat with second portion of dough. Cover with greased polythene. Leave in warm place until dough almost doubles in size. Bake in moderately hot oven, 375°F or Gas 5 (190°C) about 30 minutes. Serve fresh.

PLUM CAKE

serves 8

Roll out half the basic dough to fit well-greased tin, measuring approximately 7 by 11 by 1 inches. Cover with halved and stoned plums (about 1–1½ pounds) which have been *only half-cooked* in a little water and sugar. Place plums on dough, cut sides down. Brush with melted margarine. Sprinkle with caster sugar. Leave in warm place until dough reaches top of tin. Bake in centre of very hot oven, 450°F or Gas 8 (230°C) 20–25 minutes. Cut into portions. Serve hot or cold with custard, ice cream or dessert topping.

SCALLOPED CAKE

serves 8

To use up remaining half-risen dough (left over from previous recipe), cut into twelve pieces. Roll each into ball. Arrange in greased 7-inch sandwich tin placing nine round the edge and three in the centre. Leave in warm place, covered with greased polythene, until dough reaches top of tin and also fills it. Brush with melted margarine. Bake in centre of very hot oven, 450°F or Gas 8 (230°C) 30–40 minutes.

Cool on wire rack. Break apart when cool. Serve fresh with butter or margarine and jam, honey or lemon curd.

LIMPA BREAD

makes 1

¼ pint plus 4 tablespoons brown ale
3 level teaspoons caraway seeds
1 tablespoon malt vinegar
4 ounces black treacle
½ ounce fresh yeast
1 ounce cooking fat,
cut into small pieces
8 ounces rye flour
(available from health food shops)
1 level teaspoon salt
7 ounces plain white flour

From Sweden comes this unique, dark bread, flavoured with ale and caraway seeds and with a close and somewhat sticky texture, reminiscent of old-fashioned malt bread. Not everybody's 'cup of tea' I agree, but for those who enjoy new flavours and want something a bit unusual, this is a good one to try.

Put first four ingredients into saucepan. Heat slowly until lukewarm. (Do not overheat, or yeast will be destroyed and unable to work efficiently.) Remove from heat. Crumble in yeast. Stir until dissolved. Add fat. Mix well. Sift rye flour and salt into bowl. Add yeast liquid. Beat well. Gradually work in white flour. Turn dough on to floured surface. Knead 15–20 minutes or until smooth and elastic. Return to clean and lightly greased bowl. Cover with greased polythene. Leave to rise in warm place until double in size; 2–3 hours. Remove to floured surface. Knead lightly. Return to bowl. Cover. Leave to rise again until almost double; 45–60 minutes. Knead about 3 minutes on floured surface. Shape into round loaf. Stand on well-greased baking tray. Cover with greased polythene. Leave to rise until double in size; about 1 hour. Bake in centre of moderate oven, 350°F or Gas 4 (180°C) 30–40 minutes. Cool on wire rack. When cold, slice and spread with margarine or butter.

Spain

MOCK PAELLA

serves 4

**4 medium-sized joints roasting
chicken, skinned
3 tablespoons salad oil or melted dripping
3 rashers streaky bacon, chopped
1 garlic clove, chopped
8 ounces long grain rice
2 tomatoes, skinned and chopped
1 pint water
salt and pepper to taste
4 heaped tablespoons cooked green peas
12 bottled mussels,
soaked 1 hour in cold water**

Fry joints in hot oil or dripping until crisp and golden. Remove to plate. Add bacon and garlic to pan. Cover. Fry gently 7 minutes. Add rice. Cook further minute, stirring. Add tomatoes and water. Season. Bring to boil. Lower heat. Simmer 5 minutes. Remove from heat. Stir in peas. Transfer to casserole dish (wide rather than too deep). Place chicken joints on top. Cover. Cook in centre of moderate oven, 350°F or Gas 4 (180°C) 45 minutes. Add mussels. Return to oven. Cook, uncovered, further 15 minutes. If liked, garnish with strips of red canned pimiento before serving.

Chicken fat *If there are pieces of spare fat on chicken, remove and render down in saucepan over low heat. Use instead of oil or dripping for frying. Obliging butchers often have pieces of chicken fat available at minimal cost; it is worth asking. If chicken skin is fatty, add it to the pan as well because any fat adhering to it will also melt down.*

Saffron *This adds a traditional touch to Paella but is fairly expensive and available mainly from chemists. However, for special occasions, it should be included and this is what you do. Take two good pinches saffron stamens. (They look like golden brown threads.) Put into cup. Add 4 tablespoons boiling water. Leave overnight. Strain. When making Paella, use saffron water together with 1 pint less 4 tablespoons water. Saffron will add a golden colour to the rice and give a subtle and distinctive flavour.*

Turmeric *For golden colour without saffron flavour, add ½–1 level teaspoon turmeric powder with water. It is obtainable from most supermarkets and is cheaper than saffron.*

GAZPACHO
(CHILLED TOMATO SOUP)

serves 6

**1 pint canned tomato juice
2 tablespoons mild vinegar or lemon juice
2 tablespoons salad oil
2 ounces fresh white breadcrumbs
½ medium cucumber,
peeled and grated
2 large tomatoes, skinned and
finely chopped
1 small green pepper,
de-seeded and finely chopped
1–2 garlic cloves, crushed
1–2 level teaspoons caster sugar
salt and pepper to taste
chopped parsley**

Put all ingredients into large bowl. Stir well to combine. Cover. Chill thoroughly. Before serving, mix well. Ladle into soup bowls. Sprinkle with parsley.

Gazpacho made in blender *Put half the liquid ingredients into blender. Add vegetables and garlic. Run machine until smooth. Pour into bowl. Add all remaining ingredients. Stir well. Cover. Chill. Mix well before serving.*

Gazpacho made with tomato concentrate *To economize, put 4 level tablespoons tomato concentrate (can or tube) into bowl. Gradually stir in 1 pint warm water. If on weak side, add little more tomato concentrate.*

To skin tomatoes *Cover required number of tomatoes with boiling water. Leave 2 minutes. Drain. Cover with cold water. When cool enough to handle, slip off skins. Alternatively, spear tomatoes on to a fork. Twist over lighted gas jet; the heat will cause skin to split and it will slide off easily.*

GARLIC SOUP

serves 4

4 large tomatoes, skinned and chopped
1 pint water
4–6 garlic cloves, very finely chopped
1 large green pepper,
de-seeded and finely chopped
2 tablespoons salad oil
1 level teaspoon paprika
2 large slices white bread,
de-crusted and cubed
salt and pepper to taste

This is similar, in some respects, to Gazpacho, except that this soup is served hot, contains a vast amount of garlic and no cucumber is included. Garlic addicts will obviously love it and make it again and again ; others, doubtless, will tread more warily!

Put tomatoes and water into saucepan. Bring to boil. Add all remaining ingredients. Cook, stirring frequently, until soup is hot and fairly thick. If on thin side, add extra half slice crumbled bread.

Blender note *Put tomatoes, garlic, green pepper and oil into blender goblet. Run machine until finely chopped. Transfer to pan. Add water and remaining ingredients.*

SPANISH BAKED FISH

serves 4

4 fillets of cod or coley, each 4–6 ounces
flour
2 tablespoons salad oil
2 rashers streaky bacon, chopped
2 ounces mushrooms and stalks, chopped
1 garlic clove, chopped
1 level tablespoon flour
1 level tablespoon tomato concentrate
(can or tube)
½ pint water
salt and pepper to taste
chopped parsley

Carefully skin fillets without breaking flesh. Dust fish with flour. Heat oil in large pan. Add fish. Fry on both sides until golden. Remove to heatproof dish. Add bacon, mushrooms and garlic to remaining oil in pan. Fry slowly 5 minutes. Stir in flour and tomato concentrate. Cook 1 minute. Blend in water. Cook, stirring, until sauce comes to boil and thickens. Season. Pour over fish. Bake, uncovered, in centre of moderate oven, 350°F or Gas 4 (180°C) 30 minutes. Sprinkle with parsley before serving.

SPANISH OMELET

serves 2

2 medium onions
1 large cooked potato
2 medium tomatoes, skinned
½ small green pepper
1 ounce margarine
1 teaspoon salad oil
4 eggs
2 teaspoons cold water
salt and pepper to taste

Slice onions thinly. Separate into rings. Cube potato. chop tomatoes and green pepper finely. Heat margarine and oil in large, heavy frying pan. Add onions. Fry until golden ; about 5 minutes. Add potatoes. Fry with onion until golden, turning often. Add tomatoes and green pepper. Fry 3 minutes. Beat eggs with water. Season. Pour into pan over vegetables. Cook gently until base is set and golden and egg mixture cooked through. Do not turn. If dry top is preferred, stand pan under preheated hot grill for 1–2 minutes. Cut into two portions in pan. Slide out on to warm plates.

Potato Omelet *This is a variation of the Spanish Omelet with only potatoes added. Dice ¾–1 pound cold cooked potatoes. Fry in oil until golden. Add egg mixture. Continue as for Spanish Omelet.*

To garnish Potato Omelet *Try topping each portion of omelet with rings of fried onions. It not only looks attractive but also improves flavour.*

BAKED PORK CHOPS WITH ORANGE

serves 4

4 large pork chops, each 6 ounces
flour
1½ ounces lard or dripping
1 large onion, chopped
1–2 garlic cloves, chopped
4 medium tomatoes
skinned and chopped
¼ pint canned orange juice
or diluted squash
large pinch mixed spice
salt and pepper to taste
2 hard-boiled eggs, chopped
2 level tablespoons chopped parsley
4 black olives (optional)

Coat chops with flour. Heat lard. Add chops, 1 or 2 at a time. Fry fairly briskly until golden brown on both sides. Transfer to shallow heat-proof casserole. Add onion and garlic to remaining fat in pan. Fry gently until light gold; 5–7 minutes. Add tomatoes, orange juice and spice. Season. Bring to boil, stirring. Pour over chops. Cover dish with lid or foil. Bake in centre of moderate oven, 350°F or Gas 4 (180°C) 45 minutes. Mix egg and parsley together. Scatter over chops. Top with olives.

BAKED SYRUP BREAD

serves 4–6

1 egg, beaten
3 tablespoons milk
6 slices white bread, de-crusted
margarine for frying
golden syrup

This is something children will enjoy and is a good way of using up stale bread.

Beat egg and milk together. Quarter each bread slice. Dip into egg mixture. Fry in hot margarine until golden on both sides. Transfer to well-greased, shallow heatproof tin or dish. Coat with melted golden syrup or honey, if preferred (and 2 tablespoons water). Cook in centre of cool oven, 200°F or Gas 2 (150°C) for about 30 minutes. Good served hot with custard.

SPANISH RICE PUDDING

serves 6

1½ pints milk
(use skimmed or diluted evaporated)
8 ounces long grain rice
finely grated peel of 1 medium lemon
3 ounces caster sugar
ground cinnamon

In every country, it seems, rice pudding is made in an infinite variety of ways, and is an acceptable and popular dessert. This Spanish version, eaten cold, is quicker to make than our own baked one.

Put milk into heavy saucepan. Slowly bring to boil, stirring. Add rice. Stir twice with fork. Add lemon peel. Cover. Simmer slowly 30–40 minutes or until rice is soft and has absorbed most of the milk. Remove from heat. Stir in 2 ounces sugar. Transfer to shallow heatproof dish. Leave until cold. Sprinkle rest of sugar and cinnamon on top. Stand under hot grill until sugar is just beginning to caramelize.

Orange Milk Pudding *For flavour variation, add to above recipe finely grated peel of one orange instead of lemon.*

Banana Rice *Children like this one. Top cold pudding in dish with slices of banana. Brush with lemon juice. Sprinkle with sugar and cinnamon. Grill as directed.*

Greece

GREEK DOLMATHES

serves 6

about 18 medium-sized cabbage leaves
water

Filling

1 ounce margarine
1 large onion, very finely chopped
2 ounces long grain rice
5 ounces cold roast lamb,
finely chopped or minced
5 level tablespoons tomato concentrate
(can or tube)
1 pint beef stock (use cubes)
2 medium tomatoes, skinned and chopped
salt and pepper to taste

These are stuffed vine leaves, usually served by the Greeks as a cold starter. Vine leaves are available at speciality shops in cans, so use them if you like. I, personally, settle for young cabbage leaves which make a perfectly adequate—and cheaper—substitute.

Remove hard pieces of stalks from cabbage leaves and discard. Put leaves into bowl. Cover with near-boiling water. Leave until pliable; about 5 minutes. Drain. Dry on paper towels. To make filling, heat margarine in pan. Add onion. Fry gently until pale gold. Stir in rice, lamb and 1 tablespoon tomato concentrate. Fry further 2 minutes, stirring frequently. Pour in ¼ pint stock. Add tomatoes. Season. Bring to boil. Stir twice with fork. Lower heat. Cover. Simmer about 15 minutes or until rice grains have absorbed all the moisture. Cool to luke-warm. Put equal amounts of filling on to each cabbage leaf. Wrap up like small parcels. Stand side by side in shallow heatproof dish. Heat remaining stock with rest of tomato concentrate. Pour over cabbage parcels. Cover with lid or foil. Cook in centre of moderate oven 350°F or Gas 4 (180°C) 30 minutes. Remove from the oven and allow to cool then refrigerate, still covered, until required. Serve very cold with tomato liquor in which Dolmathes were cooked.

TARAMOSALATA

serves 8

6 ounces smoked cod's roe
(available in jars or in the piece)
3 ounces white bread, cubed
hot water
1 garlic clove, crushed
1 small onion, very finely grated
4 tablespoons salad oil
3 tablespoons lemon juice
pepper to taste

This is one of the tastiest and also one of the most delicious Greek hors d'oeuvre. And, because a little goes a long way, it is economical as well.

Put roe into bowl. (If roe is in the piece, scrape soft part away from skin and allow extra 2 ounces as skin itself is quite heavy.) Beat roe until smooth. Cover bread cubes with water. Leave 3 minutes. Squeeze dry. *Gradually* beat into cod's roe. Stir in garlic and onion. Slowly beat in oil and lemon juice alternately, adding both a few drops at a time. When mixture is smooth and thoroughly blended, season with pepper. Transfer to serving bowl. Accompany with hot toast.

AVGOLEMONO SOUP
(EGG AND LEMON SOUP)

serves 6

1½ pints chicken stock (use cubes)
½ small garlic clove
1 bay leaf
1 long strip lemon peel
2 ounces long grain rice
3 egg yolks
juice of 1 medium lemon
salt and pepper to taste
parsley for garnishing

An impressive soup, made with the simplest of ingredients.

Bring stock to boil. Tie garlic, bay leaf and lemon peel in piece of muslin. Add to stock with rice. Cover. Simmer 20 minutes. Remove muslin bag. Put egg yolks and lemon juice into warm soup tureen. Using whisk, gradually beat in hot chicken stock. Ladle into warm soup bowls. Sprinkle with chopped parsley.

Avgolemono Soup with Chicken *If liked, 1 or 2 tablespoons finely chopped cold, cooked chicken may be added to soup before serving.*

Using up chicken carcase *A good-tasting stock can easily be made from a chicken carcase and has a more authentic flavour than cubes. Put carcase into large pan. Add 3 pints water, 2 large quartered carrots, 2 large sliced onions, 2 large celery stalks, handful of parsley, pinch of mixed herbs, 2–3 level teaspoons salt and pepper to taste. Bring to boil, lower heat and cover pan. Simmer 1½ hours. Strain. Use as required.*

To pressure-cook carcase *Cook above ingredients for 30 minutes at 15 pounds pressure.*

GREEK-STYLE STUFFED LAMB BREASTS

serves 4

2 large lamb breasts, boned
6 ounces fresh white breadcrumbs
8 ounces beef sausagemeat
1 egg, beaten
1 small onion, finely grated
1 garlic clove, finely chopped
1 level tablespoon *each,*
chopped parsley and fresh mint
2 level tablespoons tomato concentrate
(can or tube)
salt and pepper to taste
milk to bind

Lamb breasts are available at almost give-away prices and if boned and stuffed, make appetizing and nutritious fare. For this recipe, the Greeks would normally use a boned shoulder but the breasts do just as well at a fraction of the cost.

Preheat oven to hot, 400°F or Gas 6 (200°C). Wash lamb breasts. Wipe dry with paper towels. Combine crumbs with all remaining ingredients except milk. Toss well to mix. Bind with milk; stuffing should be neither too wet nor too dry. Spread equal amounts over lamb breasts. Roll up *loosely* as stuffing swells up in oven. Tie at 1-inch intervals with fine string. Put into a roasting tin and roast in the centre of the oven for 45–60 minutes or until golden and crisp. Serve with gravy and vegetables to taste.

Spare stuffing *If there should be any stuffing left over, put it into a small, well-greased heatproof dish. Top with flakes of margarine or dripping. Cook with the lamb for the last 20 minutes.*

BAKED MACKEREL

serves 4

2 tablespoons salad oil
4 medium mackerel, cleaned and boned
1 large onion, finely chopped
4 small bay leaves
juice of 1 medium lemon or
2 dessertspoons mild vinegar
1 level teaspoon mixed herbs
salt and pepper to taste
2 ounces black olives

This is sometimes known as Monk's Mackerel because it is prepared in this way by the Brothers.

Preheat oven to moderate, 350°F or Gas 4 (180°C). Pour 1 tablespoon oil into shallow heatproof dish, covering base completely. Arrange fish, side by side, in dish. Heat rest of oil in pan. Add onion. Cover. Fry gently until pale gold; about 8–10 minutes. Spoon over mackerel. Top each fish with one bay leaf. Sprinkle with lemon juice or vinegar and herbs and season. Add the olives. Cover the dish with a lid or foil. Bake in the centre of the oven for 30 minutes. Serve hot with freshly cooked potatoes, showered heavily with finely chopped parsley or chives.

MOUSSAKA

serves 4–5

2 medium aubergines
salt
4 tablespoons salad oil
4 medium onions, sliced
1 garlic clove, chopped
12 ounces cold, cooked lamb,
finely minced
4 level tablespoons fresh
white breadcrumbs
2 level tablespoons tomato concentrate
(can or tube)
¼ pint hot water
salt and pepper to taste
2 eggs
5 tablespoons undiluted evaporated
milk

A worthwhile dish to make during the summer months when purple-skinned aubergines (sometimes known as eggplants) are plentiful and reasonably priced. Moussaka is incredibly filling, on the rich side and typically Balkan in character. It is also an excellent means of using up cooked lamb, left over from the weekend joint.

Wash and dry aubergines. Do not peel. Cut into ¼-inch slices. Spread out on plates. Sprinkle with salt. Leave 45 minutes. (This salting process draws out excess moisture from aubergines and stops them absorbing too much oil.) Rinse. Dry aubergines thoroughly on paper towels or in clean tea towel. Heat oil until hot. Add aubergines. Fry fairly briskly until golden on both sides. Remove to plate. Add onions and garlic to remaining oil in pan. Fry gently until pale gold. Combine meat with crumbs, tomato concentrate and water. Season. Line lightly greased, fairly shallow, heatproof dish with half the aubergine slices. Cover with meat mixture, fried onions and fried garlic. Arrange rest of aubergine slices on top. Cover. Bake in centre of moderate oven, 350°F or Gas 4 (180°C) 30 minutes. Beat eggs and milk together. Pour over top of Moussaka. Return to oven. Cook further 30 minutes or until top is golden and set like a custard.

Cheese-topped Moussaka *Make Moussaka*

as previously directed, but after 30 minutes, cover with ½ pint white sauce into which 1 egg yolk has been beaten. Sprinkle with 2–3 ounces Cheddar cheese. Return to oven. Cook further 30 minutes.

Mock Moussaka *To make this dish really economical, substitute 1½ pounds par-boiled potatoes (sliced) for the aubergines. Egg and milk, or sauce with cheese topping, may be used according to taste.*

BASIC PILAFF

serves 4–6

1¼ pints fairly concentrated chicken stock
2 ounces table margarine
8 ounces long grain rice
salt and pepper to taste

Bring stock and 1 ounce margarine to boil. Add rice. Season. Stir twice with fork. Lower heat. Cover. Simmer about 15–20 minutes or until rice grains are tender and have absorbed all the moisture. Using fork, stir in rest of margarine. Serve, instead of potatoes, with main course dishes.

Like all basic dishes. Pilaff lends itself to all sorts of variations and listed below are a few from which to choose. Notice, by the way, how easily they convert into main course dishes.

Lamb Pilaff *While Pilaff is cooking, fry or grill two meaty lamb chops until crisp. Cut into smallish pieces. Five minutes before Pilaff is ready, add lamb together with 1 small packet frozen peas. Stir well with fork while heating through. Sprinkle each portion with suspicion of chopped mint. Serves 4.*

Chicken Pilaff *Add 4–6 ounces small cubes of cold cooked chicken to Pilaff, 7 minutes before it is ready. If liked, include also 1–2 tablespoons coarsely chopped peanuts. Serves 4.*

Liver Pilaff *Fry 8 ounces chicken livers in 1 ounce margarine until golden; about 5 minutes. Add stock then proceed as for Basic Pilaff. For* flavour interest, add ½ level teaspoon finely grated orange peel and 1–2 tablespoons seedless raisins 5 minutes before Pilaff is ready. Serves 4.

Vegetable Pilaff *Add 8 ounces cooked mixed vegetables to Pilaff 5 minutes before it is ready.*

Top each portion with grated cheese. Serves 4.

Smoked Haddock and Egg Pilaff *Add 6 ounces cooked and flaked smoked haddock and 2 coarsely chopped hard-boiled eggs 5 minutes before Pilaff is ready. Sprinkle portions with finely chopped watercress. Serves 4.*

Yugoslavia

WHITE CABBAGE WITH MEAT

serves 4

2 pounds middle neck of lamb
flour
1 head white cabbage (about 2 pounds)
2 ounces dripping
1 large onion, chopped
1–2 large garlic cloves, chopped
½ pint hot water
4 level tablespoons tomato concentrate (can or tube)
1 level teaspoon paprika
salt and pepper to taste

Preheat oven to moderate, 350°F or Gas 4 (180°C). Cut lamb into neat pieces, discarding surplus fat. Coat lamb lightly with flour. Remove outer bruised and damaged leaves from cabbage. Cut cabbage into eight wedges. Heat dripping in *large* flameproof casserole. Add lamb. Fry until well-browned. Remove to plate. Add onion and garlic to remaining dripping in pan. Fry gently until pale gold. Replace lamb. Surround with cabbage wedges. Combine all remaining ingredients. Pour over lamb. Cover. Cook in centre of oven 1½–2 hours or until meat is tender. Serve with boiled barley or potatoes.

BACON WITH BARLEY AND BEANS

serves 4

8–12 ounces boiled bacon
8 ounces haricot beans, soaked overnight
4 ounces pearl barley
2 tablespoons salad oil
1 large onion, chopped
1 level tablespoon paprika

½ pint water
salt and pepper to taste
chopped parsley

Dice bacon. Drain beans. Cook in boiling salted water until tender. Do the same with barley. Heat oil in large pan. Add onion. Fry gently until gold. Add bacon. Fry little more briskly 5 minutes. Leave on one side. When beans and barley are cooked, drain and add to onions and bacon. Stir in paprika and water. Season. Cover. Simmer 30 minutes or until most of the liquid has been absorbed. Transfer to serving dish. Sprinkle heavily with parsley. Accompany with crisp salad.

LEEKS WITH RICE

serves 4

8 medium-sized leeks
boiling water
2 ounces margarine
1 medium can (about 1 pound) tomatoes
1 level tablespoon paprika
3 ounces long grain rice
¼ pint water
salt and pepper to taste
juice of 1 lemon
about 4 ounces grated Cheddar cheese

Trim leeks, leaving on as much green part as possible. Slit each in half lengthwise. Wash carefully. Cut into chunks. Put into bowl. Cover with boiling water. Leave 10 minutes. Drain *thoroughly*. Heat margarine in large pan. Add leeks. Fry very gently until pale gold; about 10 minutes. Add all remaining ingredients except lemon and cheese. Bring to boil. Cover. Simmer 15–20 minutes. Transfer to 4 warm plates. Sprinkle with lemon juice and cheese.

BACON AND CURD CHEESE PASTIES

serves 4–6

5 ounces plain flour
pinch salt
5 ounces margarine
5 ounces curd cheese
4 ounces raw bacon, finely chopped
little beaten egg
pepper
chopped parsley

A sustaining light lunch or supper dish which is equally good as a party snack.

Sift flour and salt into bowl. Cut in margarine until it is in pea-size pieces. Stir in curd cheese. With fork, mix to dough. Draw together with finger tips. Wrap in foil. Chill 1 hour. Roll out to about $\frac{1}{4}$ inch in thickness on floured surface. Cut into 2- by 3-inch pieces. Mix bacon with little egg. Put small amounts on to centres of pastry pieces. Moisten edges of pastry with water. Fold over into triangles. Using fork, press edges well together to seal. Put on to lightly greased baking tray. Brush with left-over egg. Bake in moderately hot oven, 400°F or Gas 6 (200°C), placing tray on shelf above centre for about 20 minutes. Serve hot or cold.

Alternative fillings *Chopped corned beef mixed with chopped boiled onion. Finely minced cold roast beef, lamb or pork moistened with gravy or tomato ketchup.*

WHITE FISH WITH PAPRIKA

serves 4

1½ pounds cod or coley fillet
3 tablespoons salad oil
2 large onions, finely chopped
2 pickled red pimientos
drained and chopped
salt and pepper
2 tablespoons finely chopped parsley
2 level teaspoons paprika
5 tablespoons lukewarm water

Preheat oven to moderately hot, 375°F or Gas 5 (190°C). Cut fish into large cubes. Heat oil in pan. Add onions. Fry gently until just beginning to turn golden. Add pimientos (these are available inexpensively in jars). Fry 5 minutes. Season. Stir in parsley and paprika. Remove from heat. Add water and raw fish cubes. Mix well. Transfer to heatproof dish. Cook, uncovered, in centre of oven 30 minutes. Serve with rice.

Left-over Pickled Pimiento
This may be used up in the following ways:

Salads *Chop pimiento and combine with potato, Russian or mixed salads tossed with French dressing.*

Hors d'Oeuvre *Serve strips of it with black and green olives and cubes of white Stilton cheese.*

Meat stews *Chop pimiento up finely and add to all types of stews made with beef, lamb or poultry. It adds a subtle piquancy which is very pleasant.*

Garnish *Use strips to garnish an egg mayonnaise.*

For slimmers *Chop it up finely and stir into cottage cheese with chives.*

SWEET PASTIES

The above curd cheese pastry can be used in sweet dishes. Roll out and cut into 4-inch squares. Put little jam in centre of each. Moisten edges with water. Fold over into triangles. Stand on greased tray. Brush with egg. Bake as directed in previous recipe. Because the pastry is slightly puffy, these pasties resemble Jam Turnovers made with flaky pastry.

Alternate fillings *Chopped cooking dates moistened with orange juice, lemon curd.*

Dieting on a Budget

This is not as tricky as one would suppose, for losing weight is not solely dependent on eating rump steak and salad every day! There are other, and indeed more interesting, ways of shedding those extra pounds and I hope the following low calorie recipes and suggestions will prove my point.

JELLIED TOMATO CONSOMME

serves 4

1¼ pints chicken or beef stock
1 envelope gelatine
2 level tablespoons tomato concentrate
(can or tube)
salt and pepper to taste
chopped parsley

Pour stock into pan. Add gelatine and tomato concentrate. Leave over low heat until gelatine dissolves. Stir frequently. Season. Leave in cold place until lightly set. Break up with spoon. Turn into four bowls. Sprinkle with parsley. Serve.

To increase piquancy *Include ½–1 teaspoon Worcester sauce and either shake of Tabasco or pinch cayenne pepper. Season with onion or garlic salt instead of ordinary salt.*

To make chicken stock *Dissolve appropriate number of chicken stock cubes in 1¼ pints water. Leave until cold. Cover. Refrigerate. Before using, skim off the fat that has risen to the top.*

To make beef stock *Either make as chicken stock above or dissolve 3–4 teaspoons meat extract in 1¼ pints boiling water.*

TOMATO, CAULIFLOWER AND ONION SOUP

serves 4–6

Cook 1 small cauliflower and 2 medium onions in boiling salted water until tender. If liked, include small garlic clove. Combine with 1 medium can (about 1 pound) tomatoes. Either rub vegetables and liquid through sieve or blend to smooth purée in blender goblet. Add plenty of salt and pepper to taste, dash Tabasco, 2 teaspoons Worcester sauce, squeeze of lemon juice and 1 artificial sweetener tablet (to off-set acidity of tomatoes). Slowly bring soup to boil, stirring. Thin down with little water if too thick. Serve each portion lightly sprinkled with grated cheese.

CAULIFLOWER AND ONION SOUP

serves 4

1 medium head cauliflower
2 large onions, quartered
2 level teaspoons salt
pepper to taste
3 heaped tablespoons instant
skimmed milk granules
ground nutmeg

Trim cauliflower. Break head into florets. Put into pan. Add onions. Just cover with water. Season. Bring to boil. Reduce heat. Cover. Cook until vegetables are soft. Rub vegetables and liquid through sieve to form purée. Return to pan. If too thick, thin down with little water. Stir in milk granules. Slowly bring to boil, stirring. Adjust seasoning to taste. Sprinkle each serving lightly with nutmeg.

Using a blender *Blend vegetables and liquid, a little at a time, in blender goblet until smooth. Return to saucepan. Add milk granules. Continue as in previous recipe.*

Additional flavourings *Add, according to taste, either 1–2 teaspoons Worcester sauce, ½ teaspoon yeast extract, ½ level teaspoon* mixed herbs, ½ teacup finely chopped parsley or 1–2 level teaspoons curry powder. If liked, combine one or two from this list.

To make Gazpacho without blender *Rub 1 medium can tomatoes through sieve. Put into bowl. Finely mince green pepper, cucumber, onion and garlic. Add to tomatoes with rest of ingredients. If no mincer is available, chop ingredients as finely as possible. To save time, cucumber and onions may be grated.*

TOMATO AND ORANGE SOUP

serves 4

1 medium can (about 1 pound) tomatoes
1 chicken stock cube
1 pint water
1 teaspoon Worcester sauce
salt and pepper to taste
1 small garlic clove
½ level teaspoon dried basil
finely grated peel of ½ medium orange
2 tablespoons orange juice
2 heaped tablespoons instant skimmed milk granules

Put all ingredients, *except* orange peel, orange juice and milk granules, into pan. Bring to boil. Lower heat. Cover. Simmer 15–20 minutes. Either rub through sieve or blend to smooth purée in liquidizer goblet. Return to pan. Add rest of ingredients. Reheat gently without boiling.

SLIMMERS' GAZPACHO

serves 4–5

1 large green pepper, de-seeded and chopped
½ medium cucumber, washed, unpeeled and coarsely chopped
1 large onion, sliced
1 or 2 garlic cloves
1 medium can (about 1 pound) tomatoes
1 tablespoon lemon juice
salt and pepper to taste

Blend ingredients, a little at a time, in liquidizer goblet. Pour into bowl. Cover. Chill. Stir before serving to mix ingredients.

Note Depending on taste, ingredients may be blended to fine purée, or coarse purée with some of the vegetables still in tiny pieces.

CARROT AND ONION SOUP

serves 4

Boil 2 large onions until tender. Rub through sieve with 1 medium can (about 1 pound) carrots. Add liquor from can. Alternatively, blend onions and carrots in liquidizer goblet until smooth. Return to pan. If too thick, thin down with little water. Stir in 3–4 heaped tablespoons instant skimmed milk granules. Season with salt, pepper, garlic salt (optional) and Worcester sauce. Slowly bring to boil, stirring. Serve each portion thickly topped with chopped parsley.

ONION SOUP

serves 4

Cook 2 pounds onions in boiling salted water until very soft. Rub onions through sieve. Thin down to soup-like consistency with onion liquor. Stir in 4 heaped tablespoons instant skimmed milk granules. Season to taste with salt, pepper, Worcester sauce, nutmeg, and freshly milled black pepper. Serve each portion sprinkled with paprika. If preferred, onions and cooking liquor may be blended to purée in blender goblet.

LEEK SOUP

serves 4

Make exactly as Onion Soup, using 6 large leeks instead of onions. Trim leeks (leaving on some of the green part). Slit. Wash thoroughly to remove earth and grit.

Canned and Packet Soups

Surprisingly, some of the condensed soups, when diluted with an equal amount of water, contain less calories than one would imagine. So do some of the packet soups. Therefore the following ideas may be useful for those who want a hurried, but also tasty and sustaining, snack lunch.

TOMATO SOUP SNACK
(about 225 calories)

serves 1

Heat ½ can condensed tomato soup with equal quantity of water (total ½ pint). Accompany with 1 crispbread, 2 ounces cottage cheese and 1 medium orange.

CONSOMME SNACK
(about 225 calories)

serves 1

Heat ½ can condensed consommé with equal quantity of water (total ½ pint). Accompany with 1 crispbread, 1 ounce Cheshire cheese, 4–5 leaves of lettuce sprinkled lightly with lemon juice and soy sauce and 1 medium orange.

OXTAIL SOUP SNACK
(about 253 calories)

serves 1

Cook ½ packet (1 pint size) oxtail soup with water as directed. Accompany with 1 crispbread, 1-egg omelet, 4 ounces grilled tomatoes and ½ medium grapefruit sprinkled with sugar substitute powder.

ASPARAGUS SOUP SNACK
(about 260 calories)

serves 1

Heat ½ can condensed asparagus soup with equal quantity of water (total ½ pint). Accompany with 1 small slice brown bread, 2 ounces well-drained canned tuna and approximately 12 slices cucumber.

SCOTCH BROTH SNACK
(about 225 calories)

serves 1

Cook ½ packet (1 pint size) Scotch Broth with water as directed. Accompany with 1 crispbread, 1 boiled egg and 4 ounces tomatoes.

CHICKEN NOODLE SNACK
(about 238 calories)

serves 1

Cook ½ packet (1 pint size) chicken noodle soup with water as directed. Sprinkle with ½ ounce grated Cheddar cheese. Accompany with 1 crispbread, 1 medium orange and 1 dessert pear.

SLIMMERS' MEAT LOAF

serves 4

**1 pound raw minced beef,
as lean as possible
3 level tablespoons instant skimmed
milk granules
2 tablespoons water
1 small onion, grated
1 level teaspoon *each,*
garlic salt and paprika
2 teaspoons Worcester sauce
1 teaspoon soy sauce
large pinch ground nutmeg
1 rasher lean bacon, finely chopped
pepper to taste**

Preheat oven to moderately hot, 375°F or Gas 5 (190°C). Put beef into bowl. Dissolve milk granules in water. Add to meat with all remaining ingredients. Mix thoroughly to combine. Shape into loaf. Stand on foil-lined baking tray. Cook in centre of oven about 45 minutes. Slice. Serve hot with cooked vegetables or cold with salad.

LUNCH DIP

serves 6

8 ounces curd cheese
1 ounce instant skimmed milk granules
3 tablespoons water
salt and pepper to taste

Beat cheese until smooth. Dissolve milk granules in water. Gradually beat into cheese. Season well to taste with salt and pepper. Transfer to serving bowl. Surround with 'dunks' of fresh vegetables such as carrot slices or sticks, 2-inch lengths celery, fresh button mushrooms, slices of cucumber and uncooked florets of cauliflower.

Mixed Herb Dip *Make cheese dip as above but before seasoning with salt and pepper, stir in 2–3 level tablespoons each, chopped parsley and chives. If liked, watercress may be used instead of chives.*

Piquant Dip *Make cheese dip as above but before seasoning with salt and pepper, stir in 1 level tablespoon each, chopped capers and gherkins, 2 teaspoons Worcester sauce and pinch cayenne pepper.*

Austrian Style Dip *Make cheese dip as above but before seasoning with salt and pepper, stir in 1 level teaspoon bright red paprika, 1 level teaspoon caraway seeds, 2 level teaspoons finely chopped capers and good sprinkling garlic salt.*

ALL-MEAT BEEFBURGERS

serves 2

8 ounces raw minced beef,
as lean as possible
1 small onion, grated
1 small egg, beaten
salt and pepper to taste

Combine all ingredients well together. Shape into 4 balls. Flatten into 4 thinnish cakes. Stand under preheated hot grill (in lightly greased grill pan). Grill on both sides until golden brown and cooked through. Serve with salad or green vegetables to taste. Grilled mushrooms and tomatoes also make good accompaniments.

Piquant Beefburgers *Make exactly as above but season with ½–1 level teaspoon continental mustard, 1–2 teaspoons Worcester sauce, dash of Tabasco and large pinch mixed herbs.*

Beefburgers with Garlic *As above but omit onion. Combine 8 ounces raw minced beef with 1 finely chopped garlic clove, 1 small egg and salt and pepper to taste.*

Curried Beefburgers *Make up All-Meat Beefburger recipe but include 1–4 level teaspoons curry powder. If hotter flavour is preferred, add curry powder to Piquant Beefburger mixture.*

Tomato Burgers *Make up All-Meat Beefburger recipe but include 1–2 level tablespoons tomato concentrate (can or tube) and shake of Worcester sauce.*

For extra lean meat *As ready-prepared mince has a high percentage of fat, either buy lean shin and mince it yourself or ask butcher to do this for you.*

To tenderize mince *Pass twice or three times through mincer. Alternatively, combine mince with powdered meat tenderizer as directed on container.*

MOCK VEAL CUTLETS HOLSTEIN

serves 2

4 ounces *each,* finely minced lean
beef and veal
½ level teaspoon finely grated lemon peel
1 small egg, beaten
onion salt and pepper to taste

Topping

2 freshly poached eggs

Combine meats with remaining ingredients. Shape into 2 thinnish cakes. Place in lightly oiled grill pan. Cook under preheated hot grill until cooked through and golden on both sides. Put on to two warm plates. Top each with poached egg. Accompany with salad or cooked green vegetables to taste.

LOW CALORIE COTTAGE PIE

serves 4

**1 pound raw minced beef,
as lean as possible
2 large carrots, grated
1 large onion, grated
1 medium green pepper,
de-seeded and finely chopped
¼ pint tomato juice
2 teaspoons Worcester sauce
salt and pepper to taste
1 medium cauliflower
1 ounce Edam cheese, finely grated
paprika**

Put beef into pan. Add next 5 ingredients. Season. Bring to boil, breaking up meat with fork all the time. Lower heat. Cover. Simmer 45 minutes. Uncover. Continue to simmer until mince is fairly thick; there should not be too much liquid. Meanwhile, cook cauliflower in boiling salted water until tender. Drain. Mash. Transfer mince to lightly greased serving dish. Top with cauliflower. Sprinkle with cheese and paprika. Reheat and brown towards top of hot oven, 425°F or Gas 7 (220°C) ¼ hour.

MEAT BALL CASSEROLE

serves 4

**1 pound raw minced beef
1 small onion, grated
1 egg, beaten
salt and pepper to taste
1 pound runner beans
3 large carrots
2 level teaspoons yeast extract
¼ pint boiling water**

Combine first 4 ingredients well together. Roll into small balls. Top and tail beans and cut away strings from sides. Slice beans diagonally. Coarsely grate carrots. Combine with beans. Put ½ quantity of vegetables into casserole. Top with meat balls. Cover with rest of vegetables. Dissolve yeast extract in water. Pour into dish. Sprinkle with salt and pepper. Cover with lid or foil. Cook in centre of moderate oven, 350°F or Gas 4 (180°C) 1 hour.

CHICKEN HOT-POT

serves 4

**2 large onions, chopped
2 large celery stalks, chopped
½ medium head white cabbage, shredded
4 large tomatoes, skinned and chopped
1 garlic clove, crushed
salt and pepper to taste
4 joints roasting chicken
2 level teaspoons yeast extract
¼ pint boiling water**

Put prepared vegetables, in layers, in deepish casserole, sprinkling salt and pepper between layers. Top with chicken portions, skin side uppermost. Dissolve yeast extract in water. Pour into dish over chicken and vegetables. Cover. Cook in centre of moderate oven, 350°F or Gas 4 (180°C) 1¼ hours. Uncover during last 30 minutes to brown chicken.

Chicken and Barley Hot-Pot *For those who do not follow a really strict slimming régime, follow previous recipe but add 2 ounces pearl barley or 2 ounces long grain rice with layers of vegetables. Increase water by about 5 tablespoons as barley or rice both absorb moisture.*

BEEF AND LIVER LOAF

serves 4

Simmer ½ pound ox liver in salted water until tender. Drain. Mince. Combine with ½ pound raw minced beef, 1 medium grated onion, 1 beaten egg and salt and pepper to taste. Shape into loaf. Continue as in recipe for Slimmers' Meat Loaf above.

SPANISH MEAT CAKES

serves 4

12 ounces corned beef, chopped
2 small garlic cloves, chopped
1 small onion, grated
½ small green pepper,
de-seeded and finely chopped
1 teaspoon *each*, Worcester sauce
and tomato ketchup
1 small egg, beaten
1 small can (about 8 ounces) tomatoes

A store cupboard quickie which works out at about 250 calories per portion.

Preheat oven to moderately hot, 375°F or Gas 5 (190°C). Combine all ingredients, except tomatoes, well together. Shape into 4 cakes. Put into lightly greased heatproof dish. Top with tomatoes. Cover. Cook in centre of oven 30 minutes. Uncover halfway through cooking time. Accompany with freshly cooked cabbage and carrots.

DEVILLED MARINADED CHICKEN

serves 4

2 tablespoons *each*,
vinegar and lemon juice
1 small onion, chopped
1 tablespoon Worcester sauce
4 tablespoons natural yogurt
2 tablespoons tomato ketchup
¼ level teaspoon *each*,
celery salt and mixed herbs
½–1 level teaspoon salt
shake cayenne pepper
4 joints roasting chicken

Note Choose breast portions of chicken in preference to back portions, as they have slightly less calories.

Combine all ingredients, except chicken, in glass or enamel dish. Beat well. Add chicken joints. Coat with marinade. Cover. Stand 2–3 hours in cool place, turning once. Transfer to roasting tin. Cook in centre of moderate oven, 350°F or Gas 4 (180°C) 45–60 minutes or

until chicken is tender. Serve with green vegetables to taste or accompany with baked tomatoes or salad.

PIQUANT ROAST CHICKEN

serves 4

Rub 4 joints roasting chicken with cut garlic clove. Sprinkle with salt, pepper and little ground nutmeg. Transfer to roasting tin. Sprinkle lightly with Worcester sauce, lemon juice and paprika. Cook as in previous recipe. Serve with salad or vegetables to taste.

GRILLED CHICKEN

serves 4

2 tablespoons lemon juice
1 tablespoon Worcester sauce
1 level teaspoon garlic or onion salt
4 joints roasting chicken

Combine first three ingredients and brush over chicken. Stand the joints in a lightly oiled grill pan, skin side down. Place about 2 inches below pre-heated hot grill. Grill 30–40 minutes, turning frequently. Serve with grilled mushrooms and tomato halves. Accompany with green vegetables to taste.

CHICKEN NEAPOLITAN

serves 4

4 joints roasting chicken
1 medium can (about 1 pound) tomatoes
1 large green pepper,
de-seeded and chopped
1 large onion, sliced
1 level teaspoon salt
pepper to taste
½–1 level teaspoon dried basil

Put chicken into casserole dish, skin side uppermost. Cover with tomatoes. Top with prepared vegetables. Sprinkle with salt, pepper and basil. Cover. Cook in centre of moderately hot oven 375°F or Gas 5 (190°C) 1 hour. Accompany with freshly cooked cauliflower or green salad.

CASSEROLED CHICKEN WITH MUSHROOMS

serves 4

4 joints roasting chicken
8 ounces mushrooms, sliced
1 large onion, grated
juice of 1 medium lemon
pepper to taste
1 level teaspoon marjoram
½–1 level teaspoon garlic salt
¼ pint tomato juice

Put joints into casserole. Top with mushrooms and onion. Sprinkle with lemon juice, pepper, marjoram and garlic salt. Pour the tomato juice into a dish. Cover. Cook in the centre of a moderately hot oven at 375°F or Gas 5 (190°C) 1 hour. Accompany with freshly cooked vegetables to taste.

BAKED CURRIED CHICKEN

serves 4

4 joints roasting chicken
½ pint natural yogurt
1–2 level tablespoons curry powder
1 level teaspoon paprika
1 garlic clove, chopped
1 tablespoon Worcester sauce
1–2 level teaspoons salt
squeeze of lemon juice
powdered sugar substitute to taste
1 level tablespoon desiccated coconut

Put joints into casserole. Combine all remaining ingredients except coconut. Spoon over chicken. Sprinkle with coconut. Cover. Cook in centre of moderately hot oven, 375°F or Gas 5 (190°C) 45 minutes. Uncover. Cook further 15 minutes to brown coconut. Accompany with green peas and salad.

COLD CHICKEN WITH EGG-LEMON SAUCE

serves 6

1 boiling chicken,
about 4 pounds prepared weight
water
3 large onions
2 large carrots
2 large celery stalks
1 small bay leaf
2–3 level teaspoons salt
pepper to taste
2 eggs and 1 yolk
juice of 1 medium lemon
chopped parsley

Put washed chicken (with giblets) into large pan. Cover with water. Bring to boil. Remove scum. Add all remaining ingredients except eggs, lemon juice and parsley. Lower heat. Cover. Simmer gently 2½–3 hours or until chicken is tender. Lift chicken out of stock. Carve into slices when cold. Stand on large serving plate. Put ½ pint cold chicken stock into bowl. Beat in eggs, yolk and lemon juice. Stand bowl over saucepan of gently simmering water. Cook, stirring frequently, until sauce is thick enough to coat back of spoon (rather like egg custard). Do not allow sauce to boil at any time or it will curdle. Remove basin of sauce from pan. Adjust seasoning. When cold, spoon over carved chicken. Sprinkle with parsley. Accompany with salad.

To pressure cook *Pressure cook for 30 minutes at 15 pounds pressure. Carve and coat with sauce as directed in recipe above.*

QUICKIE CHICKEN PUREE SOUP

serves 6

Put stock and vegetables remaining from above recipe into large bowl. Cover. Refrigerate overnight. Remove surface layer of fat. Discard. Either rub vegetables and stock through sieve or blend, small quantity at a time, in liquidizer goblet until smooth. Transfer to pan. If too thick, thin down with extra water. Bring to boil. Simmer gently 10 minutes. Sprinkle each portion with chopped parsley.

CHICKEN BROTH

serves 4

After refrigerating vegetables and stock (previous recipe) and discarding fat, put into saucepan with chicken carcase. Add ¼ pint water, 2 well-washed and chopped leeks, 1 small diced turnip and parsnip and seasoning to taste. Bring to boil. Remove scum as it rises to top. Lower heat. Cover. Simmer 1 hour. Remove carcase. Transfer soup and vegetables to four warm soup plates. Sprinkle each with chopped parsley or watercress.

CHEESE-STUFFED TOMATOES

serves 4

**4 really large or 8 medium tomatoes
1 small onion, chopped
4 ounces Cheddar cheese, grated
4 level tablespoons
fresh white breadcrumbs
salt, pepper and
prepared mustard to taste**

Stuffed tomatoes, hot or cold, make tasty and nutritious meals. Below are some suggestions.

Halve tomatoes. Gently scoop out pulpy centres, discarding any hard pieces. Put tomato halves upside down to drain on paper towels. Combine pulp with all remaining ingredients. Pile back into tomato halves. Stand on very lightly oiled baking tray. Cook in centre of moderately hot oven, 375°F or Gas 5 (190°C) 20 minutes. Accompany with cooked green vegetables to taste.

Meat-Stuffed Tomatoes *Prepare exactly as Cheese-Stuffed Tomatoes but combine tomato pulp with 6 ounces cold roast meat or poultry (finely chopped), 2 tablespoons cooked rice, 1 chopped garlic clove and salt and pepper to taste.*

Fish-Stuffed Tomatoes *Prepare exactly as Cheese-Stuffed Tomatoes but combine tomato pulp with 6 ounces cooked and finely flaked smoked haddock, 1 level tablespoon fresh white or brown breadcrumbs, 2 level teaspoons finely chopped parsley, 1 small grated onion and salt and pepper to taste.*

CHEESE AND MUSHROOM COCOTTES

serves 4

**8 ounces cottage cheese
4 ounces mushrooms, chopped
4 standard eggs, beaten
1 small onion, finely grated
2 level tablespoons
finely chopped parsley
salt and pepper to taste**

Preheat oven to moderately hot, 400°F or Gas 6 (200°C). Brush four individual heatproof dishes lightly with melted margarine. Mix cheese, mushrooms, eggs, onion and 1 tablespoon parsley well together. Season. Put into dishes. Stand on baking tray. Bake in centre of oven 15 minutes. Sprinkle with rest of parsley. Serve straight away.

To vary *Add 1–2 ounces finely chopped cold roast beef or poultry to other ingredients.*

Tomato-topped Cocottes *Make exactly as Cheese and Mushroom Cocottes but top mixture in dishes with thin slices of skinned tomatoes before baking. Sprinkle with parsley when cooked.*

EGG AND FISH-STUFFED TOMATOES

serves 4

**4 really large or 8 medium tomatoes
onion salt
2 hard-boiled eggs, chopped
4 ounces smoked haddock,
cooked and finely mashed
1 level tablespoon
finely chopped parsley
1–2 tablespoons milk (skimmed if liked)
salt and pepper to taste
mustard and cress**

Halve tomatoes. Gently scoop out pulpy centres with teaspoon, discarding any hard pieces. Put tomato halves upside down to drain on paper towels. Sprinkle insides lightly with onion salt. Combine tomato pulp with all remaining ingredients. Pile back into tomato halves. Sprinkle with cress. Chill lightly before serving.

Cottage Cheese-Stuffed Tomatoes *Make exactly as Egg and Fish-Stuffed Tomatoes but combine tomato pulp with 6–8 ounces cottage cheese, 6 finely chopped spring onions and plenty of salt and pepper to taste. Pile back into tomato halves. Top with thin slices of cucumber. Chill lightly before serving.*

Scrambled Egg-Stuffed Tomatoes *Make exactly as Egg and Fish-Stuffed Tomatoes but combine tomato pulp with 4 large beaten eggs, 1 tablespoon skimmed milk, 2 level tablespoons finely chopped parsley and salt and pepper to taste. Lightly scramble. Pile back into tomato halves. Chill lightly. Sprinkle with paprika and/or scissor-snipped chives before serving.*

FISH BRAISE

serves 4

1 large onion, grated
1 large carrot, grated
2 medium celery stalks, chopped
4 ounces mushrooms, sliced
2 large tomatoes, skinned and sliced
½ level teaspoon mixed herbs
salt and pepper to taste
5 tablespoons hot water
4 pieces (each 4–6 ounces) coley, haddock or cod fillet
1 ounce Cheddar cheese, finely grated

Preheat oven to moderately hot, 375°F or Gas 5 (190°C). Put all ingredients, except fish and cheese, into largish casserole. Stir well to mix. Cover. Cook in centre of oven for ½ hour. Remove from oven. Arrange fish on top. Sprinkle with salt, pepper and cheese. Return to oven. Cook, uncovered, further 20–30 minutes or until fish flakes easily with fork and cheese is golden.

To vary *If liked, rub fish with cut clove of garlic before cooking. Sprinkle with paprika in addition to cheese. Dust lightly with finely chopped parsley before serving.*

FISH IN FOIL

serves 4

4 haddock or cod steaks
1 medium onion, sliced
juice of 1 small lemon
½ level teaspoon garlic salt
1 tablespoon Worcester sauce
1 small bay leaf, crumbled

Preheat oven to moderately hot, 375°F or Gas 5 (190°C). Prepare four large squares of foil. Brush lightly with melted margarine or oil. Stand a fish steak on centre of each. Top with slices of onion, separated into rings. Sprinkle with all remaining ingredients. Wrap foil loosely round fish to form parcels, making sure joins are well secured. Stand on baking tray. Cook near top of oven 30 minutes. Transfer to warm plates. Let people unwrap their own 'parcels'. Accompany with baked tomatoes and cauliflower.

Fish with Tomato and Orange *Prepare exactly as above. Top with equal amounts of sliced tomatoes (allow about 4 skinned ones) in addition to onion. Sprinkle with ½ level teaspoon finely grated orange peel as well as all the other ingredients.*

Mackerel Fillets

These are available in flat, sardine-type tins and, when once the cotton-seed oil has been drained off, the fillets themselves are full of nourishment and rich in protein. Although the fish is high in calorific value the calories are the same kind as in meat; they build flesh and muscle and not fat and therefore are ideal for slimmers. Below are suggestions for using these tasty and very inexpensive fillets.

MACKEREL WITH CUCUMBER

serves 2

Spread 2 crispbreads very thinly with margarine. Top each with 2 well-drained mackerel fillets. Sprinkle with lemon juice and pepper to taste. Cover with cucumber slices. Sprinkle with mustard and cress or with chopped watercress.

MACKEREL AU GRATIN

serves 2

Toast 2 slices white slimming bread on one side only. Spread untoasted sides thinly with peanut butter. Top each with 2 well-drained mackerel fillets. Sprinkle lightly with vinegar and 1 ounce grated Cheddar cheese. Dust sparingly with cayenne pepper or more liberally with paprika. Brown under hot grill. Serve straight away.

MACKEREL SALAD

serves 2

Tear $\frac{1}{2}$ medium-sized lettuce into bite-size pieces. Put into bowl. Add 8 chopped spring onions, 12 sliced radishes, 1 thinly sliced and unpeeled eating apple and $\frac{1}{4}$ peeled and thinly sliced cucumber. Toss with juice of 1 medium lemon blended with 3 tablespoons natural yogurt and powdered artificial sweetener to taste. Transfer to 2 dishes or bowls. Top each with 2 well-drained mackerel fillets. Garnish with chopped hard-boiled egg.

Chopping egg can be a messy business because egg has a habit of flying all over the place! Instead, I either grate mine into a bowl on the coarse side of a grater or press whole egg through mesh sieve.

DEVILLED MACKEREL ON TOMATO SLICES

serves 2

Stand 8 large and thickish tomato slices in lightly greased grill pan. Mash 1 can well-drained mackerel fillets with 2 teaspoons vinegar, 2 teaspoons Worcester sauce, $\frac{1}{2}$ level teaspoon chili powder, shake Tabasco or pinch cayenne pepper and 1 level teaspoon curry powder. Pile equal amounts on top of tomato slices. Heat through and lightly brown under preheated hot grill. Serve with crispbreads and green vegetables to taste

TANGY MACKEREL SPREAD

serves 2

Finely mash 1 can well-drained mackerel fillets. Stir in 1 level tablespoon drained and finely chopped capers, olives or gherkins; 1 small crushed garlic clove; 1 level dessertspoon tomato concentrate (can or tube); 2 teaspoons lemon juice; pepper to taste. Spread equal amounts over 4 crispbreads. Top with shredded lettuce.

Jacket Potatoes

Curiously enough, potatoes are lower in calories than one would expect and a largish one, weighing 4 ounces, is only about 92 calories. Consequently, one can slim quite happily on potatoes, provided they are not eaten to excess or used as an accompaniment to main courses. Have them as a meal in their own right. With 1 or 2 additions, they are substantial and tasty and below are a few suggestions showing how the universally popular 'spud' can be used to good advantage in a low calorie diet.

JACKET POTATOES WITH COTTAGE CHEESE

serves 2

2 ½-pound baking potatoes
4 ounces cottage cheese
1 level tablespoon finely chopped parsley
1 tablespoon tomato ketchup
1 teaspoon Worcester sauce
1 level tablespoon chopped gherkin
1 small onion, grated
salt and pepper to taste

Preheat oven to moderately hot, 375°F or Gas 5 (190°C). Wash and scrub potatoes. Put on to lightly oiled baking tray. Bake just above centre of oven 1½–2 hours or until potatoes feel soft when gently pressed between finger and thumb. Remove from oven. Cut in half lengthwise. Remove middles. Mash finely. Add all remaining ingredients. Return to potato cases. Stand on baking tray. Return to oven. Reheat for 15 minutes. Serve with green vegetables or salad.

To prevent potatoes bursting in oven *After washing and scrubbing potatoes, prick all over with fork or make short slits in skins with sharp knife.*

Jacket Potatoes with Dutch Cheese *Make exactly as Jacket Potatoes with Cottage Cheese but this time combine mashed potatoes with 3 ounces finely grated Edam cheese, 1 tablespoon hot water, 1 level tablespoon instant skimmed milk granules, 1 level teaspoon continental mustard, 2 level teaspoons tomato concentrate (can or tube) and salt and pepper to taste. Return to potato cases. Reheat as directed.*

Jacket Potatoes with Beef *Make exactly as Jacket Potatoes with Cottage Cheese but this time combine mashed potatoes with 1 tablespoon hot water, 1 level tablespoon instant skimmed milk granules, 4 ounces finely chopped cold roast or boiled beef, 2 level teaspoons horseradish and salt and pepper to taste. Return to potato cases. Reheat as directed.*

To vary *Corned beef may be used instead of roast or boiled beef.*

Jacket Potatoes with Bacon and Onion *Make exactly as Jacket Potatoes with Cottage Cheese but this time combine mashed potatoes with 1 boiled and finely chopped onion, 3 ounces chopped and crisply fried lean bacon, 2 teaspoons hot water, 1 level tablespoon instant skimmed milk granules, large pinch ground nutmeg and salt and pepper to taste. Return to potato cases. Reheat as directed.*

Pasta

Another surprise where calories are concerned is pasta, for eggless varieties contain about 100 calories per 1 ounce raw weight. Therefore, all sorts of appetizing thoughts spring to mind; such as the following.

INSTANT MACARONI CHEESE

serves 2

4 ounces macaroni, eggless
1 egg, beaten
2 level tablespoons
instant skimmed milk granules
2 level teaspoons tomato concentrate
(can or tube)
1 ounce dry Cheddar cheese, finely grated
salt, pepper and prepared
mustard to taste

Cook macaroni in plenty of boiling salted water until just tender; 8–10 minutes. Drain, leaving behind about 2 tablespoons water. Return pan of macaroni to low heat. Add all remaining ingredients. Toss with 2 spoons until egg is lightly set. Pile on to 2 warm plates. Serve as it is or sprinkle with chopped parsley, chives or watercress.

To vary *Add 3 skinned and chopped medium tomatoes instead of concentrate.*

MACARONI WITH TOMATO SAUCE

serves 2

1 small can (about 8 ounces) tomatoes
1 level teaspoon dried basil
1 small garlic clove,
crushed or finely chopped
1 tablespoon dried pepper flakes
2-inch strip lemon peel
salt, pepper and
sugar substitute to taste
4 ounces macaroni, eggless

Put all ingredients, except macaroni, into pan. Bring to boil. Lower heat. Cover. Simmer gently 30 minutes. Bring plenty boiling salted water to boil. Add macaroni. Cook until just tender; 8–10 minutes. Drain. Put equal amounts on to 2 warm plates. Top with sauce, after first removing lemon peel. Top each portion with 1 heaped teaspoon grated Parmesan cheese.

PASTA SHELL SALAD

serves 2–3

4 ounces bow or shell-shaped
pasta, eggless
6 ounces cold roast or boiled beef
(poultry if preferred), chopped
4 tablespoons sliced raw mushrooms
4 ounces cooked green beans
2 unpeeled red-skinned apples,
cored and chopped
1 carton (¼ pint) natural yogurt
2 tablespoons fresh orange juice
½ level teaspoon onion salt
shake pepper
mustard and cress and/or
curry powder for garnishing

Cook pasta in plenty of boiling salted water until just tender; 8–10 minutes. Drain. Leave until cold. Put into bowl. Add meat, mushrooms, beans and apples. Beat yogurt, orange juice, onion salt and pepper well together. Pour on to the salad. Toss thoroughly. Transfer to a salad bowl and sprinkle with cress and/or curry powder.

SLIMMERS' TOMATO DRESSING

just under ¼ pint

2 slightly rounded tablespoons
natural yogurt
4 tablespoons tomato juice
½ teaspoon *each,* Worcester sauce
and continental mustard
shake garlic salt

An excellent dressing that may be used as a salad topping, or to replace French dressing in tossed salads.

Beat all ingredients well together.

Peppy Tomato Dressing *Make exactly as Slimmers' Tomato Dressing but include also ½–1 level teaspoon curry powder and shake of Tabasco or shake of cayenne pepper.*

Lemon Tomato Dressing *Make exactly as Slimmers' Tomato Dressing but reduce tomato juice by 1 tablespoon and replace with 1 tablespoon fresh lemon juice. Half teaspoon grated lemon may be added as well.*

Mild Tomato Dressing *Make exactly as Slimmers' Tomato Dressing but omit Worcester sauce, mustard and garlic salt. Add instead ½ level teaspoon finely grated orange peel and 2 teaspoons lemon juice.*

MOCK SALAD CREAM

serves 4

2 hard-boiled egg yolks
1 ounce instant skimmed milk granules
large pinch dry mustard
salt and pepper to taste
1 tablespoon malt vinegar
1–2 tablespoons water

Mash yolks finely. Combine with milk granules, mustard and salt and pepper. Whisk in vinegar and sufficient water to make smooth cream.

Sieving Egg Yolks *Instead of mashing the egg yolks, press them through a fine mesh sieve.*

To vary *For milder Salad Cream, use lemon juice instead of vinegar.*

Tarragon Flavoured Salad Cream *If salad cream is going to be used over egg or fish salads, tarragon flavoured vinegar adds a subtle flavour.*

Blender Salad Cream *Use the same ingredients as given in the recipe for Mock Salad Cream (page 74). Put into a liquidizer goblet and blend until smooth.*

CHEESE DRESSING

makes about ¼ pint

**4 ounces low fat cheese,
such as curd or cottage
1 level teaspoon finely chopped parsley
finely grated peel and
juice of 1 medium lemon
1 heaped tablespoon
instant skimmed milk granules
3 tablespoons water
salt and pepper to taste
artificial powdered sweetener to taste**

Mash cheese finely. (If using cottage cheese, rub through sieve.) Beat in all remaining ingredients. Chill. Spoon over mixed salads of all types.

To vary *Include 1 level tablespoon scissor-snipped chives and/or 1 level tablespoon finely chopped gherkins, olives or capers.*

Cheese Dressing for Fresh Fruit Salads *Make exactly as Cheese Dressing above, but use finely grated peel and juice of ½ lemon and juice only of 1 medium orange. Omit salt and pepper.*

STUFFED EGGS

serves 2

**4 hard-boiled eggs
1 ounce dry Cheddar cheese, finely grated
2–3 teaspoons cold milk
salt and pepper to taste
4 large lettuce leaves
Low Calorie Dressing or
Salad Cream to taste (page 74)
2 medium carrots, grated
4 black olives or gherkins**

Halve the boiled eggs lengthwise. Transfer yolks to bowl. Mash finely. Add cheese. Work to paste with milk. Season. Place in whites. Line four plates with lettuce. Top each with stuffed egg halves. Coat with Dressing or Salad Cream. Garnish with grated carrots, olives or gherkins.

Herb-Stuffed Eggs *Prepare as Stuffed Eggs but add 2 level teaspoons each, finely chopped parsley and chives to egg yolk mixture.*

Paprika-Stuffed Eggs *Follow recipe for Stuffed Eggs but omit cheese. Instead, add 1 level teaspoon paprika and 1 ounce curd or cottage cheese to yolks.*

Fish-Stuffed Eggs *Follow recipe for Stuffed Eggs but omit cheese. Add 2 ounces well-drained canned and finely mashed sardines, mackerel fillets, tuna or pink salmon to egg yolks. Include ½ level teaspoon finely grated lemon peel. Substitute lemon juice for milk.*

To shell hard-boiled eggs easily *As soon as eggs are boiled, pour off all the boiling water and cover eggs with cold water from tap. Leave until required. If eggs are left to cool off in hot water, they will be difficult to shell.*

Farm-fresh eggs *Leave about 3 days before hard-boiling otherwise they will prove extremely difficult to shell.*

To prevent eggs breaking or splitting while boiling *Add 1 or 2 teaspoons vinegar to the water. Eggs are less likely to split if at room temperature, therefore if kept in refrigerator, remove an hour or so before cooking.*

EGG AND MUSHROOM SALAD

serves 4

½ medium lettuce, washed and
leaves shaken dry
4 hard-boiled eggs, sliced
4 ounces raw mushrooms, sliced
Slimmers' Tomato Dressing (page 74)
½ bunch watercress, chopped

Line four plates with lettuce. Top with egg slices and mushrooms. Coat with dressing. Sprinkle with watercress.

To vary *Use any of the other low calorie dressings given in this section.*

MOULDED TOMATO SALAD

serves 2

¾ pint chicken or beef stock (fat skimmed)
1 envelope gelatine
2 level tablespoons tomato concentrate
(can or tube)
1 small onion, grated
salt and pepper to taste
1 small green pepper,
de-seeded and finely diced
6 ounces cold roast chicken,
coarsely chopped
1 medium carrot, grated
2 medium celery stalks, chopped
1 hard-boiled egg,
pressed through fine sieve

Pour stock into pan. Add gelatine and tomato concentrate. Stir over low heat until both have dissolved. Add onion. When cold and just beginning to thicken and set, fold in all remaining ingredients except egg. Transfer to 2-pint rinsed mould or basin. Leave until set. Unmould on to plate. Shower with egg. Serve with lettuce salad.

To vary *The green pepper may be omitted and ¼ medium chopped cucumber (peeled or unpeeled) used instead.*

ALL-IN-ONE COLESLAW

serves 4

1 medium head white cabbage
2 large carrots, grated
4 medium celery stalks, chopped
4 ounces Edam or
processed Cheddar cheese, diced
1 small whole fresh pineapple
Low Calorie Dressing or
Salad Cream to taste (page 74)

Finely shred cabbage. Put into large bowl. Add next 3 ingredients. Skin pineapple. Dice flesh. Add to rest of salad ingredients with dressing. Toss thoroughly.

TOSS-UP

serves 2

1 medium crisp lettuce,
well-washed and dried
½ small cauliflower
2 unpeeled rosy apples,
cored and sliced
¼ medium unpeeled cucumber, sliced
2 ounces Edam, cut into tiny cubes
Low Calorie Dressing or Salad Cream
to taste (page 74)
2 sliced tomatoes
2 level tablespoons cooked peas

Shred lettuce. Coarsely chop cauliflower. Put both into bowl. Add next 4 ingredients. Toss thoroughly. Transfer to two plates. Garnish with tomatoes and peas.

PARSLEY SAUCE

serves 4–5

1 ounce instant skimmed milk granules
½ pint milk
2 large eggs, beaten
1 level teaspoon cornflour
salt and pepper to taste
pinch ground nutmeg
2 heaped tablespoons
chopped parsley

Dissolve milk granules in water. Put into top of double saucepan (with simmering water underneath) or into basin standing over pan of gently boiling water. Add eggs and cornflour. Cook, stirring frequently, until sauce is thick enough to coat back of spoon, 30 minutes. (Sauce will curdle if allowed to boil.) Remove from heat. Season. Add nutmeg and parsley. Serve over poached white fish or boiled chicken.

Cheese Sauce *Make exactly as Parsley Sauce, adding 1 ounce dry, grated Cheddar cheese with eggs and cornflour. Omit nutmeg and parsley. Use ½ level teaspoon prepared mustard instead. Serves 4.*

Curry Sauce *Make exactly as Parsley Sauce, omitting nutmeg and parsley. Instead, add 2–4 level teaspoons curry powder and dash Worcester sauce with eggs and cornflour. Serves four or five.*

CAULIFLOWER CHEESE

serves 4

Make Cheese Sauce as directed above. Cook 1 largish head cauliflower in boiling salted water until tender. Drain. Transfer to heatproof dish. Coat with sauce. Sprinkle with 1 ounce grated Cheddar cheese. Brown under hot grill. Accompany with grilled tomatoes.

ONION CHEESE

serves 4

Make Cheese Sauce as directed above. Boil 4 large Spanish onions in salted water until tender when pierced with fork. Drain. Transfer to heatproof dish. Coat with sauce. Sprinkle with 1 ounce grated Cheddar cheese. Brown under hot grill. Serve with freshly cooked carrots, sprinkled with chopped parsley.

Milk Shakes

For those with blenders, fresh fruit milk shakes, plus thinly buttered crispbread, a small piece of Edam cheese and 1 or 2 whole tomatoes, make a pleasant and healthy light lunch or supper snack on warm busy days.

ORANGE MILK SHAKE

serves 1

**1 ounce instant skimmed milk granules
cold water
4 ounces fresh orange,
weighed after peeling
artificial sweetener to taste**

Make up milk granules to ½ pint with water. Put into blender goblet. Cut up orange, removing pips and pith. Add to goblet with sweetener. Blend until smooth. Pour into glass and drink straight away.

Berry Fruit Milk Shake *Make exactly as Orange Milk Shake, substituting 4 ounces raspberries, strawberries or loganberries for orange.*

Banana Milk Shake *Make exactly as Orange Milk Shake, substituting 1 medium banana for orange. Sprinkle top lightly with cinnamon or ground nutmeg.*
Diet note *If having Banana Milk Shake, omit cheese.*

Apple Milk Shake *Make exactly as Orange Milk Shake, substituting 4 ounces unpeeled eating apple (weighed after coring) for orange. If liked, flavour with powdered ginger or cinnamon. Drink straight away.*

Apple and Yogurt Shake *Shake together 1 carton (¼ pint) natural yogurt and ¼ pint apple juice. Drink straight away.*

To vary *Canned and unsweetened orange or tomato juice may be used instead of apple.*

Desserts

These tend to be a problem for slimmers with a sweet tooth, so I hope the following recipes will help to ease the burden!

MOCK WHIPPED CREAM

serves about 4

2 ounces instant skimmed milk granules
cold water
2 teaspoons fresh lemon juice, strained
powdered artificial sweetener to taste
1 teaspoon vanilla essence

Make up milk granules to ¼ pint with cold water. Using whisk, beat until stiff with all remaining ingredients. Serve over fresh fruit salad or over cold stewed fruit, sweetened to taste with artificial sweetener.

For speed *If you have a mixer, beat ingredients together with electric beaters; it saves arm ache too!*

To vary *If Mock Cream is going to be served over fresh stewed apricots, flavour cream with little almond essence instead of vanilla.*

VANILLA ICE CREAM

serves 4–6

2 ounces instant skimmed milk granules
cold water
4 large eggs, well-beaten
2 teaspoons vanilla essence
artificial sweetener to taste

A high protein but non-fattening ice cream which must surely be a rare treat for slimmers !

Set refrigerator to coldest setting at least 1 hour before making ice cream. Wash and dry 1 or 2 ice cube trays, removing dividers. Make up milk granules to 1 pint with water. Pour into pan. Bring just up to boil, stirring. Remove from heat. Beat in all remaining ingredients. Return to top of double saucepan (with gently simmering water beneath) or to basin standing over pan of gently boiling water. Cook, stirring frequently, until mixture thickens enough to coat back of spoon. (About 30–40 minutes). On no account allow mixture to boil or it will curdle. Remove from heat. Cool. Pour into trays. Put into freezing compartment of refrigerator. Leave until ice cream has frozen about ½ inch round sides of tray. Turn into bowl. Beat until smooth. Pour back into trays. Return to freezing compartment. Leave until frozen and firm, turning out and beating hard 2 or 3 times more for smooth consistency.

For speed *Heat skimmed milk in heavy-based saucepan. Add all remaining ingredients. Stir continuously over lowest possible heat until custard thickens sufficiently to coat back of spoon. Over-cooking or too high a heat will result in scrambled eggs!*

Remember *to turn refrigerator back to normal setting after ice cream has frozen, or foods in rest of cabinet may freeze up.*

Coffee Ice Cream *Make exactly as Vanilla Ice Cream but omit vanilla essence. Dissolve 2–3 heaped teaspoons instant coffee in milk while it is heating.*

Orange or Lemon Ice Cream *Make exactly as Vanilla Ice Cream but add finely grated peel and juice of 2 medium oranges or lemons to custard after it has been removed from heat. For decorative touch, reserve orange or lemon shells and fill with scoops of orange or lemon ice cream before serving. Top with fresh mint leaves for colour contrast.*

Peppermint Ice Cream *Make exactly as Vanilla Ice Cream but omit the vanilla essence. After custard has cooled, stir in peppermint essence to taste. Tint pale green with food colouring.*

Rum Ice Cream *Make exactly as Vanilla Ice Cream but omit vanilla essence and substitute rum essence instead.*

Mock Pistachio Ice Cream *Make exactly as Vanilla Ice Cream but omit vanilla essence. After custard has cooled, stir in almond essence to taste. Tint pale green with a little food colouring.*

Strawberry or Raspberry Ice Cream *Make exactly as Vanilla Ice Cream. After custard has cooled, stir in 8 ounces crushed fresh strawberries. If necessary, add little extra artificial sweetener.*

Apricot Ice Cream *Make exactly as Vanilla Ice Cream. Leave to cool. Rub about ¾ pound fresh stewed apricots (sweetened with artificial sweetener) through fine sieve to give thickish purée. Add to cooled custard with, if liked, ½–1 teaspoon almond essence.*

Slimmers' Sundaes

MELBA STYLE

serves 4–6

Put scoops of Vanilla Ice Cream into 4–6 sundae glasses. Top each with ½ peeled fresh peach. Coat with fresh raspberries, either rubbed through sieve or blended until smooth in blender goblet, and sweetened to taste with artificial sweetener.

JAMAICAN

serves 4–6

Halve 2 small pineapples lengthwise. Carefully scoop out flesh, taking care not to pierce skins. Cut flesh into small dice, discarding central cores. Return flesh to pineapple shells. Top with scoops of rum-flavoured ice cream and Mock Whipped Cream (page 78). Dust very *sparingly* with instant coffee granules.

KNICKERBOCKER GLORIES

serves 4–6

Chop up 2 cored but unpeeled rosy apples and 2 peeled and cored dessert pears. Sprinkle with lemon juice to stop browning. If in season, add 1 dozen stoned and halved cherries. Transfer to 4–6 sundae glasses. Top with scoops of Apricot Ice Cream. Decorate with Mock Whipped Cream (page 78) and *light* scattering of flaked and toasted almonds.

STRAWBERRY SPECIAL

serves 4–6

Slice 8 ounces fresh strawberries. Chop up 1 medium peeled orange. Combine both fruits. Put equal amounts into 4–6 sundae glasses. Top with scoops of Orange Ice Cream. Decorate each with 1 unpeeled orange slice—slit from centre to outside edge and shaped into twist—and sprig of mint.

BANANA SUNDAES

serves 4–6

Permissible if diet has been light through the day! Split four medium bananas lengthwise. Stand one on each plate. Sandwich together with Vanilla Ice Cream. Decorate with Mock Whipped Cream (page 78). Dust tops very *sparingly* with cocoa powder. Sprinkle with few chopped nuts or top each with ½ glacé cherry.

ORANGE WHIP

serves 4

**1 pint fresh, frozen or unsweetened canned orange juice
4 level teaspoons gelatine
2 tablespoons cold water
powdered artificial sweetener
2 egg whites
about 1 level dessertspoon
finely grated orange peel**

Put 4 tablespoons orange juice into pan. Add gelatine to cold water. Mix well. Leave 4–5 minutes. Add to juice in pan. Stir over low heat until dissolved. Stir in rest of orange juice. Sweeten to taste. Leave in cold place until just beginning to thicken and set (consistency of unbeaten egg whites). Beat egg whites to stiff snow. Beat jelly until foamy then fold in egg whites. When smooth and evenly combined, transfer to four sundae glasses. Chill until set. Sprinkle with peel before serving.

CAFE AU LAIT

serves 4–6

Put scoops of Coffee Ice Cream into 4–6 sundae glasses. Top with mounds of Mock Whipped Cream (page 78). Dust *lightly* with cocoa powder.

CORAL REEF

serves 4–6

Slice 6–8 ounces strawberries. Put equal amounts into 4–6 sundae glasses. Top with scoops of Vanilla Ice Cream. Decorate with Mock Whipped Cream (page 78) and strings of redcurrants.

Slimmers' Fruit Fools

STRAWBERRY OR RASPBERRY YOGURT FOOL

serves 4

1 level teaspoon gelatine
2 teaspoons water
½ pint strawberry or raspberry purée, made from fresh fruit
(or frozen without sugar)
powdered artificial sweetener to taste
1 carton (¼ pint) natural yogurt
1 egg white

Soften gelatine in cold water 5 minutes. Transfer to pan. Stir over low heat until dissolved. Add to fruit purée. Sweeten to taste. Leave until cold and just beginning to thicken slightly. Stir in yogurt. Beat egg white to stiff snow. Fold into fruit mixture. Pile into four sundae glasses. If liked, decorate with whole strawberries or raspberries. Serve straight away.

Banana Yogurt Fool *Make exactly as Strawberry or Raspberry Yogurt Fool, but substitute 3 large bananas for soft fruit. Mash finely with 3 teaspoons lemon juice.*

Gooseberry Yogurt Fool *Make exactly as Strawberry or Raspberry Yogurt Fool, using ½ pint gooseberry purée made from stewed gooseberries (sweetened with artificial sweetener). Tint mixture pale green with food colouring. Decorate each with mint sprig.*

Fools with Custard

If preferred, fools may be made slightly richer by combining the fruit with home-made egg custard (used when cold). Below is the recipe.

EGG CUSTARD SAUCE

serves 4

½ pint skimmed milk
3 standard eggs, beaten
1 teaspoon vanilla essence
artificial sweetener to taste

Bring milk just up to boil, stirring. Beat well together with eggs. Pour into top of double saucepan (with gently simmering water beneath) or into basin standing over saucepan of gently boiling water. Cook, stirring frequently, until mixture thickens enough to coat back of spoon; about 20–30 minutes. Stir in vanilla. Sweeten to taste. On no account allow custard to boil or it will curdle. Leave custard until completely cold, when it will thicken up.

For easy Fruit Fool *Combine Egg Custard with ½ pint fresh fruit purée, sweetened to taste with artificial sweetener.*

Warning note *Don't be tempted to make fruit purée from canned fruit, or from frozen fruit which is already sugared.*

BAKED EGG CUSTARD

serves 4

**1 pint skimmed milk
4 standard eggs and 1 or 2 extra yolks
artificial sweetener to taste
1 teaspoon vanilla essence
ground nutmeg**

Preheat oven to moderate, 325°F or Gas 3 (170°C). Lightly grease 2-pint heatproof dish. Bring milk to boil, stirring. Beat in all remaining ingredients except nutmeg. Pour into dish. Stand in roasting tin containing 2 inches cold water. Sprinkle with nutmeg. Bake in centre of oven about 45–60 minutes or until custard is set. Serve hot or cold, either by itself or with stewed fruit sweetened with artificial sweetener.

To test if custard is set   *Insert knife into centre. If it comes out clean, the custard is set.*

To avoid air bubbles   *Leave custard to stand 30 minutes before baking then tap sides of dish slightly with wooden spoon.*

Orange or Lemon Custard   *Make as Baked Egg Custard but add 1 level teaspoon finely grated orange or lemon peel to milk/egg mixture. Sprinkle with ground cinnamon or ginger before baking.*

Coffee Custard   *Make as Baked Egg Custard but dissolve 1 tablespoon instant coffee granules in milk while it is heating.*

ORANGE SORBET WITH YOGURT

serves 4–6

**2 cartons (each ¼ pint) natural yogurt
1 can frozen concentrated
orange juice, thawed
finely grated peel of 2 medium oranges
4 level teaspoons gelatine
4 tablespoons water
2 egg whites**

Set refrigerator control to coldest setting 1 hour before starting. Combine yogurt, orange juice and orange peel. Soften gelatine in 2 tablespoons water for 5 minutes. Add rest of water. Transfer to pan. Stir over low heat until dissolved. Add to yogurt mixture. When cold and just beginning to thicken, beat egg whites to stiff snow. Fold into yogurt mixture with large metal spoon. When smooth and evenly combined, transfer to dish. Put into freezing compartment of refrigerator. Freeze until firm. To serve, put scoops of sorbet into glasses. Eat straight away.

Grapefruit Sorbet   *Make exactly as previous recipe, using 1 can frozen concentrated grapefruit juice, thawed. Include finely grated peel of 1 medium grapefruit.*

Use up peeled oranges in a Citrus Cocktail Starter. Segment oranges by cutting out flesh between membranes with knife. Repeat with 1 medium grapefruit. Put both fruits, together with any juice, into bowl. Sweeten to taste with artificial sweetener. Cover and chill. Transfer to dishes before serving. Serves 2.

To prevent wastage of juice   *Segment both oranges and grapefruit over a bowl.*

APPLES AND CUSTARD

serves 4–6

As this is such a firm favourite, simply make egg custard as given in recipe above. Meanwhile, stew 1–1½ pounds peeled, cored and sliced apples with water and artificial sweetener to taste. Put hot apples into 4 or 6 bowls and top with hot custard.

Spiced Apples   *If liked, stew the apples in the above recipe with a little cinnamon and 2–3 cloves.*

Lemon Apples   *Half level teaspoon finely grated lemon peel, added to the hot stewed apples, gives it a subtle fragrance and flavour.*

Rhubarb and Custard   *Make exactly as Apples and Custard. If liked, cook rhubarb with a little ground ginger.*

BAKED APPLES AND CUSTARD

serves 4

**4 medium-sized cooking apples
(Bramleys are best)
powdered artificial sweetener to taste
4 heaped teaspoons diabetic jam
(flavour to taste)
5 tablespoons water
Egg Custard Sauce (page 80)**

Preheat oven to moderately hot, 375°F or Gas 5 (190°C). Wash and dry apples. Remove cores two-thirds of the way down each. With sharp knife, score line round each apple, about one-third of the way down from top. Sprinkle apple cavities with powdered sweetener. Fill with jam. Stand in shallow heatproof dish. Add water. Bake just above centre of oven until apples are tender and puff up like soufflés. Baste once or twice with water whilst apples are cooking. Serve apples straight away. Pass custard separately.

To vary Use apple juice instead of water. Alternatively, try 5 tablespoons low calorie ginger ale.

CHILLED LEMON CHEESE CAKE

serves 6–8

**12 ounces cottage cheese
2 egg yolks
finely grated peel of 1 lemon
3 tablespoons fresh lemon juice
1 envelope gelatine
5 tablespoons water
1 carton (¼ pint) natural yogurt
1 teaspoon vanilla essence
powdered artificial sweetener to taste
2 egg whites**

Rub cheese through sieve into bowl. Beat in yolks, lemon peel and juice. Soften gelatine in 2 tablespoons water for 5 minutes. Put into pan with rest of water. Stir over low heat until dissolved. Add to cheese mixture with yogurt and essence. Mix thoroughly. Sweeten to taste with artificial sweetener. When cold and just beginning to thicken and set, fold in stiffly beaten egg whites. Transfer to 7–8-inch cake tin, first rinsed with cold water. Chill until firm and set. Turn out on to serving plate. Cut into wedges with knife dipped in warm water. Serve with fresh berry fruits, or with stewed fruit, sweetened with artificial sweetener.

Chilled Orange Cheese Cake Make exactly as previous recipe but omit lemon peel. Instead, include finely grated peel of 1 medium orange. Add lemon juice as directed.

Alcohol

Although alcohol should be taboo when one is dieting, the occasional glass of wine may probably do more good than harm and purely for interest, I list some approximate calorific values.

1 small glass	*calories*
dry white wine	60–70
dry red wine	65–75
dry sherry	65
medium dry sherry	70
sweet sherry	75

BEER DRINKERS

Don't! But if you really can't do without, then reckon that each ½ pint mild ale is as much as 155 calories; each ½ pint strong ale or stout is 210 calories.

CHEESE AND BISCUITS

For those who prefer to finish their diet meal off with cheese and biscuits instead of a sweet, the following approximate calorific values may be of some help.

	calories
1 starch reduced roll	27
1 crispbread	30
1 medium slice starch reduced bread	30–40
1 cream cracker	40
1 water biscuit	30
1 digestive biscuit	60

Cheeses

Full-fat cheeses should be avoided whilst slimming unless they are part of a medically controlled diet. The cheeses with the *least* calories per ounce are:

Cheese	calories (approx.)
Camembert	88
Edam	88
Gouda	96
Cheese spreads	82
Cottage cheese	33

Cheeses to avoid *Cream, Stilton and Gruyère.*

Grow your Own

Many keen gardeners take immense pride and pleasure in growing their own fruits and vegetables, be it in their back garden, back yard or allotment. For all those who sometimes wonder what to do with the surplus (and, let's face it, there are limits as to how much one can off-load on to friends and neighbours), I offer a selection of jams, pickles and chutneys, which should help to solve the problem. In addition, home-made preserves, made with home-grown produce, are far cheaper than shop bought varieties and if attractively wrapped, make welcome gifts at all times of the year.

Jam-making Hints

Avoid over-ripe and wet fruit.

Choose large heavy-based saucepan. Jam rises up when boiling and can easily overflow if pan is too small.

Avoid skimming jam as it boils. This tends to be wasteful and is better done after jam has reached setting point and finished cooking. A knob of butter or margarine stirred in at end, helps to disperse any scum that remains.

Although specialists advise preserving sugar (it creates less scum), I always use granulated because it is cheaper and results are perfectly satisfactory.

Always use large wooden spoon for stirring jam. Metal ones get over-heated.

To test if jam is set, pour spoonful on to cold saucer. Leave 2 minutes. If skin forms on top and crinkles when touched, jam is ready. For those who have sugar thermometers, the temperature should reach 220°F.

Cool jam slightly before potting. Strawberry jam and marmalade should be left in pan until skin forms on top; otherwise fruit and peel will sink to bottom.

Cover with waxed discs while jam is still hot. Add Cellophane tops when jam is completely cold.

Store in *cool, dry* place and away from strong sunlight: dampness can turn jam mouldy; excess heat can cause fermentation.

PLUM OR GREENGAGE JAM

makes about 5 pounds

**3 pounds stewing plums or
greengages (or mixture)
¾ pint water
3 pounds granulated sugar**

Wash and halve fruit. Remove stones if they come out easily; otherwise leave. Put fruit and water into pan. Bring to boil. Lower heat. Cover. Simmer gently about 30 minutes or until fruit is very soft. Add sugar. Stir over low heat until dissolved. Bring to boil, stirring. Boil fairly briskly until setting point is reached, removing stones as they rise to top. Stir frequently. Remove from heat. Skim. Cool slightly. Pot and cover.

To vary *1 level teaspoon finely grated orange peel adds a distinctive flavour.*

Damson Jam *Make exactly as plum or greengage jam, using 2½ pounds damsons.*

MIXED CURRANT JAM

makes about 5 pounds

**1½ pounds blackcurrants
1 pound redcurrants
1½ pints water
3 pounds granulated sugar**

This gives a better flavoured jam than using all blackcurrants and is also less 'dry'.

Put currants into pan with water. Simmer very gently until skins are tender (about 45 minutes). Add sugar. Stir over low heat until dissolved. Bring to boil, stirring. Boil fairly briskly until setting point is reached. Stir frequently. Remove from heat. Skim. Cool slightly. Pot and cover.

Blackcurrant Jam *Make exactly as mixed currant jam, using 2½ pounds blackcurrants.*

Rhubarb

Rhubarb is an excellent additive for jam. It combines well with most fruits; it contributes little flavour of its own and therefore never dominates the jam; it is an economical 'filler'.

RHUBARB AND BLACKCURRANT JAM

makes 5 pounds

Make exactly as Mixed Currant Jam, using 2 pounds currants and 1 pound chopped-up rhubarb.

RHUBARB AND APPLE JAM

makes 5 pounds

**1¼ pounds cooking apples
(prepared weight)
1¼ pounds rhubarb
(prepared weight)
3 pounds granulated sugar
1 ounce ground ginger**

Peel, core and slice apples. Wash and cut rhubarb into chunks. Put apples into bowl, layering them with half the sugar. Repeat with rhubarb. Cover both bowls. Leave to stand 24 hours. Put both fruits—with their syrup—into saucepan. Add ginger. Bring to boil, stirring. Boil fairly briskly until setting point is reached. Stir frequently. Remove from heat. Skim. Cool slightly. Pot and cover.

RHUBARB AND STRAWBERRY JAM

makes between 4–5 pounds

**1½ pounds rhubarb
(weight after trimming)
4 tablespoons water
1½ pounds smallish strawberries
2¾ pounds granulated sugar**

Cut rhubarb into chunks. Put into pan. Add water and strawberries. Slowly bring to boil.

Lower heat. Cover. Simmer 15 minutes. Add sugar. Stir over low heat until dissolved. Bring to boil, stirring. Boil fairly briskly until setting point is reached. Stir frequently. Remove from heat. Skim. Cool slightly. Pot and cover.

Rhubarb and Raspberry Jam *Make exactly as Rhubarb and Strawberry Jam, substituting raspberries for strawberries.*

RHUBARB AND BLACKBERRY JAM

makes 5 pounds

1½ pounds rhubarb
(weight after trimming)
1½ pounds firm blackberries
(not over-ripe)
4 tablespoons water
3 pounds granulated sugar

Chop rhubarb. Put into pan. Add berries and water. Bring to boil. Lower heat. Cover. Simmer slowly until fruit is very soft. Add sugar. Stir over low heat until dissolved. Bring to boil, stirring. Boil fairly briskly until setting point is reached. Stir frequently. Remove from heat. Skim. Cool slightly. Pot and cover.

FIGGY RHUBARB JAM

makes about 9 pounds

1 pound dried figs
4 pounds rhubarb
(prepared weight)
1 pound cooking apples or gooseberries
(prepared weight)
finely grated peel and
juice of 2 medium lemons
finely grated peel and
juice of 1 orange
4½ pounds granulated sugar

An old-fashioned recipe which produces an interesting and unusual preserve.

Wash figs well. Soak overnight in plenty of water. Next day, drain. Reserve ¾ pint liquor.

Coarsely chop figs. Cut rhubarb into chunks. Peel, core and slice apples or top and tail gooseberries. Put all fruit into pan with peel and juice of lemons and orange. Bring to boil. Lower heat. Cover pan. Simmer 15–20 minutes or until fruit is very soft. Add sugar. Stir over low heat until dissolved. Bring to boil. Boil fairly briskly until setting point is reached. Stir frequently. Remove from heat. Skim. Cool slightly. Pot and cover.

RASPBERRY AND APPLE JAM

makes about 5 pounds

This jam is a good keeper and the seeds of the raspberries are less noticeable than in jam made only from raspberries.

Use 1½ pounds raspberries and 1½ pounds peeled, cored and sliced cooking apples. Cook until very soft in ¼ pint water. Add 3 pounds granulated sugar then follow recipe for Raspberry and Redcurrant Jam.

RASPBERRY AND REDCURRANT JAM

makes about 5 pounds

1½ pounds raspberries
1½ pounds redcurrants
½ pint water
3 pounds granulated sugar

Crush raspberries. Put currants into saucepan with water. Bring to boil. Lower heat. Cover. Simmer 20 minutes or until skins are very tender. Add raspberries and sugar. Stir over low heat until sugar has dissolved. Bring to boil, stirring. Boil fairly briskly until setting point is reached. Stir frequently. Remove from heat. Skim. Cool slightly. Pot and cover.

Raspberry and Blackcurrant Jam *Make exactly as Raspberry and Redcurrant Jam, substituting blackcurrants for red. Simmer currants about 30 minutes before adding raspberries and sugar.*

Raspberry and Gooseberry Jam *Make exactly as Raspberry and Redcurrant Jam, substituting topped and tailed gooseberries for redcurrants. Simmer for same length of time before adding raspberries and sugar.*

RASPBERRY JAM (1)

makes about 5 pounds

**2½ pounds raspberries,
as fresh as possible
3 pounds granulated sugar,
warmed in moderate oven
1 tablespoon strained lemon juice**

Put raspberries into heavy pan. Simmer very gently over low heat until juice begins to run. Bring slowly to boil. Boil 7 minutes. Add warm sugar and lemon juice. Leave over low heat until sugar dissolves, stirring. Bring to boil. Boil briskly *2 minutes only.* Remove from heat. Skim. Leave to cool slightly. Pot and cover.

Keeping raspberry jam *Due to short boiling time, this jam has a light set and is apt to deteriorate more quickly than raspberry jam made in the traditional way. Therefore I store mine in the least cold part of the refrigerator. The main advantage of this jam is its beautifully fresh raspberry flavour and brilliant colour.*

RASPBERRY JAM (2)

makes about 5 pounds

**3 pounds raspberries
3 pounds granulated sugar**

Put raspberries into heavy pan. Crush fruit over medium heat. Add sugar. Stir until dissolved. Slowly bring to boil, stirring. Boil briskly until setting point is reached. Remove from heat. Skim. Leave to cool slightly. Pot and cover.

Loganberry Jam *Make exactly as Raspberry Jam, 1 or 2.*

GOOSEBERRY JAM

makes about 5 pounds

**2½ pounds gooseberries,
(topped and tailed)
1 pint water
3 pounds granulated sugar**

Put gooseberries into saucepan with water. Bring to boil. Lower heat. Cover. Simmer until fruit is very soft. Add sugar. Stir over low heat until dissolved. Bring to boil. Boil briskly until setting point is reached. Stir frequently. Remove from heat. Skim. Cool slightly. Pot and cover.

Gooseberry and Strawberry Jam *Make exactly as Gooseberry Jam, using 1½ pounds topped and tailed gooseberries and 1½ pounds small strawberries.*

STRAWBERRY JAM

makes 5 pounds

**3½ pounds strawberries
3 tablespoons lemon juice
3 pounds granulated sugar**

Put strawberries into pan with lemon juice. Simmer slowly 30 minutes. Add sugar. Stir over low heat until dissolved. Bring to boil. Boil briskly until setting point is reached. Remove from heat. Skim. Leave until skin forms on surface. Stir. Pot and cover.

To vary *Use ½ ounce tartaric or citric acid (available from chemists) instead of lemon juice. Increase strawberries and sugar by ½ pound each. Cook exactly as directed for Strawberry Jam. Yield is between 5–6 pounds.*

STRAWBERRY AND REDCURRANT JAM

makes about 5 pounds

1½ pounds redcurrants
1½ pounds strawberries
¼ pint water
3 pounds granulated sugar

Put fruit into pan with water. Bring to boil. Lower heat. Cover. Simmer until fruit is very soft (20–30 minutes). Add sugar. Stir over low heat until sugar dissolves. Bring to boil. Boil briskly until setting point is reached. Stir frequently. Remove from heat. Skim. Leave until skin forms on surface. Stir. Pot and cover.

BLACKBERRY JAM

makes about 5 pounds

3 pounds blackberries
juice of 1 lemon
4 tablespoons water
3 pounds granulated sugar

Put blackberries into pan with lemon juice and water. Bring to boil. Lower heat. Cover. Simmer slowly, about 30 minutes or until fruit is very soft. Add sugar. Stir over low heat until dissolved. Bring to boil. Boil briskly until setting point is reached. Stir frequently. Remove from heat. Skim. Cool slightly. Pot and cover.

To vary *Use 1 level teaspoon tartaric acid instead of lemon juice.*

BLACKBERRY AND APPLE JAM

makes about 5 pounds

1½ pounds blackberries
1½ pounds cooking apples
(weight after peeling and coring)
½ pint water
3 pounds granulated sugar

Put blackberries into saucepan. Slice apples. Add to pan with water. Bring to boil. Lower heat. Cover. Simmer gently until fruit is very soft. Add sugar. Stir over low heat until dissolved. Bring to boil. Boil briskly until setting point is reached. Stir frequently. Remove from heat. Cool slightly. Pot and cover.

Seedless Blackberry and Apple Jam *To make seedless jam, cook both fruits to pulp with water. Rub through sieve. To each pint purée, allow 1 pound granulated sugar. Cook over low heat until sugar dissolves. Proceed as in previous recipe.*

BLACK CHERRY JAM

makes about 5 pounds

3 pounds dark cherries
(weight after stoning)
¼ pound redcurrants
juice of 2 medium lemons
¼ pint water
3 pounds granulated sugar

Put cherries into pan with currants, lemon juice and water. Bring to boil. Lower heat. Cover. Simmer gently until fruit is very soft. Add sugar. Stir over low heat until dissolved. Bring to boil. Boil briskly until setting point is reached. Stir frequently. Remove from heat. Cool slightly. Pot and cover.

CHERRY AND GOOSEBERRY JAM

makes about 5 pounds

2 pounds cherries
(weight after stoning)
1 pound gooseberries, topped and tailed
¼ pint water
3 pounds granulated sugar

Put fruit into pan with water. Bring to boil. Lower heat. Cover. Simmer gently until fruit is very soft. Add sugar. Stir over low heat until dissolved. Bring to boil. Boil fairly briskly until setting point is reached. Stir frequently. Remove from heat. Cool slightly. Pot and cover.

Cherry and Redcurrant Jam *If preferred, use 1 pound redcurrants instead of gooseberries.*

APRICOT JAM

makes about 5 pounds

**3 pounds fresh apricots
½ pint water
juice of 1 lemon
3 pounds granulated sugar**

Halve and stone fruit. Put into pan with water and lemon juice. Bring to boil. Lower heat. Cover. Simmer until fruit is very soft. Add sugar. Stir over low heat until dissolved. Bring to boil. Boil fairly briskly until setting point is reached. Stir frequently. Remove from heat. Skim. Leave until skin forms on top. Stir. Pot and cover.

Apricot and Orange Jam *As above but add grated peel and juice of 1 large orange with water and lemon.*

Apricot kernels *If time permits and you have a co-operative husband, ask him to crack some of the apricot stones. (This needs a strong hand and reliable hammer!) Put kernels into boiling water. Leave 2 minutes. Drain. Slide off skins. Stir kernels into jam after removing pan from heat.*

Apricot and Almond Jam *This has an intriguing fragrance and flavour. After removing Apricot Jam from heat add almond essence to taste and about 1 ounce flaked almonds.*

MIXED FRUIT JAM

makes about 5 pounds

**3-pound mixture of strawberries, black- or redcurrants, gooseberries, stoned cherries, plums, etc.
¼ pint water
3 pounds granulated sugar**

Put prepared fruit into pan with water. Bring to boil. Lower heat. Cover. Simmer gently until fruits are very soft. Add sugar. Stir over low heat until dissolved. Bring to boil. Boil fairly briskly until setting point is reached. Stir frequently. Remove from heat. Cool slightly. Pot and cover.

MULBERRY AND RHUBARB JAM

makes about 5 pounds

**1 pound prepared rhubarb
¼ pint water
3 pounds mulberries
3 pounds granulated sugar
finely grated peel and
juice of 2 medium lemons**

Cut rhubarb into chunks. Put into saucepan with water. Add mulberries. Bring to boil. Lower heat. Cover. Simmer gently until fruit is very soft. Add sugar and lemon peel and juice. Stir over low heat until dissolved. Bring to boil. Boil fairly briskly until setting point is reached. Stir frequently. Remove from heat. Skim. Pot and cover.

Mulberry and Apple Jam *Use 1 pound cooking apples (weight after peeling) or gooseberries instead of rhubarb.*

QUINCE JAM

makes 5 pounds

**2 pounds quinces
(weight after peeling and coring)
juice of 1 lemon
1 pint water
3 pounds granulated sugar**

Slice quinces. Put into pan with lemon juice and water. Bring to boil. Cover. Simmer gently until fruit is very soft. Add sugar. Stir over low heat until dissolved. Bring to boil. Boil fairly briskly until setting point is reached. Stir frequently. Remove from heat. Skim. Pot and cover.

MARROW AND GINGER JAM

makes about 5 pounds

3 pounds marrow (prepared weight)
3 pounds granulated sugar
1 ounce root ginger
3 large lemons

Cube marrow. Put into large bowl. Add half the sugar. Mix thoroughly. Cover. Leave overnight. Transfer to saucepan. Bruise ginger by hitting it gently with hammer. Peel lemons thinly. Tie ginger and lemon peel in piece of muslin. Add to pan with lemon juice. Stir over low heat until sugar dissolves. Simmer 30 minutes. Add rest of sugar. Stir until dissolved. Continue to simmer until marrow is transparent (about 20–30 minutes). Remove from heat. Skim. Leave until luke-warm. Pot and cover.
Note This jam never has a firm set and is more like a syrupy conserve.

Fruit Jellies

These are made from cooked fruit juice (as opposed to whole fruit) and sugar. The usual proportion is 1 pound granulated sugar to 1 pint juice.

APPLE JELLY

Wash and dry as many apples as are required. Remove stalks and bruised pieces and discard. Cut fruit into thick pieces without peeling or coring. Put into pan, allowing ½ pint water and juice of ½ lemon to every pound of fruit. Cook slowly, covered, until fruit is soft and pulpy. Strain through jelly bag or large piece of sheeting into bowl. Do not squeeze at any time as pieces of fruit can be forced through and in turn make jelly cloudy. Measure fruit juice. Put into saucepan with 1 pound sugar to each pint. Stir over low heat until sugar dissolves. Bring to boil. Boil fairly briskly until setting point is reached, stirring frequently. Remove from heat. Cool slightly. Pot and cover.

Apple and Blackberry Jelly *Make exactly as Apple Jelly, using half apples and half blackberries.*

Crab-apple Jelly *Make exactly as Apple Jelly.*

Minted Apple Jelly *Add handful of mint (tied in muslin bag) to Apple Jelly while it is boiling. If liked, colour jelly pale green with food colouring before potting.*

Spicy Apple Jelly *Add 1 cinnamon stick and between 2–6 cloves to apples while cooking.*

Apple and Orange Jelly *Make exactly as Apple Jelly, adding 2 level teaspoons finely grated orange peel to apples while cooking.*

Apple and Elderberry Jelly *Make as Apple Jelly, using half apples and half elderberries. Allow only ¼ pint water to each pound fruit.*

Apple and Ginger Jelly *Make exactly as Apple Jelly, adding 1 ounce bruised root ginger to every 4 pound apples.*

Redcurrant Jelly *Make as Apple Jelly.*

Blackcurrant Jelly *Make exactly as Apple Jelly but use an extra 4 tablespoons water to every pound fruit.*

Bramble Jelly (Blackberry Jelly) *Make exactly as Apple Jelly but use only 4 tablespoons water and juice of ½ medium lemon to every pound fruit.*

Gooseberry Jelly *Make exactly as Apple Jelly. If liked, flavour jelly with finely grated peel of 1 small lemon.*

Marmalade

As the cost of oranges, lemons and grapefruits has increased so much, I have become less inclined to make marmalade in recent years. Its preparation is bothersome and there is very little saving—if any—by comparison with the many excellent shop-bought varieties available. Occasionally, when I'm in the mood, I compromise and buy a 1¾-pound can of ready-to-use marmalade oranges and make it up as directed. With 3 pounds of sugar, I get about 5 pounds of good-tasting marmalade, and not much effort involved. However, for those who like chunky marmalade or mixed flavours here is how I adapt my 'canned' marmalade.

CHUNKY ORANGE

Wash and peel 2 large oranges. Cut peel into short, stubby pieces. Cook in water until softish. Drain. Add to marmalade while it is boiling.

GRAPEFRUIT OR LEMON

Wash and finely grate peel of 1 medium grapefruit or 2 medium lemons. Add to marmalade while it is boiling.

Home Freezing

Before freezing fruit and vegetables in a domestic deep freeze, a certain amount of preliminary preparation is required to prevent the action of particular enzymes which would spoil colour, flavour, texture and nutritive value. This takes the form of blanching, details of which are given below.

HINTS ON HOME FREEZING

It is advisable to check the instruction manual which comes with the freezer before you start freezing food, but here are some general hints which may be found useful.

Fruits and vegetables selected for freezing should be as fresh as possible; ideally freshly picked from the garden.

After being prepared, they should be packed in polythene bags (the thicker the better), lengths of polythene sheeting, heavy duty aluminium foil or double thickness of ordinary, waxed containers (which may be used several times), foil dishes or plastic tubs. Bags and wrappings should be pressed round vegetables and fruits—so that as much air as possible is excluded—and then closed firmly with plastic-coated wire ties. Joins should be held in place with special freezer tape; ordinary tape works loose at low temperatures. If containers have lids, these should be put on and the joins also sealed with tape. Containers without lids may be covered with foil and then taped.

In order to know what is what, all packages and cartons should be labelled with contents and date. Special labels are available from freezer shops and should be filled in with a wax pencil.

When packing vegetables in purée form (tomatoes for example) 1 inch head-room should be left at top of container as liquids expand on freezing.

BLANCHING

To Blanch Fill large pan with 8 pints water. Bring to boil.

Put 1 pound prepared vegetables into wire basket or sieve. Lower into water.

Blanch for length of time given for each vegetable (see below), timing the process after water in pan has returned to rapid boil.

Remove vegetables and rinse under cold running water.

Drain thoroughly.

Blanching water may be used 6—8 times before changing.

VEGETABLES

Broad Beans *Shell. Blanch 3 minutes. Drain. Rinse. Pack and seal. Store up to 1 year.*

French Beans *Top and tail. Wash thoroughly. Leave whole. Blanch 3 minutes. Drain. Rinse. Pack and seal. Store up to 1 year.*

Runner Beans *Top and tail. Cut away stringy sides. Wash. Slice diagonally. Blanch for 3 minutes. Drain. Rinse. Pack and seal. Store up to 1 year.*

Brussels Sprouts *Choose tightly closed and small sprouts. Remove outer leaves. Wash sprouts. Blanch 4 minutes. Drain. Rinse. Pack and seal. Store up to 1 year.*

Cabbage *Remove discoloured leaves and discard. Wash cabbage. Shred. Blanch for 1½ minutes. Drain. Rinse. Pack and seal. Store up to 6 months.*

Carrots *Choose small ones. Peel or scrape. Top and tail. Wash. Blanch 5 minutes. Drain. Rinse. Pack and seal. Store up to 6 months.*

Cauliflower *Break head into florets. Wash. Blanch 3½ minutes. Drain. Rinse. Store up to 8 months.*

Corn-on-the-Cob *Choose young ones. Remove husk and silk. Blanch 6 minutes. Drain. Rinse. Pack and seal. Store up to 1 year.*

Peas *Shell. Blanch 1½ minutes. Drain. Rinse. Pack and seal. Store up to 1 year.*

Potatoes *These do not freeze well when raw, and should either be creamed, packed in cartons, sealed and frozen (up to 3 months only), or cut into chips, fried until pale gold, drained, cooled, packed and sealed. Chips freeze satisfactorily up to 3 months but must be partially thawed before being re-fried in hot oil or fat.*

Root Vegetables *These include parsnips, swedes and turnips, etc. Peel and dice. Blanch 3 minutes. Drain. Rinse. Pack and seal. Store up to 6 months.*

Spinach *Wash very thoroughly. Remove stalks. Blanch each 2 ounces of leaves for 2 minutes. Drain. Rinse. Pack and seal. Store up to 1 year.*

Tomatoes *These freeze best in purée form. Skin tomatoes as directed on page 55. Either rub through sieve or liquidize in blender goblet. Combine every 2 pints purée with 1 level teaspoon salt. Pack and seal. Store up to 1 year.*

Garden Herbs (1) *These do not need blanching. Simply chop leaves or leave in sprays. Wrap and seal. Store up to 1 year.*

Garden Herbs (2) *Wash herbs. Chop finely. Three-quarter fill ice cube tray (filled with usual dividers) with herbs. Top up with water. Freeze. When solid, transfer herb ice cubes to polythene bag. Pack and seal. To use, thaw as many cubes as required. Strain. Chopped herbs are then ready for use.*

FRUITS

Some fruits are best frozen in syrup and these include stoned apricots, plums, greengages, damsons, cherries, cubes of melon, peeled and sliced fresh peaches (for how to skin, see skinning tomatoes page 55), peeled and quartered pears and halved and de-seeded grapes.

Allow approximately ½ pint syrup to every pound prepared fruit and make it by slowly dissolving 8–10 ounces granulated sugar in 1 pint water. Leave until completely cold before using. Pack fruit and syrup into containers, leaving 1 inch headroom at top of each for expansion. Cover, seal and label. Store all fruits up to 1 year. Thaw in containers before using.

Important note regarding peaches and pears *To prevent browning, brush slices with lemon juice before packing with syrup.*

Soft Berry Fruits, Red- and Blackcurrants and Gooseberries *These may be packed in syrup as directed above or in dry sugar. Toss every pound of fruit with approximately 4 ounces caster sugar. Pack into cartons, leaving 1 inch headroom at top of each for expansion if in syrup; 1½ inches if in dry sugar. Cover, seal and label. Store up to 1 year. Serve fruit just before it has completely thawed.*

Apple Purée *Cook peeled, cored and sliced cooking apples with small amount of water until very soft. Beat to purée. Sweeten to taste (or liquidize cooked apples and sugar in blender goblet). Pack into cartons, leaving 1 inch headroom at top for expansion. Cover, seal and label. Store up to 1 year. Thaw before using.*

Gooseberry Purée *Make and prepare for freezing exactly as Apple Purée.*

Bottling Fruit

It is essential to invest in proper jars before attempting to bottle fruits. These are glass, wide-necked and come in 1- and 2-pound sizes. Each should have a heat-resistant glass disc cover with rubber band and screw-band to hold the discs in place. Jars, glass discs and screw-bands may be used repeatedly; new rubber bands must be used every time for seal to be effective.

Before bottling, make sure jars are very clean. After washing, rinse thoroughly under hot running water and do not dry the insides.

SYRUP FOR BOTTLING FRUIT

Although water is sometimes used for bottling fruit, it is much less satisfactory than syrup in that it contributes neither to the flavour nor to the colour of the fruit. Therefore I recommend the following syrup; dissolve 8 ounces granulated sugar in 1 pint water. Bring to boil. Boil 1 minute.

PREPARING THE FRUIT

Prepare soft fruits by removing hulls and/or skins. *Do not* wash *raspberries, loganberries* or *mulberries.* Do not bottle *strawberries*; they are rarely successful. Top, tail and wash *gooseberries*; prick each slightly to prevent shrivelling. Hull *blackberries* and wash well. Stalk *cherries* and wash; stone with cherry stoner if liked. Bottle washed *apricots* and *plums* either whole or first halved and stoned. Wash *damsons* and bottle unstoned. Peel and quarter *dessert pears* and gently remove cores; to prevent browning, put into cold water containing 2 teaspoons salt and $\frac{1}{4}$ ounce citric acid to every 2 pints. Rinse well before bottling. *Hard cooking pears* should be peeled, quartered and cored and stewed until tender in syrup (4–6 ounces granulated sugar to 1 pint water) before being drained and bottled. Peel, core and slice *apples* and drop into salted water to prevent browning; rinse before bottling. Cut trimmed *rhubarb* into 2-inch lengths.

PACKING THE FRUIT

Spoon fruit carefully into jars, packing it as closely as possible but at same time taking care not to bruise or crush it. If loosely packed, fruit, which inevitably shrinks after heating, may rise in the jars.

TO STERILIZE FRUIT IN OVEN

Make sure one shelf is centrally placed inside oven. Preheat oven to cool, 300°F or Gas 2 (150°C). Line large solid baking sheet with newspaper to catch juice which may boil over. Fill fruit-packed jars carefully with boiling syrup to within 1 inch of top. Put on rubber rings and glass discs. *Do not* place screw-bands in position. Stand jars about 2 inches apart on baking sheet. Place carefully in centre of oven.

TIME TO ALLOW IN OVEN

Cherries, damsons, whole plums, greengages, currants, blackberries, loganberries, mulberries, raspberries, gooseberries, rhubarb and apples:

1–4 pounds	40–50 minutes
5–10 pounds	55 minutes–70 minutes

Apricots and halved plums:

1–4 pounds	50 minutes–60 minutes
5–10 pounds	65 minutes–80 minutes

Pears:

1–4 pounds	60 minutes–70 minutes
5–10 pounds	75 minutes–90 minutes

TO CHECK BOTTLING

When ready, remove one bottle at a time from oven. Stand on wooden surface or on folded tea-towel resting on heatproof surface. Screw metal band on firmly. When cold, unscrew metal bands and try to lift bottles gently up by heat-resistant glass sealing disc. If disc remains firmly on bottle, this indicates that a vacuum has been formed, the seal is satisfactory and the fruit will remain in good condition. If the disc comes off, there may be a fault in the rim of the bottle, the rubber band or the cap. If all the discs come off, then the processing was incorrectly carried out. Either use up the fruit in cooking as soon as possible or re-process fruit in clean bottles with new fittings.

WATER-BATH METHOD

This is a more complicated method than the oven one and requires special equipment plus a sugar thermometer. Those who already bottle fruit by this method will probably have all the necessary apparatus and know exactly what they are doing. My advice to those who are new to fruit bottling is to stick to the above method which is comparatively trouble-free and relatively reliable. In addition, you will not be the victim of a steamy kitchen!

Fruit 'Cheeses'

These are thick preserves made from fruit purée and sugars and are worth making if you happen to have a glut of fruit in the garden and want a change from jam. 'Cheeses' make excellent spreads on breads, biscuits and scones and I like them with hot roast pork, lamb and all kinds of poultry. To make, simply cook any quantity of peeled, cored and sliced apples, crab-apples, damsons, quinces, stemmed black- or redcurrants or topped and tailed gooseberries with enough water to prevent fruit from sticking. When very soft, rub fruit and liquid through fine sieve. Measure carefully. To every pint of purée, allow 1 pound granulated sugar. Put purée and sugar into pan. Stir over low heat until sugar dissolves. Simmer gently until mixture becomes *very* thick, which can take anything up to 1½–2 hours. Stir frequently, in figure of eight movement with wooden spoon. The cheese is ready when spoon, drawn across surface, leaves straight, clean line. Transfer to small pots. Cover while still hot. Leave to mature 2–3 months before using.

QUINCE CHEESE

Add 1 level teaspoon citric acid and 1 level teaspoon finely grated lemon peel to every 3 pounds fruit.

SPICED APPLE OR CRAB-APPLE CHEESE

Add 3–4 cloves and 1–2 level teaspoons cinnamon to every 3 pounds apples while they are cooking with water.

GINGER APPLE OR CRAB-APPLE CHEESE

Add 1–2 level teaspoons ground ginger to every 3 pounds apples while they are cooking.

Pickles and Chutneys

PICKLED RED CABBAGE

**1 large head red cabbage
salt
spiced vinegar (see below)**

Remove any discoloured outer leaves from cabbage. Shred head finely. Put layers of cabbage and salt into large bowl. Cover. Leave overnight. Rinse. Drain well. Pack loosely into jars. Fill with cold spiced vinegar, leaving 1 inch headroom at top of each jar. Cover securely. Leave 1 week before using. Use up within 1 month as cabbage tends to lose crispness and colour if left any longer.

SPICED VINEGAR

Put 2 pints white vinegar into pan. Add 2 level tablespoons pickling spice, 1 cinnamon stick, 12 cloves, 1 blade mace and 1 bay leaf. Bring to boil. Simmer 5 minutes. Leave to stand overnight. Drain. Use as required.

PICKLED BEETROOT

Loosely pack jars with small boiled and skinned beetroots or larger ones, first sliced or cubed. Fill with cold spiced vinegar, leaving 1 inch headroom at top of each jar. Cover securely. Leave 1–2 weeks before using.

PICKLED ONIONS OR SHALLOTS

Peel as many onions or shallots as are required. Leave to soak in brine 36 hours. Drain and rinse. Loosely pack into jars. Fill with cold spiced vinegar. Cover securely. Leave 2–3 months before using.

Brine *Dissolve ½ pound salt in 4 pints water.*

APPLE CHUTNEY

makes about 5 pounds

4 pounds apples, peeled, cored and sliced
2 pounds onions, chopped
1–3 garlic cloves, chopped (optional)
1 pound cooking dates, chopped
2 pints malt vinegar
1½ pounds brown sugar
2 level teaspoons *each,*
salt and ground ginger
1 level teaspoon cinnamon

1 level tablespoon pickling spice ⎫
6 cloves
2 bay leaves
last three tied together in piece of cloth or muslin bag

Put apples, onions, garlic and dates into pan with half vinegar. Slowly bring to boil. Lower heat. Cover. Simmer ½ hour or until apples and onions are soft. Add all remaining ingredients. Stir over low heat until sugar dissolves. Cook, uncovered, until chutney thickens to jam-like consistency. Stir frequently. Remove from heat. Take out bag of spices. Pot and cover.

For speed *If preferred, apples, onions, garlic and dates may be coarsely minced instead of chopped.*

To vary *Use any other type of dried fruit instead of dates such as sultanas, stoned prunes or seedless raisins.*

Apple and Plum Chutney *Make exactly as Apple Chutney, using half cooking apples and half cooking plums. To allow for weight of stones, use approximately ¼ pound extra plums.*

Damson Chutney *Make exactly as Apple Chutney, using 4 pounds damsons and 1 pound cooking apples. Remove damson stones either before cooking or just before potting the chutney.*

Gooseberry, Plum and Apple Chutney *Make exactly as Apple Chutney, using 2 pounds topped and tailed gooseberries, 1 pound stoned cooking plums and 1 pound peeled, cored and sliced apples.*

Green Tomato Chutney *Make exactly as Apple Chutney, using 5 pounds chopped-up green tomatoes and only 1 pound onions.*

Red Tomato Chutney *Make exactly as Apple Chutney, using 5 pounds chopped-up red tomatoes and only 1 pound onions. Include 2 level tablespoons tomato concentrate (can or tube) and 1 tablespoon Worcester sauce.*

When Time is Money

Since so many of us these days are out working and running a home simultaneously, there comes a point when time is money. Thus, in this section, I have included fairly quick dishes of all kinds which incorporate dried, frozen and canned convenience foods. I admit this is not the cheapest way of cooking, but it does cut down on precious time and energy. In addition, the recipes (all tried out on my own family) are tasty, nourishing and, I hope, interesting. My own wish is that they will give the over-worked and over-rushed housewife a little more leisure.

QUICK ITALIAN SAUCE

serves 4–6

1 can (1 pound)
minced steak and onions in gravy
2–3 level tablespoons tomato concentrate
(can or tube)
1 garlic clove, chopped
1 level teaspoon *each,*
sugar and mixed herbs or basil
dash Worcester sauce
1 small can peeled tomatoes
salt and pepper to taste

Put all ingredients into pan. Bring to boil, stirring. Lower heat. Cover. Simmer gently 30 minutes. Stir once or twice. Serve over freshly boiled macaroni or spaghetti. Pass grated cheese separately.

MOCK BOLOGNESE SAUCE

serves 4–6

1 pound raw minced beef
1 pint water
1 packet minestrone soup mix
(1½ pint size)
salt and pepper to taste
grated cheese

Put minced beef into pan. Fry over medium heat until well-browned, breaking it up with fork all the time. Add water and soup powder.

Stir well to mix. Season. Bring to boil, stirring. Lower heat. Cover. Simmer gently 30 minutes. Serve with freshly boiled spaghetti or macaroni. Pass grated cheese separately.

QUICK CHILI CON CARNE

serves 4–5

1 can (about 1 pound)
minced steak and onions in gravy
1 can (about 1 pound)
baked beans in tomato sauce
1 small garlic clove, crushed
1 level dessertspoon
dried red and green pepper flakes
½–1 level teaspoon
carraway seeds (optional)
2–4 level dessertspoons chili powder
salt and pepper to taste

Put all ingredients into saucepan. Bring slowly to boil, stirring. Cover. Reduce heat. Simmer gently 30 minutes, stirring once or twice. Accompany with freshly boiled long grain rice (2–3 ounces raw weight per person) and either green vegetables to taste or salad.

Chili powder *is a purple-cum-brown pepper which is less fierce than Cayenne but more potent than paprika. If peppery foods are not appreciated in your house, it is wise to take the precaution of adding chili powder teaspoon by teaspoon.*

95

EASY SHEPHERD'S PIE

serves 4–5

1 can (about 1 pound) minced steak
1 teaspoon Worcester sauce
1 packet instant mashed potato
(about 4 servings)
about ½ ounce margarine

Turn minced steak into greased heatproof dish. Stir in Worcester sauce. Make up mash as directed. Spoon over steak. 'Rough up' with fork. Top with flakes of margarine. Reheat and brown towards top of hot oven, 425°F or Gas 7 (220°C) 15–20 minutes.

STEAK, CORN AND POTATO PIE

serves 4

1 can (about 1 pound) minced steak
1 level tablespoon dried onion flakes
1 small packet frozen sweetcorn
1 pound cold cooked potatoes
½ ounce margarine

Put steak, onion flakes and sweetcorn into greased heatproof dish. Stir well. Slice potatoes thinly. Arrange attractively on top of meat, etc. Top with flakes of margarine. Reheat and brown towards top of hot oven, 425°F or Gas 7 (220°C) 15–20 minutes.

Cheese-topped Pie *Make exactly as previous recipe but sprinkle potato slices with 2 ounces grated Cheddar cheese instead of dotting with margarine. Reheat as directed.*

CRISPY-TOPPED STEAK PIE

serves 4–5

Tip 1 can (1 pound) minced steak into greased heatproof dish. Crush 2 packets potato crisps (or use about ¼ of a family sized packet). Scatter over steak. Reheat towards top of moderately hot oven, 400°F or Gas 6 (200°C) about 20 minutes.

CRUMBLE STEAK PIE

serves 4

1 can (about 1 pound) stewed steak
1 level tablespoon dried onion flakes
4 tablespoons water
4 ounces plain flour
pinch salt
2 ounces margarine
½ level teaspoon mixed herbs

Preheat oven to moderate, 350°F or Gas 4 (180°C). Heat steak with onion flakes and water. Turn into fairly deep, greased pie-dish. Sift flour and salt into bowl. Rub in margarine. Add herbs. Toss ingredients lightly together to mix. Sprinkle thickly over steak mixture in dish. Bake in centre of oven 30 minutes. Serve with vegetables to taste.

To vary *Add 1–2 level tablespoons coarsely chopped salted peanuts to crumble mixture.*

Storing rubbed-in or crumble mixtures *These can be kept well in a polythene bag in the refrigerator and it is therefore practical to make up a large batch of rubbed-in mixture in one go (say 2 pounds flour and 1 pound fat). It can afterwards, and at a moment's notice, be turned into sweet or savoury crumble toppings, biscuits or short-crust pastry.*

MEAT AND VEGETABLE PIE

serves 4–5

1 can (1 pound) minced steak
1 level dessertspoon dried onion flakes
½ pound cooked mixed vegetables
(frozen or canned)
4 ounces rolled oats
2 ounces grated Cheddar cheese
1 level teaspoon paprika
3 ounces margarine, melted
salt and pepper

Tip meat into greased heatproof dish. Add onion flakes and vegetables. Stir well to mix. Combine oats, cheese and paprika. Stir in margarine with fork. Season. Sprinkle over meat. Reheat and brown towards top of moderately hot oven, 375°F or Gas 5 (190°C) 20–30 minutes.

MEAT AND VEGETABLE PIE
(WITH PASTRY)

serves 4–5

Follow recipe for crunchy-topped Meat and Vegetable Pie, but put steak, onion flakes and vegetables into greased pie-dish with rim. Moisten rim with water. Cover with 1 small packet (about ½ pound) frozen puff pastry (thawed), rolled out to fit top of dish. Brush with beaten egg or milk. Bake near top of hot oven, 425°F or Gas 7 (220°C) 15–20 minutes.

Covering a pie-dish *For best results, line dampened rim of dish with strip of pastry. Moisten strip with more water. Cover with pastry lid. Press edges well together to seal. Flake up edges by knocking them up with back of knife. If pie is to cook for long time, make one or two slits in top to allow steam to escape. Brush with egg and/or milk. Bake as directed in specific recipe.*

STEAK COBBLER PIE

serves 4

1 can (about 1 pound) stewed steak
1 level tablespoon dried onion flakes
½ level tablespoon dried celery flakes
2 tablespoons tomato juice
6 ounces self-raising flour
½ level teaspoon salt
1½ ounces lard or cooking fat
6 tablespoons cold milk
little beaten egg
(or left-over yolk or white)

Preheat oven to hot, 425°F or Gas 7 (220°C). Heat steak in saucepan with onion and celery flakes. Add tomato juice. Put into well-greased pie-dish. Sift flour and salt into bowl. Rub in fat. Mix to soft but not sticky dough with milk. Turn on to floured surface. Knead lightly until smooth. Roll out to ½ inch in thickness. Cut into twelve rounds with 2-inch biscuit cutter, re-kneading, rolling and cutting trimmings as

well. Stand on top of steak mixture, leaving a little room between each as they spread slightly. Brush with egg. Bake near top of oven 20 minutes or until cobbler topping is well-risen and golden. Serve with green vegetables to taste.

ALL-IN-ONE COBBLER PIE

serves 4

Add 8–12 ounces cooked mixed vegetables to stewed steak in saucepan. Include onion flakes and tomato juice. Omit celery flakes. Use slightly larger dish.

SPEEDY TOPPED STEAK PIE

serves 4

Prepare steak as in Steak Cobbler Pie and heat until very hot. Transfer to pie dish. Top with squares or triangles of bread, first spread with margarine. Sprinkle with grated Cheddar cheese. Brown under hot grill.

CREOLE-STYLE STEAK

serves 4

2 tablespoons dried onion flakes
1 tablespoon dried red and
green pepper flakes
boiling water
1 ounce margarine
1 can (10 ounces) condensed tomato soup
½ pint water
1 can ready-to-serve
cream of mushroom soup
4 ounces long grain rice
1 can (about 1 pound) stewed steak
salt and pepper to taste

Put vegetable flakes into bowl. Cover with boiling water. Leave 5 minutes. Drain. Heat margarine in pan. Add vegetable flakes. Fry 7 minutes or until pale gold. Add all remaining ingredients. Stir over low heat until very well combined. Cover. Simmer 15–20 minutes or until rice grains are tender. Serve with potatoes and green vegetables or green salad to taste.

To vary *Instead of dried vegetable flakes, 1 medium grated onion and 1 finely chopped, de-seeded green pepper may be used if preferred.*

SALMON PATE

serves 8

1 can (about 7 ounces) pink salmon
2 ounces fresh white breadcrumbs
2 ounces table margarine, melted
½ level teaspoon
finely grated lemon peel
juice of ½ medium lemon
1 small onion, very finely grated
pinch nutmeg
1 tablespoon cider, stock or water
1 egg, beaten
salt and pepper to taste

A pleasant change from liver pâté and excellent as a summer starter.

Preheat oven to moderate, 325°F or Gas 3 (170°C). Mash salmon and liquor finely after first removing bones. Add all remaining ingredients. Mix very thoroughly. Transfer to foil-lined 1-pound loaf tin. Smooth over the top with a knife. Cover with foil. Bake in the centre of the oven for 1–1¼ hours or until firm and set. Remove from the tin when cold. Slice and serve with hot toast.

To make removal of the pâté from the tin easier *Brush the foil lining heavily with some melted margarine.*

TUNA PATE

serves 8

Make exactly as salmon pâté, using 1 can (also about 7 ounces) tuna instead of salmon. If garlic flavour is appreciated, crush 1 small clove and add as well.

MOCK SWEET-SOUR PORK

serves 4

1½ ounces margarine
1 large onion, chopped
1 garlic clove, chopped
4 ounces mushrooms and stalks, sliced
12 ounces pork luncheon meat
6 ounces cooked green beans
(frozen or canned)
4 ounces cooked green peas
(frozen or canned)
1 medium can pineapple chunks
1 level tablespoon cornflour
1 level tablespoon soft brown sugar
3 tablespoons mild vinegar
¾–1 pound (raw weight)
ribbon noodles, freshly cooked

Heat margarine in large pan. Add onion and garlic. Fry gently until soft and pale gold. Add mushrooms. Fry over low heat 5 minutes. Cut luncheon meat into strips measuring 2 by ½ inch. Add to pan. Fry slowly 5 minutes, turning frequently. Add beans, peas and all but 8 pineapple chunks. (Reserve syrup from can.) Mix cornflour and sugar to smooth paste with vinegar and pineapple syrup. Add to pan of vegetables and luncheon meat, etc. Slowly bring to boil, stirring. Cover. Lower heat. Simmer 5 minutes. Line serving dish with noodles. Pile sweet-sour mixture in centre. Garnish with the eight pineapple chunks.

COD THERMIDOR

serves 4

4 cod steaks
1 packet cheese sauce mix
½ pint milk (skimmed or diluted evaporated if liked)
1 level teaspoon prepared mustard
2 ounces Cheddar cheese, grated
1 level tablespoon toasted breadcrumbs
2 medium tomatoes,
skinned and dried
½ ounce margarine

Using shallow pan, poach fish in very gently boiling water about 7–12 minutes, depending on thickness. Meanwhile make up cheese sauce as directed on packet, using ½ pint milk. Stir in mustard and 1 ounce cheese. Arrange drained fish in lightly greased shallow heatproof dish. Coat with hot sauce. Sprinkle rest of cheese and crumbs on top. Garnish with tomato slices. Add flakes of margarine. Brown under hot grill. Serve with creamed potatoes and vegetables to taste.

To vary *Use 4-6 ounce pieces of cod, coley or haddock fillet (skinned) instead of cod.*

COD FLORENTINE

serves 4

Poach cod as directed in recipe for Cod Thermidor. Make up 1 packet cheese sauce with ½ pint milk as directed. Heat 1 medium can spinach purée with ½ ounce margarine. Put into greased heatproof dish. Arrange cod steaks on top. Coat with hot sauce. Sprinkle with 2 ounces grated Cheddar cheese. Brown under preheated hot grill.

Eggs Florentine *Make exactly as Cod Florentine, substituting four lightly poached eggs for cod steaks.*

CURRIED CORNED BEEF

serves 4

Make up 1 packet white sauce mix with ½ pint milk as directed. Stir in 1–2 level tablespoons curry powder, 1 tablespoon tomato ketchup and 1 tablespoon seedless raisins. Season to taste. Cube 12 ounces corned beef. Add to hot sauce. Heat through thoroughly. Serve with freshly boiled rice and chutney.

To slice corned beef easily *If in can, leave in refrigerator overnight before opening and slicing. Corned beef is too soft to cut cleanly at room temperature; it tends to crumble.*

Instead of corned beef *Use 12 ounces sliced luncheon meat, breakfast sausage or slices of boiled bacon.*

LIVER 'SANDWICHES'

serves 4

**8 thinnish slices lambs' liver
1 ounce margarine
2 ounces fat bacon, chopped
½ packet sage and onion stuffing
(made up as directed)
flour
1 packet white sauce mix
½ pint milk
1 level tablespoon toasted breadcrumbs
½ ounce margarine**

Preheat oven to hot, 425°F or Gas 7 (220°C). Wash liver. Dry with paper towel. Heat margarine in pan. Add bacon. Fry gently until fat runs. Remove bacon. Add to stuffing, mixing it in well. Sandwich liver slices together, in pairs, with equal amounts of stuffing. Coat 'sandwiches' lightly on both sides with flour. Fry briskly in remaining margarine/bacon fat. Transfer to greased casserole. Make up white sauce mix with ½ pint milk as directed. Pour over liver. Sprinkle with crumbs. Dot with flakes of margarine. Reheat towards top of oven 15–20 minutes.

LUXURY LIVER

serves 4

**1 pound chicken livers
(available in tubs from supermarkets)
2 level tablespoons flour
1 ounce margarine
1 large onion, grated
¼ pint dry cider
salt and pepper to taste
¼ pint soured cream**

Wash livers. Dry on paper towels. Coat with flour. Heat margarine in pan. Add onion. Fry gently until soft and pale gold. Add livers. Fry little more briskly until well-browned. Add cider. Slowly bring to boil, stirring. Season. Lower heat. Cover. Simmer very gently 15 minutes. Stir in soured cream. Reheat without boiling. Accompany with freshly boiled rice and salad.

If livers are frozen *Make sure they are completely thawed before using.*

BAKED SAUSAGES IN CURRY SAUCE

serves 4

1½ pounds pork sausages
1 level tablespoon *each,*
flour and curry powder
1 ounce dripping or lard
1–2 ounces sultanas
1 cooking apple, peeled and grated
1 level tablespoon dried onion flakes
1 medium can
ready-to-serve mulligatawny soup
1 level tablespoon desiccated coconut

Preheat oven to hot, 425°F or Gas 7 (220°C). Coat sausages with mixture of flour and curry powder. Fry in hot dripping until crisp and golden. Put into heatproof casserole. Scatter with sultanas, apple and onion flakes. Pour soup into dish over sausages, etc. Sprinkle with coconut. Bake, uncovered, near top of oven 15–20 minutes or until heated through and coconut is just beginning to turn golden.

CHICKEN AND MUSHROOM CASSEROLE

serves 4

4 large par-boiled potatoes, sliced
8 ounces cooked mixed vegetables
(frozen or canned)
4 portions roasting chicken
1 can (10 ounces)
condensed cream of mushroom soup
¼ pint water
large pinch mace or nutmeg
pepper to taste

Preheat oven to moderate, 350°F or Gas 4 (180°C). Arrange potatoes over base of large, greased shallow casserole. Sprinkle with mixed vegetables. Arrange chicken on top, skin sides uppermost. Heat soup and water well together, beating lightly until smooth. Season with mace or nutmeg and pepper. Pour over chicken. Cover with lid or foil. Bake in centre of oven 1–1¼ hours or until chicken is tender. Accompany with salad.

Chicken and Tomato Casserole *Make exactly as Chicken and Mushroom Casserole, but use 1 can condensed tomato soup instead of the mushroom soup.*

CORNED BEEF AU GRATIN

serves 4

1 ounce margarine
1 medium onion, chopped
1–1½ pounds cold cooked potatoes
(or canned)
12 ounces corned beef (in one piece)
1 packet cheese sauce mix
¾ pint milk
shake Worcester sauce
½ level teaspoon
prepared English mustard
2 ounces Cheddar cheese, grated
1 level tablespoon toasted breadcrumbs

Preheat oven to moderately hot, 400°F or Gas 6 (200°C). Heat margarine in pan. Add onion. Fry gently, with lid on pan, 5–7 minutes or until pale gold. Cut potatoes into thickish slices. Slice corned beef. Make up cheese sauce mix with ¾ pint milk, as directed on packet. Season with Worcester sauce and mustard. Fill 2-pint greased casserole with layers of potatoes, beef and sauce, ending with layer of sauce. Combine cheese and crumbs well together. Sprinkle over sauce. Reheat and brown towards top of oven 20–30 minutes or until top is golden brown.

MEDITERRANEAN LAMB

serves 4

8 chump ends of lamb
1 ounce margarine
2 large onions, grated
1–2 garlic cloves, crushed
1–2 level tablespoons
dry red and green pepper flakes
1 can (10 ounces)
condensed tomato soup
1 strip lemon peel,
about 3 inches long

Preheat oven to moderate, 350°F or Gas 4 (180°C). Put chump ends into large casserole dish. Heat margarine in pan. Add onions and garlic. Fry gently until pale gold. Spoon over lamb in dish. Sprinkle with pepper flakes. Top with tomato soup, heated through gently. Place strip of lemon peel on top. Cover with lid or foil. Cook in centre of oven 1–1¼ hours. Serve with freshly boiled rice, macaroni or potatoes. Accompany with green salad.

EGGS IN CELERY CHEESE SAUCE

serves 4

6 hard-boiled eggs, freshly cooked
1 can (10 ounces) condensed celery soup
6 ounces Cheddar cheese, finely grated
3 tablespoons milk
2 level tablespoons finely chopped parsley
salt and pepper to taste
1 level tablespoon toasted breadcrumbs
½ level teaspoon paprika

Shell and halve eggs. Arrange in shallow, greased heatproof dish. In saucepan, combine soup with 4 ounces cheese and the milk. Whisk over low heat until sauce is creamy and smooth. Stir in parsley. Season. Pour over eggs in dish. Top with rest of cheese, breadcrumbs and paprika. Brown under hot grill. Serve with freshly made toast.

EASY BOEUF BOURGUIGNONNE

serves 4

1½ pounds beef shin
3 ounces unsmoked streaky bacon
1 ounce margarine
2 large onions, grated
2 level tablespoons flour
¼ pint stock
4 tablespoons red wine
1 can (10 ounces)
condensed tomato soup
1 level teaspoon mixed herbs
2 ounces mushrooms and stalks, sliced

With ordinary red wine, *Vin Ordinaire*, as cheap as it is at most supermarket chains, a few tablespoons added to Boeuf Bourguignonne is hardly an extravagance, especially as the rest of the bottle will undoubtedly be drunk with the meal itself!

Cube beef. Coarsely chop bacon. Fry bacon slowly in heavy saucepan until fat runs. Add margarine and melt. Add beef cubes. Fry little more briskly until golden brown. Remove to plate. Add onions to remaining fat in pan. Fry until pale gold. Stir in flour. Cook 1 minute. Gradually blend in stock, wine, soup and herbs. Bring to boil, stirring. Replace beef. Add mushrooms. Cover. Lower heat. Simmer over very low heat about 2 hours or until meat is tender. Stir frequently. Add little extra water if gravy appears to be thickening up too much. Serve with boiled potatoes and green vegetables to taste.

To pressure cook *Pressure cook Boeuf Bourguignonne for 15 minutes at 15 pounds pressure.*

Oven-cooked Boeuf Bourguignonne *Boeuf Bourguignonne will cook quite happily in the oven and can therefore be forgotten about for a good 3–4 hours; ideal for a busy hostess. Prepare as directed. Transfer contents of pan to heavy casserole. Cover closely. Cook in centre of cool oven, 300°F or Gas 2 (150°C) 3–3½ hours or until meat is tender.*

To freeze Boeuf Bourguignonne *Often it is a good idea to treble the quantity and freeze what is left. Transfer Boeuf Bourguignonne to suitable containers, leaving 1 inch headroom at top of each. Cover, seal and label. Freeze up to 2 months. Thaw in container, either overnight in refrigerator or about 2 hours at room temperature. Reheat before serving by boiling gently, 15–20 minutes.*

15 minutes in centre of oven. Remove. Carefully lift out foil. Meanwhile cook onions as directed on packet. Add 3 ounces cheese and egg yolks. Beat egg whites to stiff snow. Fold into sauce mixture. Season. Pour into flan case. Sprinkle rest of cheese on top. Bake near top of oven 25 minutes or until golden and puffy. Serve straight away. Accompany with salad.

BEEF BALLS IN PIQUANT SAUCE

serves 4–5

1 can (10 ounces) condensed tomato soup
3 tablespoons water
1 tablespoon salad cream or mayonnaise
1 level tablespoon sweet pickle
1 teaspoon Worcester sauce
3 teaspoons vinegar
1 pound lean minced beef
3 ounces fresh white breadcrumbs
1 small onion, grated
1 egg, beaten
salt and pepper to taste

Put soup, water, salad cream, pickle, Worcester sauce and vinegar into pan. Slowly bring to boil, stirring. Lower heat. To make meat balls, combine mince with remaining ingredients. Mix thoroughly. Shape into small balls. Drop into soup. Cover. Simmer 20 minutes. Serve with mashed potatoes and green vegetables.

CHEESE AND ONION PUFF FLAN

serves 4–5

1 packet (about ½ pound)
frozen shortcrust pastry, thawed
1 packet (½ pound)
frozen small onions in cream sauce
4 ounces Cheddar cheese, grated
2 eggs, separated
salt and pepper to taste

Preheat oven to moderately hot, 400°F or Gas 6 (200°C). Roll out pastry. Use to line 8-inch flan ring standing on lightly greased baking tray. Prick lightly all over. Line with foil to prevent pastry from rising as it cooks. Bake

102

MIXED MEAT LOAF

serves 6

1 pound raw minced beef
8 ounces pork or beef sausagemeat
3 level tablespoons porridge oats or
fresh white breadcrumbs
1 large onion, finely grated
1 egg, lightly beaten
1 level teaspoon mixed herbs
2 teaspoons ketchup or Worcester sauce

Preheat oven to moderately hot, 400°F or Gas 6 (200°C). Combine all ingredients well together. Shape into loaf on foil-lined baking tray (lightly greased first). Bake in centre of oven 1 hour. Slice. Serve hot with chips or creamed potatoes and green vegetables to taste.

Alpine Meat Loaf *After the above loaf has been cooking 45 minutes, remove from oven. Cover completely with 1 packet instant mashed potatoes (4–5 servings) made as directed on packet. Sprinkle with 1 ounce grated cheese. Return to hot oven, 425°F or Gas 7 (220°C) and cook further 15 minutes or until potatoes are lightly flecked with gold.*
To vary Top with lightly fried onions instead of cheese.

Meat Loaf Surprise *Make up Mixed Meat Loaf mixture exactly as directed above. Shape into loaf. Make two deep indentations and put in 2 hard-boiled eggs. Bring meat mixture over eggs so that they are well embedded in centre. Bake as directed. Very good cold with salad.*

Hamburgers *Make up mixed meat loaf mixture as directed. Shape into twelve cakes. Fry or grill about 7–10 minutes (depending on thickness), turning twice.*

All-beef Hamburgers *Make up mixture as given for mixed meat loaf but omit sausage-meat. All other ingredients remain unchanged. Serves 4.*

TOMATO MEAT LOAF

serves 6

1 can (10 ounces) condensed tomato soup
3 tablespoons water
2 ounces fresh white bread, diced
1 medium onion, finely grated
2 level tablespoons
finely chopped parsley
1 egg, lightly beaten
1½ pounds raw minced beef

Preheat oven to moderate, 350°F or Gas 4 (180°C). Put soup into pan with water. Heat to lukewarm. Mix 8 tablespoons with bread, onion, parsley and egg. Leave to stand 10 minutes. Combine with meat, mixing very thoroughly. Shape into loaf on foil-lined baking tray (grease foil first). Bake in centre of oven 1–1¼ hours. Serve hot with vegetables to taste. Accompany with tomato sauce, made by heating up rest of soup until hot. If liked, soup may be seasoned with a little Worcester sauce.

Left-over Meat Loaf *Wrap in foil and refrigerate. When cold, cut into slices and use as sandwich filling.*

SAVOURY SUPPER PIE

serves 4–5

1 large packet (about ¾ pound)
frozen puff pastry, thawed
1 ounce margarine
1 large onion, thinly sliced
1 garlic clove, crushed
1 large tomato, skinned and sliced
8 ounces skinless pork sausages,
halved lengthwise
2 eggs
salt and pepper
1 level tablespoon finely chopped parsley

Preheat oven to hot, 425°F or Gas 7 (220°C). Roll out two-thirds pastry and use to line fairly shallow 8–9-inch pie plate. Heat margarine in pan. Add onion and garlic. Fry gently until gold. Sprinkle over base of flan. Cover with tomato slices and sausages. Lightly beat eggs with salt and pepper. Pour over other ingredients in flan, reserving little egg for brushing. Sprinkle with parsley. Moisten edges of pastry with water. Cover with lid, rolled from rest of pastry. Press edges well together to seal. Brush top with egg. Bake just above centre of oven 30 minutes or until golden brown. Serve hot or cold.

Supper Pie with Bacon *Make exactly as previous recipe, replacing sausages with eight lightly fried or grilled streaky bacon rashers.*

SILVERSIDE WITH MOCK ROBERT SAUCE

serves 6

1 can (10 ounces) condensed oxtail soup
3 tablespoons water
1 level tablespoon tomato concentrate
(can or tube)
4 teaspoons vinegar
2 level teaspoons continental mustard
1 bay leaf
12 ounces sliced cooked silverside of
beef (or cooked brisket)

Put all ingredients, except meat, into saucepan. Cook slowly, whisking continuously, until sauce is smooth. Lower heat. Cover. Simmer gently 15 minutes. Remove bay leaf. Arrange meat on four hot dinner plates. Coat with sauce. Serve straight away with creamed potatoes and green vegetables to taste.

Reheating meat *It is inadvisable to reheat meat; warmth from plate and sauce will be ample.*

To freeze left-over sauce *Transfer to small container leaving 1 inch headroom at top. Cover, seal and label. Freeze up to 2 months. Store in container. Reheat gently before serving, adding little extra water if sauce is on thick side.*

SCALLOPED TUNA AND SWEETCORN

serves 4

1 can (12 ounces) sweetcorn kernels
1 can (7 ounces) tuna, drained and flaked
1 medium onion, grated
½ pint milk
3 eggs
pinch nutmeg
salt and pepper to taste
1 level tablespoon toasted breadcrumbs
½ ounce margarine

Preheat oven to moderate, 350°F or Gas 4 (180°C). Combine sweetcorn with tuna and onion. Beat milk and eggs well together. Add nutmeg. Season. Stir into tuna and corn mixture. Transfer to greased casserole. Sprinkle with crumbs. Dot top with flakes of margarine. Cook in centre of oven 30 minutes or until golden brown and set. Accompany with green vegetables to taste and chips.

Scalloped Haddock Casserole *Make exactly as above, using 8 ounces cooked and flaked smoked haddock instead of tuna.*

CHINESE PORK AND BROCCOLI

serves 4

1 large packet frozen broccoli, thawed
2 tablespoons salad oil
1 level teaspoon
finely chopped preserved ginger
½ level teaspoon salt
1 garlic clove, finely chopped
2 tablespoons soy sauce
1 level dessertspoon cornflour
3 tablespoons hot water
8 ounces pork luncheon meat, cubed
1–2 dessertspoons vinegar or lemon juice

Cut broccoli into 1-inch lengths. Heat oil in heavy frying pan. Add broccoli. Fry briskly 2 minutes, shaking pan gently all the time. Add ginger, salt, garlic and soy sauce. Cover. Simmer 5 minutes. Mix cornflour to smooth paste with water. Add cubes of luncheon meat to pan. Cover. Fry 5 minutes, shaking pan frequently. Stir cornflour mixture into ingredients in pan. Bring to boil, stirring. Add vinegar or lemon juice to taste. Serve very hot with freshly boiled rice or noodles.

To vary *Instead of luncheon meat, use 8 ounces cold roast chicken, lamb or beef instead. Cut into ½-inch cubes.*

QUICK IRISH STEW

serves 4

1 packet thick Devon onion soup
(1 pint size)
1½ pints water
1 level tablespoon dried onion flakes
2 pounds stewing lamb,
cut into neat pieces
1½ pounds potatoes, thinly sliced
salt and pepper to taste
2 level tablespoons chopped parsley

Make up soup as directed on packet, using 1½ pints water. Add all remaining ingredients except parsley. Bring to boil. Lower heat. Cover. Simmer gently 1½ hours or until meat is tender. Stir occasionally. Serve each portion sprinkled with parsley.

CHICKEN A LA KING

serves 3–4

2 ounces mushrooms
½ ounce margarine
1 packet white sauce mix
½ pint milk
8 ounces cold roast chicken, diced
1 level tablespoon dry red and
green pepper flakes
boiling water
2 tablespoons top of milk
1 egg yolk
salt and pepper to taste

Slice mushrooms. Fry in margarine 5 minutes. Make up sauce with milk as directed. Add mushrooms and chicken. Cover. Simmer 15 minutes. Meanwhile, cover pepper flakes with boiling water. Leave 10 minutes. Drain. Add to sauce mixture. Simmer further 7 minutes. Beat milk and egg yolk together. Stir into chicken mixture. Reheat without boiling. Season. Serve with freshly made toast or boiled rice.

To vary *Use any other poultry, or cold roast veal, instead of chicken.*

MACARONI MUSHROOM CHEESE

serves 4

**6–8 ounces quick-cooking macaroni
1 can (10 ounces)
condensed mushroom soup
½ soup can macaroni water
3–4 ounces Cheddar cheese, grated
pepper to taste
2 level tablespoons toasted breadcrumbs**

Cook macaroni in boiling unsalted water (soup contributes sufficient) until tender. Drain, reserving ¼ pint water. Bring soup and water to boil, whisking gently. Add 2–3 ounces cheese. Stir until melted. Season to taste with pepper. Add macaroni. Heat through, stirring. Transfer to greased heatproof dish. Sprinkle top with remaining cheese and crumbs. Brown under hot grill. Serve with green vegetables to taste.

Macaroni Tomato Cheese *Make exactly as Macaroni Mushroom Cheese, but use condensed tomato soup instead of mushroom.*

Macaroni Cheese Extravaganza *Make up either of the two previous recipes. While reheating with macaroni, add 4 rashers chopped and freshly fried streaky bacon, 4 tablespoons cooked peas and 1 small onion, chopped and lightly fried first in a little margarine or dripping.*

SHORT-CUT STEAK AND KIDNEY

serves 4

**2 level tablespoons dried onion flakes
boiling water
1 ounce margarine
1 pound shin of beef, cubed
1 can (10 ounces) condensed kidney soup
1 soup can water
1 teaspoon Worcester sauce**

Cover onion flakes with boiling water. Leave 10 minutes. Drain. Heat margarine in pan. Add onions. Fry gently until soft and pale gold. Move to one side of pan. Add beef. Fry little more briskly until well-sealed and brown. Add rest of ingredients. Slowly bring to boil, stirring. Lower heat and cover. Simmer gently 2–2½ hours or until meat is tender. Stir occasionally. Top up with extra water if gravy seems to be thickening up too much.

To pressure cook *Pressure cook 20 minutes at 15 pounds pressure.*

Short-cut Steak and Kidney Pie *When steak and kidney mixture is cold, turn into pie dish with rim. Cover with lid, cut and rolled from one small packet frozen and thawed puff pastry. Brush with beaten egg. Cook near top of hot oven, 425°F or Gas 7 (220°C) 20–25 minutes or until pastry is well-puffed and golden. Accompany with vegetables to taste.*

Croissant Steak and Kidney Pie *For a novelty touch, turn hot steak and kidney mixture into pie dish and top with four ready-made croissants (French style flaky rolls, available from some supermarkets), first warmed through under the grill or in the oven. It saves making a pastry topping!*

Steak and Kidney with Mustard Dumplings *Combine 4 ounces self-raising flour with large pinch salt, 1 level teaspoon dry mustard and 2 ounces packeted beef suet (already shredded). Mix to stiffish dough with 4–5 tablespoons cold water. With floured hands, shape into eight dumplings. Drop into steak and kidney about 15 minutes before it is ready.*

FISH AND POTATO CASSEROLE

serves 4

1 pound cold cooked potatoes
(or canned), sliced
4 tablespoons cooked sweetcorn
1 packet (1 pound) frozen fish fillets
1 can (10 ounces)
condensed mushroom or celery soup
2 ounces Cheddar cheese, grated
2 level tablespoons toasted breadcrumbs

Preheat oven to moderately hot, 375°F or Gas 5 (190°C). Line shallow, greased casserole dish with sliced potatoes. Sprinkle with sweetcorn. Arrange fish on top. Coat with undiluted soup. Sprinkle with cheese and breadcrumbs. Cook, uncovered, just above centre of oven 30 minutes. Accompany with salad.

Using frozen fish fingers *Line dish with potatoes as directed in previous recipe. Coat potatoes with 1 can undiluted condensed mushroom or celery soup. Top with twelve fish fingers. Sprinkle with 2 ounces grated Cheddar cheese. Reheat and brown towards top of moderately hot oven, 400°F or Gas 6 (200°C) 20–25 minutes.*

Thawing *It is unnecessary to thaw fish fingers first.*

CRISPY FISH CASSEROLE

serves 4

1 can (7 ounces) tuna
1 packet cheese sauce mix
½ pint milk
salt and pepper to taste
4 slices bread
2–3 ounces bacon dripping
celery salt

Preheat oven to hot, 425°F or Gas 7 (220°C). Drain tuna. Flake fish with fork. Make up sauce with milk as directed on packet. Stir in tuna. Season. Transfer to greased heatproof dish. Cube bread. Fry in dripping until golden. Pile

on top of tuna mixture. Sprinkle lightly with celery salt. Reheat towards top of hot oven, 425°F or Gas 7 (220°C), 10 minutes. Serve with salad or green vegetables.

Savoury Pancakes

Usually served sprinkled with sugar and lemon, pancakes are equally good if stuffed with savoury fillings and served piping hot with gravy or sauce.

BASIC PANCAKE RECIPE

makes 8

4 ounces flour
(use either plain or self-raising)
pinch of salt
1 standard egg
½ pint milk (skimmed if preferred)

Sift flour and salt into bowl. Mix to smooth, thick and creamy batter with egg and half the milk. Beat a good 5 minutes. Gently fold in rest of milk. Brush base of heavy, smooth-based 7–8-inch frying pan with cooking fat or salad oil. Heat until hot. Pour in sufficient batter to cover base of pan *thinly*. Fry until golden. Turn or toss over. Fry until golden. Repeat with rest of mixture.

Velvety Pancakes *Beat in 1 or 2 teaspoons melted margarine or salad oil with egg and first amount of milk.*

Blender Pancakes *Put all ingredients into blender goblet. Run machine until batter is smooth.*

Different-sized pancakes *From same quantity of batter, you will be able to make twelve pancakes in 5-inch pan and ten pancakes in 6-inch pan.*

To store pancakes *Stack, one on top of the other, with sheets of greaseproof paper between* each. *Wrap in foil or place in air-tight tin. Refrigerate up to 3 days.*

To freeze pancakes *Stack pancakes in same way as suggested above. Wrap closely in heavy duty foil. Seal securely and label. Store up to 2 months. Leave to thaw 2–3 hours at room temperature before use.*

CURRIED HADDOCK PANCAKES

serves 4

Make up 1 packet white sauce mix with ½ pint milk as directed. Stir in 1–2 tablespoons curry powder, 8 ounces cooked and flaked smoked haddock and 1 tablespoon raisins. Put equal amounts on to pancakes. Roll up. Stand in greased heatproof dish. Cover closely with foil. Reheat in centre of hot oven, 425°F or Gas 7 (220°C) 20 minutes. Serve with gravy, additional white sauce or condensed canned soup to taste, heated through until very hot with 1 or 2 tablespoons water.

CHICKEN AND MUSHROOM PANCAKES

serves 4

Heat ½ can condensed cream of mushroom soup with 2 tablespoons milk. Stir in ½–¾ pound cold chopped roast chicken, ½ level teaspoon finely grated lemon peel, squeeze lemon juice, pinch nutmeg and 1 level tablespoon chopped parsley. Divide equally between pancakes. Roll up. Reheat as directed in recipe for Curried Haddock Pancakes. Serve with sauce made from rest of mushroom soup, heated through with 2 or 3 tablespoons water.

SPINACH AND HAM PANCAKES

serves 4

Put 1 packet (14 ounces) frozen chopped spinach into saucepan containing ½ ounce melted margarine. Cover. Cook over brisk heat 6 minutes, shaking pan frequently. Uncover. Cook until most of the liquid has evaporated, stirring. Make up 1 packet cheese sauce mix as directed on packet with ½ pint milk. Stir in spinach, 2 ounces chopped ham, salt and pepper to taste and shake of nutmeg. Mix thoroughly. Divide equally between pancakes. Roll up. Arrange in greased heatproof dish. Moisten with 4–5 tablespoons chicken stock. Cover. Reheat as directed in Curried Haddock Pancakes.

EGG, ANCHOVY AND ONION PANCAKES

serves 4

Make up 1 packet white sauce mix as directed with ½ pint milk. Add 4 chopped hard-boiled eggs, 6–8 finely chopped anchovy fillets and 1 small finely grated onion. Season to taste. Divide equally between pancakes. Roll up. Arrange in greased heatproof dish. Moisten with 4–5 tablespoons chicken stock. Cover. Reheat as directed in Curried Haddock Pancakes above.

BACON, ONION AND OXTAIL PANCAKES

serves 4

Fry 4 rashers chopped streaky bacon in 1 ounce margarine for 3 minutes. Add 1 medium grated onion. Fry gently until pale gold. Stir in ½ can condensed oxtail soup. Mix well. Divide equally between pancakes. Roll up. Arrange in greased heatproof dish. Cover. Reheat as directed in Curried Haddock Pancakes above. Serve with sauce made by heating rest of soup with 2 tablespoons water.

STEAK AND TOMATO PANCAKES

serves 4

Divide 1 can (approximately 1 pound) minced steak between pancakes. Roll up. Transfer to greased heatproof dish. Coat with 1 can condensed tomato soup heated with ½ soup can water. Cover. Reheat as directed in Curried Haddock Pancakes above, allowing extra 5 minutes.

EASY MOCK-LASAGNE

serves 4

Cut eight cooked pancakes into quarters (or make twelve small ones in 5-inch pan). Fill greased heatproof dish with layers of pancakes, mock Bolognese Sauce (page 95) and 1 packet cheese sauce mix made up as directed on packet with ½ pint milk. Sprinkle thickly with 2–3 ounces grated Cheddar cheese. Reheat and brown towards top of hot oven, 425°F or Gas 7 (220°C) 15–20 minutes.

FRUIT LAYER PUDDING

serves 6

1 can (15 ounces) fruit-pie filling
6 ounces luxury margarine
6 ounces caster sugar
3 large eggs
1 level teaspoon finely grated lemon peel
6 ounces self-raising flour
1 level teaspoon baking powder
large pinch salt

Well grease 2-pint pudding basin. Put 3 tablespoons fruit-pie filling into the base. Beat all the remaining ingredients for 2–3 minutes or until smooth. Put into basin on top of the pie filling. Cover securely with double thickness greased greaseproof paper or foil. Stand in saucepan, half-filled with boiling water. Cover with lid. Steam 1¾ hours. Turn out on to warm plate. Accompany with rest of pie filling, heated through until hot.

QUICK FRUIT MERINGUE FLAN

serves 6

1 bought sponge flan case
1 can (15 ounces) fruit-pie filling
2 egg whites
pinch cream of tartar or
squeeze lemon juice
3 ounces caster sugar

Preheat oven to moderately hot, 400°F or Gas 6 (200°C). Stand flan case on heatproof plate. Fill with fruit-pie filling. Put egg whites and cream of tartar or lemon juice into clean, dry bowl. Beat until stiff. Gradually add half sugar. Continue beating until meringue is very thick and shiny, and stands in firm peaks. Gently fold in rest of sugar. Pile over pie filling. Bake in centre of oven about 15–20 minutes or until meringue is pale gold. Serve hot.

FRUIT TRIFLE

serves 6

6 trifle sponge cakes
red jam
4 tablespoons diluted orange squash
rum or sherry essence
1 can (15 ounces) fruit-pie filling
1 large can custard
4 tablespoons double cream
2 teaspoons milk
chocolate vermicelli to decorate

Split sponge cakes. Sandwich together with jam. Put into shallow serving dish. Flavour squash with essence to taste. Pour over cakes. Top with fruit filling. Cover completely with custard. Refrigerate. Just before serving, whip cream until thick with milk. Spoon mounds on top of custard. Sprinkle cream with vermicelli.

To vary *Use dessert topping instead of cream.*

CHOCOLATE ROLL TRIFLE

serves 6

Slice one chocolate Swiss roll and use to line base of serving dish. Moisten with 4 tablespoons diluted orange squash flavoured to taste with rum or sherry essence. Top with 1 can (15 ounces) apricot fruit filling. Coat completely with 1 large can custard. Decorate with whipped cream or dessert topping. Sprinkle with grated chocolate, 'hundreds and thousands' or chocolate vermicelli.

CREAM CHEESE FRUIT DESSERT

serves 4

**8 ounces cream cheese
2 tablespoons golden syrup or clear honey
1 can (15 ounces)
raspberries or strawberries**

Beat cream cheese until smooth with syrup or honey. Drain fruit. Reserve syrup. Rub fruit through sieve (or liquidize in blender goblet). Gently fold fruit into cream cheese mixture. Transfer to four sundae glasses. Refrigerate 3–4 hours or until thoroughly chilled. Gently pour reserved syrup over each.

QUICK FRUIT FOOL

serves 4–6

Beat 1 small can chilled evaporated milk with 1–2 tablespoons bottled lemon juice until really thick, with consistency of whipped cream. Combine with $\frac{1}{2}$–$\frac{3}{4}$ pint thick fruit purée made from stewed, canned or frozen fruit. Divide between 4–6 sundae glasses. Chill lightly before serving. If liked, decorate each with blobs of red jam or sprinkle with chocolate vermicelli.

SUGAR AND SPICE SLICE

makes 8 slices

**1 packet ($\frac{3}{4}$ pound)
frozen shortcrust pastry, thawed
2 eggs
6 ounces caster sugar
6 ounces cooking dates, finely chopped
2 level teaspoons mixed spice
2 ounces margarine, melted
2 teaspoons vinegar**

Preheat oven to moderately hot, 400°F or Gas 6 (200°C). Roll out pastry. Use to line lightly greased Swiss roll tin measuring about 12 by 8 inches. Beat eggs and sugar together until light, fluffy and as thick as whipped cream. (A slow job by hand, 7–10 minutes with mixer.)

Stir in remaining ingredients. Spread over pastry in tin. Bake in centre of oven 30 minutes. Cut into eight slices. Serve while still warm.

For those without mixers *Beat eggs and sugar in basin standing over saucepan of hot water; the mixture thickens up fairly quickly.*

GOLDEN CRUMB ORANGE PIE

serves 4–6

**1 packet (about $\frac{1}{2}$ pound)
frozen shortcrust pastry, thawed
2 ounces margarine
2 ounces caster sugar
1 egg, separated
$\frac{1}{2}$ can frozen
orange juice concentrate, thawed
4 ounces stale plain cake crumbs or
crushed biscuit crumbs**

Preheat oven to moderate, 350°F or Gas 4 (180°C). Roll out pastry. Use to line 8-inch flan ring standing on lightly greased baking tray. Cream margarine and sugar until light and fluffy. Beat in egg yolk. Add orange juice (mixture will curdle but this has no affect). Blend in crumbs. Beat egg whites until stiff. Fold into crumb mixture. Transfer to pastry case. Bake in centre of oven 35–40 minutes. Serve hot.

Using rest of orange juice *Dilute rest of orange juice as directed, using $\frac{1}{2}$ water only. Chill. Serve as a drink.*

APPLES AND CUSTARD

serves 4–6

Divide 1 can apple-pie filling between 4–6 sundae glasses. Top with canned custard. Sprinkle lightly with cinnamon. Accompany with shortbread biscuits.

APRICOT SHORTBREAD CRUNCH

serves 4–5

**1 can (about 1 pound) apricots
2 cartons (each ¼ pint) natural yogurt
sifted icing sugar to taste
about 6 shortbread biscuits, crushed**

Drain apricots. Either sieve fruit itself or liquidize in blender goblet until thick and smooth. Beat in yogurt then sweeten to taste with sugar (if necessary). Put a few crushed biscuits into 4–5 sundae glasses. Fill with apricot mixture. Sprinkle rest of biscuit crumbs on top of each.

BROWN MOUSSE

serves 4

**½ pint milk
2 large eggs, separated
2 ounces caster sugar
1 teaspoon vanilla essence
4 ounces brown breadcrumbs
2 level teaspoons gelatine
2 tablespoons cold water**

An unusual and deliciously flavoured mousse made with, of all things, brown breadcrumbs! Useful if there is left-over brown bread in the house and also if one wants an interesting dessert that is easy on the budget.

Bring milk (skimmed or diluted evaporated if liked) to boil, stirring. Beat into egg yolks and sugar. Pour into top of double saucepan or into basin standing over pan of gently boiling water. Cook, stirring continuously, until mixture thickens enough to coat back of spoon. Add essence. Cool. Stir in crumbs. Put gelatine into small pan. Add cold water. Leave to soften 10 minutes. Stand over low heat. Stir until gelatine dissolves. Stir into crumb mixture. Fold in egg whites, beaten to stiff snow. Pour into 1-pint wetted mould. Refrigerate until set. Turn out. Serve with stewed or canned fruit.

BUTTERSCOTCH SAUCE

**1 small can evaporated milk
4 ounces soft brown sugar
1 teaspoon vanilla essence
2 ounces table margarine
(preferably with percentage of butter)**

An easy sauce which can be used in several different ways.

Put all ingredients into heavy pan. Leave over low heat until sugar dissolves and margarine melts. Stir continuously. Bring to boil. Boil steadily 10 minutes, stirring occasionally. Use as suggested below.

BUTTERSCOTCH BANANA SUNDAES

serves 4

Put scoops of vanilla ice cream into four sundae glasses. Top each with slices of banana. Coat with sauce. Sprinkle with chopped nuts or glacé cherries. Serve straight away.

BUTTERSCOTCH SPONGE SUNDAE

serves 4

Half-fill four sundae glasses with stale plain cake, first broken up. Moisten with syrup from can of peach halves. Top each with two peach halves and scoop of chocolate ice cream. Coat with sauce. Serve straight away.

BUTTERSCOTCH MANDARIN SUNDAES

serves 4

Make up either chocolate blancmange or any of the chocolate flavoured instant desserts with 1 pint milk. Divide between four sundae dishes. Top with well-drained canned mandarins. Chill lightly. Before serving, coat with hot butterscotch sauce. Serve straight away.

To vary butterscotch *Before bringing sauce to boil, add 2–4 level teaspoons instant coffee granules.*

To keep left-over sauce *Put into basin. Cover with foil. Reheat gently before serving. Add extra teaspoon or so of milk if sauce is too thick.*

MANDARIN JELLY FLIP

serves 4

Make up 1 orange jelly to ¾ pint with syrup from 1 can mandarins and water mixed. Dissolve over low heat. When cold and just beginning to thicken and set, whisk jelly until foamy. Beat in 4 tablespoons single cream or undiluted evaporated milk and 1 egg yolk. Stiffly whip egg white. Fold into jelly mixture. When smooth and evenly combined, spoon into four sundae glasses. Chill until firm. Top each portion with equal amounts of mandarins.

SPICED PINEAPPLE UPSIDE-DOWN CAKE

serves 6

Base

2 ounces luxury margarine
4 ounces soft brown sugar
1 8-ounce can pineapple rings
2 glacé or canned, stoned cherries, halved

Cake

4 ounces self-raising flour
½ level teaspoon *each,* baking powder, mixed spice and finely grated lemon peel
4 ounces luxury margarine
4 ounces caster sugar
2 large eggs
juice of 1 small lemon

Preheat oven to moderate 350°F or Gas 4 (180°C). Melt first 2 ounces margarine. Stir in sugar. Spread over the base of a 7-inch well-greased round cake tin. Drain pineapple rings. Reserve syrup. Arrange pineapple rings over base of tin. Put half cherry into centre of each, cut sides uppermost. Put all remaining ingredients (except lemon juice) into bowl. Beat

until smooth. Continue to beat further 2–3 minutes. Transfer to tin. Spread top evenly with knife. Bake in centre of oven about 45 minutes or until wooden cocktail stick, inserted into centre, comes out clean. Turn out on to plate. Serve hot. Accompany with pineapple syrup from can, heated through with juice of lemon.

To vary *Use four canned pear or peach halves instead of pineapple. Increase cherries to 8, cut in half and stand in between fruit.*

FRUIT SHORTCAKES

serves 6

8 ounces self-raising flour
½ level teaspoon baking powder
pinch salt
2 ounces table margarine
1 level tablespoon caster sugar
¼ pint milk
(skimmed gives excellent results)
table margarine or butter
1 medium can (about 1 pound)
canned pears, peaches, apricots or mandarins, drained

These are cheap to make, quick to bake, American in style and super to eat on almost any occasion.

Preheat oven to very hot, 450°F or Gas 8 (230°C). Sift flour, baking powder and salt into bowl. Rub in margarine. Stir in sugar. Add milk all at once. Using round-tipped knife, mix to soft but not sticky dough. Turn on to floured surface. Knead lightly until smooth. Roll out to ½ inch in thickness. Cut into six rounds with 3–4-inch cutter. Put on to greased tray. Bake towards top of oven 10 minutes or until well risen and golden. Transfer to wire rack. Split each apart with fingers. Spread fairly thickly with margarine or butter. Sandwich together with drained canned fruit. Top each with whipped cream for extravagance; dessert topping for economy.

Warning note *Do not cut warm scones with knife or they will become doughy.*

Fresh Fruit Shortcakes *Instead of canned fruits, use soft summer fruits, halved strawberries, raspberries or loganberries, when they are in season and at their cheapest.*

To freeze unfilled shortcakes *Make and bake shortcakes in advance. When cold, transfer to polythene bag. Seal. Freeze immediately. Store up to 6 months. Thaw, unopened, at room temperature 1–2 hours. Warm through in moderately hot oven, 400°F or Gas 6 (200°C) 7–8 minutes before splitting and filling as suggested in previous recipe.*

Budget Celebrations

No one likes to *have* to budget at Christmas, Easter and other festive occasions such as birthdays, anniversaries and christenings, but sometimes the need to economize exists, and here are a few ways round it.

HOME-MADE MINCEMEAT

makes about 4½ pounds

½ pound soft brown sugar
½ pound *each,* currants,
sultanas and seedless raisins
½ pound dried apricots,
washed but unsoaked
½ pound finely shredded suet
½ pound mixed chopped peel
½ pound cooking apples,
peeled, cored and grated
1 ounce almonds,
blanched and finely chopped
1 level teaspoon *each,*
mixed spice and cinnamon
½ level teaspoon ground ginger
juice of 3 lemons and
3 medium oranges, strained
4–5 tablespoons sherry

Not only is home-made mincemeat better flavoured than many of the bought varieties, but it works out cheaper in larger quantities.

Not, perhaps, a practical proposition for small families but well worthwhile if catering for large gatherings.

Put sugar into large bowl. Coarsely mince currants, sultanas, raisins and apricots. Add all remaining ingredients. Mix thoroughly. Cover. Leave to stand 2 days before potting. (This prevents mincemeat fermenting later.) Stir occasionally while standing.

To vary *The apricots, which absorb surplus juice, may be replaced with unsoaked but stoned prunes if preferred.*

Vegetarian Mincemeat *For vegetarians and others who, for health reasons, are unable to tolerate suet, 8 ounces melted margarine may be added to mincemeat instead.*

To blanch almonds *Put almonds into small basin. Cover with boiling water. Leave 5 minutes. Drain. When cool enough to handle, slide off skins.*

MINCEMEAT PIES

makes 24

1 pound self-raising flour
1½ level teaspoons salt
2 level tablespoons caster sugar
5 ounces cooking fat or lard
(taken straight from refrigerator)
4 ounces table margarine,
(taken straight from refrigerator)
6–8 tablespoons cold milk to mix
1½ pounds mincemeat
beaten egg for brushing
icing sugar

Flaky is the ideal pastry to use for these but home-made flaky requires time, patience and a good deal of fat and it may or may not work to your satisfaction. Frozen pastry is an admirable alternative but it can hardly be considered an economy if bought in large quantities. Therefore I have developed a pastry which is a cross between short crust and flaky; melt-in-the-mouth and perfect, in fact, for every kind of pie. And unproblematic to make as well!

Preheat oven to hot, 425°F or Gas 7 (220°C). Sift flour, salt and sugar into bowl. Cut in fats until they are in pieces no larger than peas. Using round-topped knife, mix to stiff dough with milk. Draw together with finger tips. Wrap in foil. Chill 1 hour. Turn on to floured surface. Knead lightly until smooth. Roll out fairly thinly with well-floured rolling pin. Cut into 24 rounds with 3½-inch cutter and same number of rounds with 2½-inch cutter. Use larger rounds to line 24 deepish bun tins. Fill with mincemeat. Top with remaining pastry rounds. Brush with egg. Bake just above centre of oven until golden; 20–25 minutes. Remove from tins. Sprinkle icing sugar over tops. Serve warm or cold.

If pastry is used for savoury dishes *Omit sugar.*

To store mincemeat pies *Put into air-tight tin. They remain in good condition up to 2 weeks. If liked, reheat in slow oven, 300°F or Gas 2 (150°C) about 15 minutes before serving.*

MINCEMEAT CRUMBLE TART

serves 8–9

Make up *half* the pastry as directed in recipe for mincemeat pies. Line 8-inch tart or enamel plate. Fill with mincemeat. Sift 3 ounces plain flour into bowl. Rub in 1½ ounces margarine. Add 1 level tablespoon caster sugar. Toss ingredients lightly together to mix. Sprinkle over mincemeat. Bake exactly as Mincemeat Tart.

To vary *Sift 1 level teaspoon cinnamon or mixed spice with flour. Use soft brown sugar instead of white. Include, if liked, 2 tablespoons desiccated coconut or same amount of chopped unsalted peanuts.*

MINCEMEAT UPSIDE-DOWN PUDDING

serves 6

¾ pound mincemeat
3 ounces margarine, softened
3 ounces caster sugar
2 standard eggs
4 ounces self-raising flour
pinch salt
6 teaspoons milk

Preheat oven to moderate, 350°F or Gas 4 (180°C). Well grease 2-pint heatproof dish. Cover base with mincemeat. Cream margarine and sugar together until light and fluffy. Beat in eggs, one at a time, adding tablespoon of flour with each to prevent mixture curdling. Fold in rest of flour alternately with milk. Spread evenly over mincemeat. Bake in centre of oven 1–1¼ hours until well-risen and firm or until wooden cocktail stick, inserted into centre, comes out clean. Turn out on to plate. Serve with custard or Vanilla Sauce (see below).

MINCEMEAT TART

serves 8–9

Make up pastry as in recipe for Mincemeat Pies, using 12 ounces flour, 1 level teaspoon

113

salt, 6 teaspoons caster sugar, 6½ ounces combination fat and margarine and 5–6 tablespoons cold milk. Wrap and chill. Divide in two, making 1 piece slightly larger than the other. Use larger piece to line 8-inch greased heatproof tart or enamel plate. Fill with 1–1½ pounds mincemeat. Moisten edges of pastry with water. Cover with lid, rolled and cut from rest of pastry. Press edges well together to seal. Brush with egg. Bake in centre of oven about 30 minutes. Dust with sifted icing sugar. Serve hot with custard.

SPEEDY VANILLA SAUCE

serves 6

1 level tablespoon cornflour
2 level tablespoons caster sugar
2 heaped tablespoons
instant skimmed milk granules
½ pint cold water
knob butter or margarine
1 teaspoon vanilla essence

Put first 3 ingredients into pan. Mix to smooth cream with some of the cold water. Blend in rest of water. Cook, stirring, until sauce comes to boil and thickens. Simmer 1 minute from heat. Stir in butter and essence.

Rum Sauce *Make as above, but substitute rum essence for vanilla. If preferred, other alcoholic flavouring or essences may be used instead.*

THE CHRISTMAS CAKE

family size

8 ounces plain flour
pinch salt
1 level teaspoon mixed spice
½ level teaspoon *each,*
cinnamon and ground ginger
6 ounces table margarine
6 ounces soft brown sugar
3 standard eggs
1 tablespoon black treacle
1½ pounds mixed dried fruit
4 ounces *each,* chopped cooking dates
and mixed chopped peel
2 tablespoons cold milk

Have all ingredients at room temperature. Brush 7-inch round or 6-inch square tin with melted cooking fat. Line base and sides with double thickness greaseproof paper. Brush paper with more fat. To prevent scorching, tie strip of newspaper (treble thickness and same depth as sides) round outside of tin. Sift dry ingredients into bowl. In separate bowl, cream margarine and sugar until light, pale in colour and fluffy. Beat in eggs, one at a time, adding tablespoon sifted dry ingredients with each to stop mixture curdling. Beat in treacle. Stir in fruits and peel. With large metal spoon, gently fold in rest of dry ingredients with milk. When well-combined, transfer to prepared tin. Spread evenly with knife. Hollow out centre slightly to prevent doming. Stand cake on newspaper-lined baking tray. Place in centre of oven. Bake in centre of cool oven, 300°F or Gas 2 (150°C) about 3½ hours or until cake has shrunk slightly away from sides of tin, and wooden cocktail stick, inserted into centre, comes out clean. Leave in tin at least 30 minutes. Turn out on to wire cooling rack.

To vary *The grated peel of 1 orange improves the flavour and should be added with the dried fruit. If liked, 1 or 2 ounces blanched, chopped almonds or shelled walnut halves may be included as well.*

To store *Leave lining paper on cake. When completely cold, wrap in foil. Leave in air-tight tin. Keep at least 1 week before covering with almond paste.*

ECONOMICAL ALMOND PASTE

4 ounces *each,*
caster and sifted icing sugar
4 ounces ground almonds
½ teaspoon *each,*
almond and vanilla essences
2 egg yolks to bind
(reserve whites for Royal Icing)
little lemon juice

Covering a cake completely with Almond Paste —even with this economical version which has double quantity of sugar to almonds—is somewhat of an extravagance, especially as it always seems to be this part and the white icing that gets left! I, myself, cover only the top with Almond Paste and icing and settle for a seasonal cake frill round the sides. It still makes a gay and attractive centre piece and certainly saves money.

Put sugars and almonds into bowl. Add essences. Mix to *stiff* paste with egg yolks and little juice. Draw together with finger tips. Turn out on to surface dusted with icing sugar. Knead lightly until smooth. Roll out into round or square large enough to fit top of cake, keeping rolling pin well-dusted with sugar.

To cover top *To make Almond Paste adhere to top of cake, brush cake first with little golden syrup or melted jam. Press paste on to cake. For smooth finish, run rolling pin lightly over top.*

To store *Leave cake in cool place until Almond Paste is firm (about 8 hours). Afterwards wrap loosely in foil and leave about 3 days before topping with Royal Icing. (If iced immediately, oil from nuts might seep through and turn icing yellow.)*

ROYAL ICING

2 egg whites
pinch cream of tartar
1 pound icing sugar, sifted
1 teaspoon glycerine
(available from chemists)

Lightly beat together egg whites and cream of tartar. Gradually beat in sugar. Continue beating until icing is very white and stiff enough to form smallish peaks when whisk—or beaters—are lifted out of bowl. Beat in glycerine.

Why glycerine? *This has no effect whatsoever on flavour but prevents icing from becoming brittle, rock hard and difficult to cut.*

Flavourings *Royal Icing tends to have a bland flavour so if liked, flavour with few drops of almond or vanilla essence, beating it in with glycerine.*

Icing the cake *Spread icing over top of cake with knife. For snow effect, either swirl icing with back of teaspoon or press back of spoon*

into icing and lift up. This forms attractive peaks. Stand Christmas decorations to taste on top. Tie frill round sides when icing has set.

DIFFERENT CAKE SIZES

For 8-inch round or 7-inch square cake

9 ounces flour
$\frac{1}{4}$ level teaspoon salt
1$\frac{1}{2}$ level teaspoons mixed spice
$\frac{1}{2}$ level teaspoon *each*,
cinnamon and ground ginger
8 ounces *each*, fat and sugar
4 eggs
1$\frac{1}{2}$ level tablespoons black treacle
1$\frac{3}{4}$ pounds mixed dried fruit
8 ounces chopped cooking dates
4–6 ounces mixed chopped peel
2 tablespoons milk

Bake for about 4 hours at same temperature as given for smaller cake.

For 9-inch round or 8-inch square cake

11 ounces flour
$\frac{1}{2}$ level teaspoon salt
2 level teaspoons mixed spice
1 teaspoon *each*,
cinnamon and ground ginger
10 ounces *each*, fat and sugar
5 eggs
2 tablespoons black treacle
2$\frac{1}{4}$ pounds mixed dried fruit
8 ounces chopped dates
8 ounces mixed chopped peel
3 tablespoons milk

Bake for about 4$\frac{1}{2}$ hours at same temperature as given for smaller cake.

Quantities of Almond Paste *For 8-inch round or 7-inch square cake, use 1$\frac{1}{2}$ times recipe given for smaller cake. For 9-inch round or 8-inch square, use double quantity of ingredients listed on page 114.*

Quantities of Royal Icing *For 8-inch round or 7-inch square cake, use 3 egg whites, large pinch cream of tartar, 1$\frac{1}{2}$ lb sifted icing sugar and 1$\frac{1}{2}$ teaspoons glycerine. For 9-inch round* *or 8-inch square, keep quantity the same as for 8-inch round or 7-inch square.*

BIRTHDAY OR CHRISTENING CAKE

Make exactly as Christmas Cake but keep Royal Icing on top smooth. Make up little extra icing and use to pipe on decorations, names, etc. If liked, colour extra icing pink, yellow, green, blue, etc., with appropriate food colourings. Tie band (same depth as cake) of Cellophane paper round sides of cake. Repeat with wide width of ribbon, finishing it off with a bow. If used for a Christening, stand appropriate ornament on top.

Why Cellophane? *To prevent fat from cake coming through to ribbon and staining it.*

To cover cake completely with Almond Paste *Make up double quantity of almond paste. Brush top and sides of cake with melted jam or syrup before covering with paste.*

To cover cake completely with Royal Icing *Make up double quantity of Royal Icing. Stand cake on cake board. Cover top and sides with icing, smoothing it on with palette or other large, flat-bladed knife, dipped in hot water. Left-over icing can be kept for decorations and/or piping.*

Self-made cake board *Cut a piece of heavy cardboard 1½ inches larger all the way round than size of cake. Cover board completely with foil, holding it in place at the back with sticky tape or glue.*

SEMI-RICH CHRISTMAS CAKE

8 ounces plain flour
2 level teaspoons baking powder
pinch salt
5 ounces margarine (easy cream)
5 ounces caster sugar
2 standard eggs
8 ounces dried fruit (either sultanas, raisins or currants or combination)
6–7 tablespoons cold milk to mix

Not everybody likes heavy, dark fruit cake, so for those who don't, here is a lighter version.

Have all ingredients at room temperature. Preheat oven to moderate, 325°F or Gas 3 (170°C). Brush 7-inch round cake tin with melted fat. Line base and sides with greaseproof paper. Brush paper with more fat. Sift dry ingredients into bowl. Cream margarine and sugar together until light and fluffy. Beat in eggs, one at a time, adding tablespoon sifted dry ingredients with each to prevent curdling. Stir in fruit. Mix to stiff dropping consistency by gently folding in dry ingredients alternately with milk. Transfer to prepared tin. Spread evenly with knife. Hollow out centre slightly to prevent doming. Place in centre of oven. Bake until well-risen and golden; 1¾–2 hours or until wooden cocktail stick, inserted into centre, comes out clean. Leave in tin 5 minutes. Turn out and cool on wire rack. Store in air-tight container until required. This cake may also be topped and/or covered with Almond Paste and Royal Icing.

To test for stiff dropping consistency *Lift up heaped tablespoon of mixture. If it drops off spoon after giving it a brisk shake, consistency is correct.*

For deeper colour *Use soft brown sugar instead of caster. Beat in 1 level tablespoon black treacle with eggs. Use 1 tablespoon less milk.*

For flavour variation *Sift 1–2 level teaspoons mixed spice with flour. Cream fat and sugar with either ½ teaspoon almond essence or 1 level teaspoon finely grated orange or lemon peel.*

For fruit variation *Use half mixed chopped peel and half dates, instead of other dried fruits suggested. For prettily coloured cake (which shows when cut), omit suggested fruit and add instead 2 ounces chopped dried apricots (soaked overnight and well-dried first), 2 ounces chopped angelica, 2 ounces glacé cherries and 2 ounces chopped dates.*

NO-BAKE FRUIT CAKE

serves 12–14

4 ounces margarine
2 ounces marshmallows
1 pound digestive biscuits, finely crushed
1 level teaspoon mixed spice
½ level teaspoon *each,*
cinnamon and ground ginger
juice of 2 large lemons
1 level teaspoon finely grated lemon peel
8 ounces cooking dates, chopped
4 ounces sultanas
2 ounces *each,* chopped mixed peel
and chopped glacé cherries
2 ounces unsalted peanuts, chopped

This is a great time and money saver and one of my own especial Christmas favourites.

Line base and sides of 2-pound loaf tin with foil. Brush with melted margarine. Put margarine and marshmallows into saucepan. Melt over low heat. Put crumbs and spices into bowl. Add melted margarine and marshmallows with lemon juice and remaining ingredients. Work together with finger tips. Press mixture into prepared tin. Cover. Chill overnight when cake should be firm. Turn out of tin. Peel away paper. Cut into thin slices.

CHOCOLATE NO-BAKE CAKE

serves about 8–10

1 ounce sultanas
about 2 tablespoons warm orange juice
2 ounces glacé cherries
1 ounce angelica or mixed chopped peel
3 level tablespoons golden syrup, melted
4 ounces luxury margarine, melted
2 level tablespoons
drinking chocolate powder
8 ounces digestive biscuits,
coarsely crushed

Another uncooked cake which is deliciously rich and fruity. For lovers of chocolate, a perfect substitute for the more traditional Christmas cakes and for the over-worked housewife, simplicity itself to make and comparatively inexpensive.

Line base and sides of 1-pound loaf tin with foil. Brush lightly with melted margarine. Put sultanas into small bowl. Add orange juice. Leave to stand 10 minutes. Chop cherries and angelica (if used). Combine melted syrup and margarine. Remove from heat. Stir in drained sultanas, rest of fruit, drinking chocolate and biscuits. Press into prepared tin. Smooth top with knife. Cover. Chill overnight. Before serving, carefully lift out of tin and peel away paper. Cut into thin slices. Keep left-over cake in the fridge as it softens at room temperature.

To decorate *As soon as mixture has been transferred to tin, stud top with border of halved glacé cherries and chocolate buttons, pressing them into mixture slightly so that they stay in position.*

CHRISTMAS PUDDING

makes 2, each enough for about 8

6 ounces self-raising flour
1 level teaspoon mixed spice
½ level teaspoon nutmeg
1 level tablespoon cocoa powder
6 ounces fresh white breadcrumbs
8 ounces finely shredded suet
8 ounces soft brown sugar
1 pound mixed dried fruit
8 ounces cooking dates, chopped
4 ounces mixed chopped peel
4 standard eggs, beaten
2 level tablespoons black treacle
5–6 tablespoons brown ale or stout

Sift flour, spices and cocoa powder into bowl. Add crumbs, suet, sugar, fruit, dates and peel. Toss well together. Mix to fairly stiff mixture with rest of ingredients. Stir thoroughly. Transfer to two largish, well-greased pudding basins. Cover securely with double thickness of greased greaseproof paper or foil. Steam, covered, in two pans of steadily boiling water 6 hours.

Warning note *Do not allow water in pans to boil away. Every so often, top up with extra boiling water.*

To store *Turn pudding out of basins when lukewarm. Wrap in foil when cold. Store in dark, dry and airy place until wanted.*

To reheat *Transfer cooked puddings to prepared basins. Cover securely. Steam about 2 hours before serving.*

DEVIL'S FOOD CAKE

serves 10

6 ounces plain flour
pinch salt
¼ level teaspoon baking powder
1 level teaspoon bicarbonate of soda
2 ounces cocoa powder
4 ounces margarine
10 ounces caster sugar
1 teaspoon vanilla essence
2 standard eggs
¼ pint and 4 tablespoons water

Filling

1½ ounces margarine
2 ounces icing sugar
1½ ounces plain chocolate
few drops vanilla essence

Frosting

1 pound granulated sugar
¼ pint water
2 egg whites

Preheat oven to moderate, 350°F or Gas 4 (180°C). Well grease two 8-inch sandwich tins. Line bases with rounds of greaseproof paper. Brush paper with more fat. For cake, sift together first five dry ingredients. Beat margarine until light and creamy. Gradually beat in sugar and vanilla. When fluffy, beat in eggs, one at a time, adding tablespoon sifted dry ingredients with each. Fold in rest of dry ingredients alternately with water. When evenly combined, transfer to prepared tins. Smooth tops with knife. Bake in centre of oven about 1 hour or until well-risen and firm. Turn out and cool on wire rack. Peel away lining paper.

To make filling, cream margarine and sugar together until light and fluffy. Melt chocolate in basin standing over pan of hot water. Leave until cool. Beat into creamed mixture with vanilla. Sandwich cold cakes together with chocolate filling.

To make frosting, put sugar and water into pan. Leave over low heat until sugar dissolves, stirring. Bring to boil. Boil rapidly until a little of the syrup, when dropped into cup of cold water, forms soft ball, leaving water clear. Beat egg whites to stiff snow. Still beating continuously, pour syrup very slowly on to beaten whites. Continue beating until thick, heavy and creamy. Cover with damp greaseproof paper. Leave to stand 5 minutes. Swirl over top and sides of cake. Leave in cool place about 4 hours to give icing a chance to set.

Now two recipes for those who prefer a lighter ending to their Christmas dinners.

SPICY YULE PUDDING

serves 8

3 ounces self-raising flour
1 level teaspoon bicarbonate of soda
½–1 level teaspoon mixed spice
pinch salt
6 ounces soft brown sugar
¾ pound mixed dried fruit
2 ounces chopped mixed peel
4 trifle sponge cakes, crumbled
6 ounces finely shredded suet
6 ounces cooking apples, grated
(prepared weight)
3 ounces carrots, grated
1 tablespoon milk
1 large egg, beaten

Well grease 2-pint pudding basin. Sift first four ingredients into bowl. Add sugar, fruit, peel, sponge cakes, suets, apples and carrots. Stir in milk and egg. Mix all ingredients thoroughly together. Transfer to prepared basin. Cover securely with double thickness greaseproof paper or aluminium foil. Steam steadily 5 hours. Turn out and serve with custard or Rum or Vanilla Sauces (page 114).

To pressure cook puddings *This is obviously a great time saver but is only suitable if the basins used are fairly small so that there is sufficient clearance at top and round sides of cooker, to prevent centre vent from becoming* *blocked. Stand pudding on trivet in pan. Half-fill with boiling water. Steam, without pressure, about 1–1½ hours, keeping water well topped up. Afterwards cook 45 minutes at 15 pounds pressure. Allow pressure to reduce at room temperature. Turn out puddings, cool, wrap and store as previously directed.*

LIGHT CHRISTMAS PUDDING

serves 8–10

8 ounces self-raising flour
1 level teaspoon mixed spice
pinch salt
8 ounces fresh white breadcrumbs
6 ounces soft brown sugar
6 ounces finely shredded suet
6 ounces mixed dried fruit
2 large eggs, beaten
cold milk to mix (skimmed if liked)

Sift flour, spice and salt into bowl. Add next four ingredients. Mix to softish batter with eggs and milk. Turn into 4-pint well-greased pudding basin or into two 2-pint ones. Cover securely with greased greaseproof paper or foil, using double thickness. Steam larger pudding steadily 4½ hours; smaller puddings, 2½–3 hours. Turn out and serve with custard or Vanilla Sauce (page 114).

Here are two cold desserts which have a festive air and are ideal for Boxing Day.

APRICOT CREAM WHIP

serves 10

2 lemon jellies
boiling water
½ pint thick apricot purée,
made from canned fruit
3 eggs, separated
¼ pint double cream
1 tablespoon milk
dessert topping
chocolate vermicelli or
hundreds and thousands

Make up jellies to 1¼ pints with boiling water. Stir until dissolved. Blend in apricot purée. When cold and just beginning to thicken, beat in egg yolks. Whisk egg whites to stiff snow. Beat cream and milk together until thick. Fold beaten whites and cream gently into jelly mixture. When smooth and evenly combined, transfer to serving dish. Refrigerate until firm and set. Before serving, decorate with dessert topping. Sprinkle with chocolate vermicelli or hundreds and thousands.

CREAM AND NUT APPLE TRIFLE

serves 12

8 trifle sponge cakes
red jam
4–5 tablespoons diluted orange squash
sherry or cider
½ pint orange jelly,
made little stiffer than usual
2 pounds stewed and sweetened apples
(fairly thick)
2 cans (each about 1 pound) custard
1 medium can cream,
refrigerated overnight
1 ounce walnuts, chopped
1 ounce glacé cherries, chopped

Halve trifle cakes. Sandwich together with jam. Halve each. Put into shallow serving dish. Moisten with orange squash and 1 or 2 tablespoons sherry or cider. When jelly just begins to thicken (consistency of unbeaten egg whites), combine with apples. Spoon over sponge cakes. Leave until set. Coat with cans of custard. Open cream and pour off liquid. Transfer cream to icing syringe or icing bag fitted with star-shaped tube. Pipe cream round edge of trifle. Sprinkle with nuts and cherries.

The Turkey

Quite obviously, the larger the turkey the better the value because there is a higher proportion of meat to bone than there is on a smaller bird, and it is therefore a more economical and advantageous buy. Small families, who want poultry just for one meal, are better off with a large chicken or capon—which can be stuffed, cooked, eaten and forgotten about—than with a mini-turkey. Ducks, although much cheaper than they were, still have to be ruled out because each one serves only four at the most and not even stuffing 'stretches' it adequately to make it a practical proposition for those having to watch the pennies.

For turkeys weighing 16 pounds and over, allow $\frac{1}{2}$ pound *raw, oven-ready* weight per person. Theoretically, this size of bird should therefore serve 32 people, once round. For smaller sized turkeys and chickens, allow $\frac{3}{4}$ pounds *raw, oven-ready* weight per person. Therefore if 10 people are expected for any celebration meal, a turkey of about 8 pounds minimum weight should be allowed; where chicken is concerned, 2 birds of about 4 pounds *raw, oven-ready* weight should suffice.

To thaw frozen bird *The quicker the better and my technique is to plunge into sink filled with hot water and leave it until flesh feels soft and pliable.*

Draining *Drain bird thoroughly. Wipe inside dry with paper towels; not dish cloth.*

Giblet bag *Remember to remove this before cooking bird. So many people don't and lose valuable stock ingredients!*

STUFFINGS

Stuffings, always popular, not only add flavour to the bird and keep it a good shape, but are also inexpensive to make and filling, enabling one to give slightly smaller portions of chicken or turkey and get away with it!

Quantities *Allow 3 ounces stuffing for every pound of bird. Therefore if stuffing a 10-pound bird, just under 2 pounds stuffing would be sufficient.*

To pack stuffing *Pack stuffing loosely into bird, bearing in mind that a stuffing with a breadcrumb base swells up during cooking.*

120

For variety, two different stuffings may be used in 1 bird; one type in the crop and another in body cavity.

When to stuff *This is very important. Stuff bird immediately before roasting; not a night or several hours before. The reason for this is that the inside of the bird—even if refrigerated—together with the stuffing may be just warm and moist enough to cause the growth of harmful bacteria, which remain active even after the bird has been roasted. The result—tummy upsets.*

BASIC BREAD STUFFING

6 ounces fresh white or brown breadcrumbs, or mixture
1 level teaspoon mixed herbs
2 level teaspoons chopped parsley (more if liked)
$\frac{1}{2}$ teaspoon finely grated lemon peel
1 small onion, grated (optional)
salt and pepper to taste
1$\frac{1}{2}$ ounces margarine or bacon dripping, melted
2–3 dessertspoons beaten egg or milk to bind

Combine crumbs, herbs, parsley and lemon peel in bowl. Add onion if used. Season. Bind with margarine or dripping and egg or milk. Stuffing should be neither too wet nor too dry, so add liquid gradually.

Egg versus milk *Egg in stuffing makes it fairly close and firm; milk gives a looser, somewhat softer texture.*

To vary *If preferred, 2 ounces finely shredded suet may be added to dry ingredients instead of margarine or dripping. It will then be necessary to increase egg or milk slightly.*

Tomato and Peanut Stuffing *Make exactly as Basic Stuffing but omit lemon peel. Add to dry ingredients, 3 skinned and chopped tomatoes and 2 ounces coarsely chopped salted peanuts. If necessary, reduce egg or milk slightly.*

Orange and Raisin Stuffing *Make exactly as Basic Stuffing, substituting orange peel for* *lemon. Add 1–2 ounces seedless raisins to dry ingredients.*

Bacon and Fried Onion Stuffing *Combine crumbs with herbs and parsley. Chop 3–4 streaky bacon rashers. Fry with 2 medium chopped onions in 2 ounces margarine until soft and pale gold; about 7 minutes. Stir into dry ingredients with seasoning to taste. If necessary, bind with little egg or milk.*

PORK SAUSAGEMEAT STUFFING

8 ounces pork sausagemeat
8 ounces fresh white or brown
breadcrumbs, or mixture
½ level teaspoon mixed herbs
¼ level teaspoon ground nutmeg
1 small onion, grated
salt and pepper to taste
3 tablespoons cold milk

Put all ingredients into bowl. Knead well together with finger tips. Use as required.

To vary above stuffing *Include 1 crushed garlic clove with other ingredients.*

RICE STUFFING

1 ounce margarine or dripping
1 medium onion, chopped
4 ounces long grain rice
½ pint chicken stock or water
salt and pepper to taste

Heat margarine in pan. Add onion. Fry gently until pale gold. Stir in rice. Fry further minute. Add stock or water. Season. Bring to boil. Stir once with fork. Cover. Lower heat. Simmer 15–20 minutes or until rice grains are tender and fluffy and have absorbed all the moisture. Leave until completely cold before packing loosely into body cavity of bird.

Rice, Bacon and Pineapple Stuffing *Make exactly as Rice Stuffing but fry 4 chopped streaky bacon rashers with onion. Stir 2–3 tablespoons chopped canned pineapple into cooked rice mixture, making sure pineapple is well-drained first.*

Mexican Rice Stuffing *Make exactly as Rice Stuffing, using tomato juice instead of stock or water. Season to taste with chili powder instead of ordinary pepper. Stir 4 tablespoons sweetcorn kernels and 1 small de-seeded and chopped green pepper into cooked rice mixture.*

Rice Stuffing with Orange and Nuts *Make exactly as Rice Stuffing but chop up chicken or turkey liver and fry with onion. Half-way through cooking time, add ½–1 level teaspoon finely grated orange peel. When rice is cooked, stir in 1 ounce finely chopped walnuts.*

ROASTING

Stand stuffed or unstuffed bird in roasting tin. Brush with melted margarine or dripping. Cover loosely with foil, tucking it under bird. Roast for required amount of time (based on weight calculations below), uncovering bird during last 30 minutes to brown the breast.

Preheat oven to very hot, 450°F or Gas 8 (230°C). As soon as bird is put into oven, reduce temperature to moderate, 325°F or Gas 3 (170°C).

Allow 25 minutes per pound for turkey and chicken weighing 4–12 pounds.

Allow 20 minutes per pound for turkeys weighing 12–16 pounds.

Allow 15–18 minutes per pound for turkeys weighing 16–25 pounds.

For stuffed birds, allow about 2 minutes longer per pound roasting time.

Carving *To give flesh a chance to 'firm-up' and make carving easier and more economical, leave bird to stand at least 5 minutes after removing from oven.*

Accompaniments *Traditional ones are Bread Sauce, Cranberry Sauce, Bacon Rolls, Chipolata sausages, roast and boiled potatoes and sprouts.*

GRAVY

enough for about 12

After removing bird, pour off all but 2 tablespoons fat from roasting tin. (Remainder should be poured into bowl and reserved as it makes excellent dripping for later use.) Stand tin over medium heat. Stir in 2 level tablespoons cornflour. Cook 2 minutes. Gradually blend in 1 pint stock or water and gravy cube. Bring slowly to boil, stirring and scraping base of tin continuously to incorporate the crispy bits. Simmer further minute or so. Pour into gravy boat or jug.

If too thick *Stir in little extra stock or water.*

Instead of gravy cube *Flavour and colour gravy with 2 level teaspoons Bovril or Marmite.*

BREAD SAUCE

serves 6

**4 cloves
1 medium peeled onion
1 blade mace
pinch ground nutmeg
½ small bay leaf
½ pint milk (skimmed reduces calories)
2 ounces fresh white breadcrumbs
salt and pepper to taste
knob margarine or butter**

Press cloves into onion. Put into saucepan. Add mace, nutmeg, bay leaf and milk. Cover. Heat slowly 20 minutes. Strain. Return flavoured milk to pan. Add crumbs. Season. Stir over low heat until fairly thick.

To increase quantities *Double quantities for 12; treble for 18.*

QUICKIE BREAD SAUCE

serves 6

This is cheating a bit but it does save time and has excellent flavour. Make up ½ packet thick

122

Devon onion soup as directed on packet, using ½ pint milk or water. When cooked, stir in 2–3 ounces fresh white breadcrumbs and knob butter or margarine. Adjust seasoning to taste.

Left-Over Turkey

This invariably happens if the bird is a very large one. After one day hot and one day cold, one starts wondering what to do with the remainders, so here are a few suggestions.

TURKEY IN SAUCE

serves 6–8

Make up 1 pint white sauce using 2 ounces margarine, 2 ounces flour and 1 pint milk which may be skimmed if liked. Alternatively, use 2 packets white sauce mix with 1 pint milk. Season well to taste with salt, pepper and nutmeg. Chop up 1–1½ pounds turkey remains coarsely. Add to sauce with 1 teacup cooked peas and 1 teacup diced carrots. Reheat about 10 minutes, stirring often. Serve with freshly boiled rice or noodles, with Risotto or with Pilaff (pages 14, 60).

TURKEY AU GRATIN

serves 6–8

Make up exactly as Turkey in Sauce, but add 3 ounces finely grated dry Cheddar cheese to sauce. Turn mixture into large, greased heatproof dish. Sprinkle top with 2 more ounces grated cheese and 3 level tablespoons toasted breadcrumbs. Brown under hot grill. Serve with hot toast.

TURKEY PIE

serves 8

Make exactly as Turkey in Sauce above. When mixture is completely cold, transfer to large, greased pie-dish, doming it up in centre. Cover with lid of frozen or home-made puff or short-crust pastry. Brush with little beaten egg. Bake just above centre of hot oven, 425°F or Gas 7 (220°C) 20 minutes or so until pastry is golden brown.

CURRIED TURKEY

serves 6–8

Make up white sauce exactly as given in previous recipe, adding 2–4 level tablespoons curry powder with the flour or to the packet mixture. Add turkey as previously directed but include one or more of the following: well-drained canned mandarins (quantity to taste); few tablespoons seedless raisins; 2–3 table-spoons chutney. Make ring of freshly boiled rice on large warm serving plate. Fill centre with curry mixture. Sprinkle with desiccated coconut, which has been lightly toasted under the grill.

CRISPY FRIED TURKEY

serves 6

Cut six large slices off breast. Coat with beaten egg and crumbs. Fry quickly in hot, but not smoking, fat until golden and crisp. Lift out of pan. Drain on paper towels. Serve hot with chips or jacket potatoes and assorted veget-ables to taste.

To vary *Include 1 or 2 level tablespoons grated Parmesan cheese with crumbs. Instead of crumbs, use finely crushed cornflakes.*

TONGUE

1 ox tongue (about 5 pounds)
1 large onion
2 medium carrots
2 medium celery stalks
1 bay leaf
6 peppercorns
about 1 teacup parsley

This is useful for any festive occasion and is very little trouble to prepare. In addition, a whole tongue, sliced thinly when cold, goes a long way and is a worthwhile buy. If served as a main meal, allow about 4 ounces *raw* weight per person, so that an average 5 pound tongue —which has to be skinned—will serve up to about 16 people.

Wash tongue. Put into large pan. Cover with cold water. Bring to boil. Simmer 5 minutes. Drain. Cover with fresh water. Add remaining ingredients. Bring to boil. Remove scum. Lower heat. Cover. Simmer 3–3½ hours or until tongue is tender. Drain. When cool enough to handle, strip off skin. Remove windpipe, gristle and bones from root end. Curl tongue round into saucepan, pressing it down well and mak-ing sure it covers base of pan completely. Stand plate on top. Weigh down with heavy garden stone. Refrigerate overnight. To carve, remove from pan and cut into thin slices with sharp knife.

To serve hot tongue *Slice tongue as directed and transfer to hot plates. Coat with freshly made gravy. Serve straight away. Do not reheat tongue in slow oven as this can lead to tummy upsets. Accompany with boiled potatoes and green vegetables to taste.*

To pressure cook tongue *Pressure cook tongue with recommended additions, for 1–1¼ hours at 15 pounds pressure.*

Tongue with Sherry Sauce *Follow directions for serving hot tongue, but flavour gravy with 1 or 2 tablespoons sherry.*

Bacon

A piece of boiled bacon is a useful standby to have in the house on any occasion. Gammon, the most expensive cut, is a great favourite but a good piece of collar comes a close second and is a lot easier on the purse strings!

GLAZED COLLAR

serves 10–12

4–5 pounds collar joint
cold water
2 cloves
1 large onion
1 bay leaf
2 ounces soft brown sugar
extra cloves
6 tablespoons syrup from can of
apricots or pineapples

Put collar into large pan. Cover with cold water. Bring to boil. Drain. Repeat. (This reduces saltiness.) Cover collar with fresh cold water. Add cloves, onion and bay leaf. Bring to boil. Remove scum. Lower heat. Cover. Simmer gently $1\frac{3}{4}$–2 hours or until bacon is tender. Drain. Stand on work surface. When joint is cool enough to handle, strip off rind. Score fat into large diamond pattern with sharp knife. Cover fat with brown sugar, pressing it well on with back of spoon. Press clove into each diamond. Stand in roasting tin. Pour fruit syrup around joint. Cook in centre of moderate oven, 350°F or Gas 4 (180°C) 45 minutes, basting at least twice with syrup. Serve hot or cold.

BACON LOAF

serves 10–12

3 pounds boned bacon
2 large onions
6 ounces fresh white breadcrumbs
$\frac{1}{2}$ level teaspoon sage
$\frac{1}{4}$–$\frac{1}{2}$ level teaspoon nutmeg
2 level tablespoons finely chopped parsley
pepper to taste
3 large eggs, beaten
3 tablespoons milk

Cover bacon with cold water; this can be knuckle, end of collar or any other inexpensive cut. Bring to boil. Drain. Repeat. (This reduces saltiness.) Leave bacon until cold. Line large loaf tin or oblong baking dish with foil. Grease heavily. Finely mince bacon (removing rind first) with onions. Put into bowl. Add all re-

maining ingredients. Mix thoroughly. Transfer to prepared tin or dish. Cover with foil. Bake in centre of moderate oven, 325°F or Gas 3 (170°C) about 2–$2\frac{1}{2}$ hours or until firm and set. Remove from oven. Uncover. Leave in tin until cold before turning out. Serve sliced with vegetables to taste and gravy.

To decorate *Stand Bacon Loaf on parsley-lined plate, or use lettuce or cress. Garnish top with either well-drained canned pineapple rings, rows of mandarins, canned apricot halves or with slices of hard-boiled egg and tomato.*

IMITATION SAGE AND ONION GOOSE

serves 6

1 pound ox liver, sliced
2 medium onions, sliced
2 ounces bacon dripping or margarine
1 level teaspoon dried sage
2 level teaspoons salt
pepper to taste
2 beaten eggs
1 pound freshly creamed potatoes

A real economy measure—but tasty all the same.

Fry liver and onions slowly in dripping or margarine 5 minutes. Lift out of pan. Mince. Combine with sage, salt, pepper and eggs. Press into 1-pound loaf tin lined with greased foil. Cover with potatoes. Trickle any remaining fat from pan over top. Bake towards top of moderately hot oven, 400°F or Gas 6 (200°C) 30 minutes. Slice or scoop out of tin, whichever is easier. Serve hot with gravy and vegetables.

Seasonal Gifts

Here are a few goodies which may be made for Christmas, Easter and birthdays—in fact for any festive occasion. A home-made cake or attractively wrapped box of candies or biscuits make a welcome gift, or can be offered to people when they pop in for a drink or a coffee.

SHORTBREAD

makes 10 wedges

2 ounces caster sugar
2 ounces *each*, butter and margarine
6 ounces plain flour
pinch salt

Cream sugar and fats well together. Sift flour and salt together and gradually work in with fork. Press into 7-inch sandwich tin. Smooth top with knife. Prick all over, and ridge edges with prongs of fork. Bake in centre of cool oven, 300°F or Gas 2 (150°C) about 50 minutes to 1 hour or until colour of pale straw. Remove from oven. Cut into wedges while still warm. Cool on wire rack. Store in air-tight tin.

Alternative method of making *Rub fat into sifted flour and salt. Add sugar. Draw mixture together with finger tips. Press into tin. Prick and ridge, etc. Bake exactly as above.*

For slightly crisper shortbread *Substitute 1 ounce semolina for 1 ounce flour.*

CRUNCHY DATE FINGERS

cuts into about 20 pieces

8 ounces cooking dates, chopped
1 level tablespoon golden syrup
4 tablespoons water
1 tablespoon lemon juice
6 ounces self-raising wholemeal flour
6 ounces fine semolina
6 ounces margarine
3 ounces caster sugar

Brush 7-inch square tin with melted fat. Line base and sides with greaseproof paper. Brush

with more fat. Put first four ingredients into pan. Cook slowly, stirring often, until mixture is thick. Sift flour and semolina. Melt margarine in pan. Add sugar. Using fork, stir into dry ingredients. Press half mixture (which will be on crumbly side) into tin. Cover with *cooled* date mixture. Press remaining flour mixture lightly on top. Bake in centre of moderately hot oven, 400°F or Gas 6 (200°C) 30 minutes. Cut into squares. Remove from tin when cold. Store in air-tight tin.

To vary *Use 1 tablespoon clear honey instead of syrup.*

DATE AND ORANGE LOAF

serves about 10

9 ounces self-raising flour
1 level teaspoon *each*,
mixed spice and cinnamon
pinch salt
3 ounces margarine or cooking fat
4 ounces soft brown sugar
6 ounces cooking dates, finely chopped
finely grated peel of 1 medium orange
1 tablespoon golden syrup or clear honey
½ pint cold milk
1 standard egg, beaten

An easily prepared cake which may be eaten as it is or sliced and spread with margarine or butter. Prettily iced, and studded with cherries and pieces of angelica, it is an attractive gift for neighbours and friends.

Preheat oven to moderately hot, 375°F or Gas 5 (190°C). Brush 2-pound loaf tin with melted fat. Line base and sides with greaseproof paper. Brush paper with more fat. Sift first three dry ingredients into bowl. Rub in margarine or fat. Add sugar, dates and peel. Gradually mix to batter with remaining ingredients. When evenly combined, transfer to prepared tin. Bake in centre of oven 1½ hours. Leave in tin 10 minutes before turning out on to wire cooling rack. Store in air-tight tin when cold.

To decorate *Sift 12 ounces icing sugar into bowl. Mix to stiffish icing with strained orange juice, adding it teaspoon by teaspoon. Pour over cake, allowing it to trickle down sides in uneven lines. Leave to set. Decorate with central line of sliced glacé cherries and diamond shapes, cut from strips of angelica.*

To cut angelica easily *Soak angelica first in a little hot water to remove sugar and make it pliable.*

GINGERBREAD

cuts into about 20 pieces

4 ounces cooking fat or lard
4 ounces golden syrup
2 ounces black treacle
8 ounces plain flour
¼ level teaspoon salt
1 level teaspoon cinnamon
1 level teaspoon mixed spice
2 level teaspoons ground ginger
1 level teaspoon bicarbonate of soda
2 ounces soft brown sugar
2 large eggs, beaten
¼ pint milk

Preheat oven to cool, 300°F or Gas 2 (150°C). Brush 7- or 8-inch square tin with melted fat. Line base and sides with greaseproof paper. Brush with more fat. Put fat, syrup and treacle into pan. Leave over low heat until melted. Sift dry ingredients into bowl. Add sugar. Toss ingredients lightly together. Make a well in the centre. Pour in melted ingredients with eggs and milk. Using wooden spoon, combine well together, stirring briskly without beating. Transfer to prepared tin. Smooth top with knife. Bake in centre of oven until well-risen and firm or until wooden cocktail stick, inserted into centre, comes out clean. Leave in tin 10 minutes. Turn out on to wire cooling rack. Store in air-tight tin when cold. Leave 1 day before cutting.

Fruited Gingerbread *Add either 4 ounces chopped dates, 4 ounces mixed chopped peel or 4 ounces seedless raisins to dry ingredients with sugar.*

Cherry and Nut Gingerbread *Well wash and dry 2–3 ounces glacé cherries. Chop. Chop 1 ounce unsalted peanuts or walnuts. Add both to dry ingredients with sugar.*

Orange Gingerbread *Reduce syrup by 2 ounces. Add 2 ounces coarse cut marmalade instead.*

Wholemeal Gingerbread *Use half wholemeal flour and half white flour.*

Crumble-topped Gingerbread *After smoothing top with knife, cover with crumble made by sifting 2 ounces flour and 1 level teaspoon cinnamon into bowl, rubbing in 1 ounce butter or margarine then tossing with 1½–2 ounces soft brown sugar.*

BANANA NUT CAKE

serves about 8–10

6 ounces self-raising flour
pinch salt
1 level teaspoon mixed spice
½ level teaspoon cinnamon
4 ounces caster sugar
1½ ounces unsalted peanuts, chopped
2 medium ripe bananas
1 standard egg, well-beaten
1 ounce margarine, melted

A speedily-made cake that tastes best freshly baked.

Preheat oven to moderate, 350°F or Gas 4 (180°C). Sift flour, salt, spice and cinnamon into bowl. Add sugar and nuts. Toss ingredients lightly together. Mash bananas thoroughly. Add to dry ingredients with egg and melted margarine. Stir briskly to combine. Transfer to greased and lined 6-inch cake tin or 1-pound loaf tin. Bake in centre of oven 1 hour, when cake should be well-risen and firm. Leave in tin 5 minutes. Turn out and cool on wire rack. Cut into wedges or slices when cold. Spread with butter or margarine before serving.

Decoration *If liked, cake may be covered with same icing as given for Date and Orange Loaf (page 125), but icing should be mixed with lemon juice instead of orange. A sprinkling of currants makes a pretty finish.*

TEA-TIME MALT BREAD

family size

3 ounces malt extract
2 ounces soft brown sugar
1 ounce margarine
8 ounces wholemeal flour
1 level teaspoon mixed spice
2 level teaspoons baking powder
large pinch of salt
6 ounces mixed dried fruit
$\frac{1}{4}$ pint milk

A fruity, old-fashioned flavoured loaf that is delicious to have at tea-time round the fire or to give with steaming mugs of cocoa to home-coming carol singers.

Preheat oven to moderate, 325°F or Gas 3 (170°C). Put malt extract, sugar and margarine into pan. Melt slowly over low heat. Leave to cool off slightly. Sift dry ingredients into bowl. Add fruit. Make well in centre. Add melted malt, etc., with milk. Mix thoroughly. Transfer to greased and paper-lined 1-pound loaf tin. Bake in centre of oven $1\frac{1}{4}$–$1\frac{1}{2}$ hours or until wooden cocktail stick, inserted into centre, comes out clean. Leave in tin 5 minutes. Turn out and cool on wire rack. Store in air-tight tin when cold.

To glaze *As soon as bread comes out of oven, brush with little melted golden syrup.*

CHOCOLATE BROWNIES

makes about 15 squares

4 ounces plain flour
pinch salt
2 ounces cocoa powder
$\frac{1}{2}$ level teaspoon baking powder
4 ounces margarine
8 ounces soft brown sugar
1 teaspoon vanilla essence
2 large eggs

Brush Swiss roll tin (about 10 by 7 inches) with melted fat. Line base and sides with greaseproof paper. Brush with more fat. Sift together first four dry ingredients. Cream margarine, sugar and essence until light and fluffy. Beat in eggs, one at a time, adding tablespoon of dry ingredients with each. Fold in rest of dry ingredients with metal spoon. Spread mixture evenly into prepared tin. Bake in centre of moderate oven, 350°F or Gas 4 (180°C) 25–30 minutes. Cool to lukewarm. Cut into squares. Remove from tin. Leave on wire rack until cold. Store in air-tight tin.

To vary *From 1–3 ounces chopped walnuts may be added to creamed mixture before folding in sifted dry ingredients.*

IRISH TEA LOAF

serves about 10

$\frac{1}{4}$ pint and 4 tablespoons
cold tea, strained
1 pound mixed dried fruit
6 ounces soft brown sugar
1 egg, lightly beaten
1 ounce margarine, melted
9 ounces plain flour
1 level teaspoon mixed spice
$\frac{1}{2}$ level teaspoon bicarbonate of soda

Put tea, fruit and sugar into bowl. Leave overnight, covered. Stir in egg and margarine. Mix well. Sift remaining ingredients together. Stir into tea mixture. When evenly combined, transfer to greased and paper-lined 2-pound loaf tin. Smooth top with knife. Bake in centre of moderate oven, 350°F or Gas 4 (180°C) $1\frac{1}{2}$ hours or until wooden cocktail stick, inserted into centre, comes out clean. Leave in tin 5 minutes. Turn out and cool on wire rack. Store in air-tight tin when cold. To serve, cut into slices and spread with margarine or butter.

To vary *Use mixture of dates, prunes and glacé cherries (all chopped), instead of other suggested fruits.*

FRUITED CIDER BREAD

¼ pint dry cider
12 ounces mixed dried fruit
4 ounces cooking dates, chopped
5 ounces soft brown sugar
1 large egg, beaten
8 ounces plain flour
pinch salt
½–1 level teaspoon cinnamon
2 level teaspoons baking powder

A mellow tasting loaf, subtly flavoured with cider and just right for Christmas and Easter.

Pour cider into bowl. Add dried fruit and dates. Cover. Soak overnight. Preheat oven to moderate, 325°F or Gas 3 (175°C). Add sugar and egg to fruit mixture. Stir well. Sift dry ingredients together and fold in. Transfer to greased and paper-lined 2-pound loaf tin. Bake in centre of oven 1½–1¾ hours. Leave in tin 15 minutes. Turn out and cool on wire rack. When cold, wrap cake in foil. Store in air-tight tin 2–3 days before cutting.

APPLE PUREE FRUIT CAKE

serves about 12

12 ounces self-raising flour
1 level teaspoon *each,*
salt, cinnamon and mixed spice
6 ounces margarine
6 ounces soft brown sugar
4 ounces sultanas
4 ounces cooking dates, chopped
2 ounces mixed chopped peel
1½ level teaspoons bicarbonate of soda
3 tablespoons milk
½ pint fairly thick apple purée,
made from stewed fruit

Brush 2-pound loaf tin with melted fat. Line base and sides with greaseproof paper. Brush with more fat. Sift dry ingredients into bowl. Rub in margarine. Add sugar, fruit and peel. Dissolve bicarbonate of soda in milk. Add to dry ingredients with apple purée. Mix well until evenly combined. Transfer to prepared tin. Smooth top with knife. Bake in centre of moderately hot oven, 375°F or Gas 5 (190°C)

1 hour or until wooden cocktail stick, inserted into centre, comes out clean. Turn out and cool on wire rack. Store in air-tight tin when cold.

For glazed surface *Dissolve 2 ounces caster sugar in 2 tablespoons cold water. Bring to boil. Boil 3 minutes. Brush over surface of cake after it has been baking ¾ hour. Return to oven further 15 minutes.*

FLORENTINES

makes about 16

3 ounces margarine
4 tablespoons milk
4 ounces icing sugar, sifted
1½ ounces plain flour
2 ounces mixed chopped peel
2 ounces currants
1 ounce glacé cherries, finely chopped
3 ounces flaked almonds
4 ounces plain or cooking chocolate

These are elegant and delicious fruity chocolate biscuits which are simple to make and far, far cheaper than shop-bought varieties.

Line two ungreased baking trays with rice paper. Put first 3 ingredients into pan. Stir over low heat until margarine melts. Remove from heat. Stir in all remaining ingredients except chocolate. Leave until cold. Spoon about 8 heaped teaspoons on to each tray, leaving plenty of room between each as they spread. Bake just above centre of moderately hot oven, 375°F or Gas 5 (190°C) 10 minutes or until pale gold. Remove from oven. Lift off trays when firm, trimming away rice paper round edges. Stand on wire cooling rack. Leave until cold. Break up chocolate. Melt over basin of hot water. Spread over rice paper sides of Florentines. Leave until half-set. Mark in wavy lines with fork. Leave until chocolate is firm before serving.

To vary *If preferred, Florentines can be left plain and not covered with chocolate.*

CHOCOLATE POTATOES

makes 36

2 ounces margarine
4 level tablespoons golden syrup
2 ounces soft brown sugar
2 teaspoons vanilla essence
7 ounces instant skimmed milk granules
cocoa powder

A good tasting sweetmeat which is nourishing as well and therefore ideal for children.

Put first three ingredients into pan. Leave over low heat until melted. Remove from heat. Add essence. Gradually stir in milk granules. Leave until mixture is cool enough to handle. Break off 36 pieces. Roll into balls. Toss in cocoa. If liked, stand in paper sweet cases. Store in airtight tin.

To vary *'Potatoes' may be flavoured with 1 teaspoon oil of peppermint (available from chemists) instead of vanilla.*

CHOCOLATE TRUFFLES

makes 18

2 ounces plain or cooking chocolate
knob margarine
3 tablespoons undiluted evaporated milk
2 teaspoons vanilla essence
8 ounces icing sugar, sifted
cocoa powder

Break up chocolate. Put into basin standing over pan of hot water. Leave until melted. Remove basin from pan. Beat in margarine, milk and essence. Gradually stir in icing sugar. Leave in cool place until firm. Break off 18 pieces. Shape into balls. Roll in cocoa. Put into paper sweet cases. Make and eat within 2 days.

If truffle mixture remains soft *Add up to 2 ounces extra sifted icing sugar.*

Rum Truffles *Make exactly as Chocolate Truffles, using rum essence instead of vanilla.*

Coffee Truffles *Make exactly as Chocolate Truffles, but melt 2 heaped teaspoons instant coffee powder or granules with chocolate.*

COCOA TRUFFLES

makes about 20

2 ounces margarine
2 ounces caster sugar
1 teaspoon almond essence
1 ounce ground almonds
1 level tablespoon cocoa powder, sifted
1 level tablespoon golden syrup
stale cake crumbs (from plain cake)
drinking chocolate powder

Cream margarine, sugar and essence together until light and fluffy. Beat in almonds, cocoa, syrup and sufficient cake crumbs to form stiff paste. Break off about 20 pieces. Roll into balls. Toss in drinking chocolate powder. Leave in cool place to harden. If liked, transfer to paper sweet cases.

HONEYCOMB

makes about 1 pound

6 level tablespoons clear honey
10 ounces granulated sugar
¼ pint water
1 ounce margarine
1 teaspoon vinegar
1 level teaspoon bicarbonate of soda

Put all ingredients except soda into *large* pan. Leave over low heat until sugar has melted, stirring occasionally. Bring to boil. Cover. Boil gently 2 minutes. Uncover. Boil briskly, without stirring, for 10–15 minutes or until a little of the mixture, when dropped into a cup of cold water, forms hard, brittle threads. Move pan away from heat. Stir in soda. (Mixture will rise up in pan.) Pour into greased tin. Leave until set. Break up into uneven pieces.

Keeping Honeycomb *As Honeycomb gets sticky quickly, it is advisable to make it and eat it on same day.*

COCONUT ICE

makes about 60 pieces

$\frac{1}{4}$ pint *each,* water and milk
2 pounds granulated sugar
1 ounce margarine
8 ounces desiccated coconut
2 teaspoons vanilla essence

Put water, milk, sugar, and margarine into large pan. Stir over low heat until sugar dissolves. Bring to boil. Cover. Boil gently 2 minutes. Uncover. Boil briskly, stirring occasionally, about 10 minutes or until a little of the mixture, when dropped into cup of cold water, forms soft ball when rolled between finger and thumb and leaves water clear. Remove from heat. Add coconut and vanilla. Beat briskly (fairly hard work) until mixture is thick and creamy. Transfer to 8-inch greased square tin. Leave in cool place until firm and set. Cut into squares. Store in air-tight tin.

Pink and White Coconut Ice *Make exactly as Coconut Ice. Spread half mixture into prepared tin. Quickly beat few drops red food colouring into remainder. Spread over white layer. Cut up when firm and set.*

PEPPERMINT CREAMS

makes about 40

1 pound icing sugar
2 ounces glucose powder
(available from chemists)
1 egg white
1 tablespoon water
1–2 teaspoons oil of peppermint
$\frac{1}{2}$ teaspoon green food colouring

Sift sugar and glucose into bowl. Beat egg white until it just begins to look foamy. Mix water with peppermint oil and colouring. Add sugar and glucose to beaten white alternately with flavoured and coloured water. Mixture by now should be fairly stiff. If not, fork in little extra sifted icing sugar. Turn out on to work surface dusted with sifted icing sugar. Roll out to $\frac{1}{4}$ inch in thickness, sprinkling rolling pin with icing sugar. Cut into 1-inch rounds with biscuit cutter. Leave in cool place until firm. If liked, transfer to paper sweet cases. Store in air-tight tin.

To vary *Colouring may be omitted. If liked, a chocolate button may be pressed on to each cream before it has set.*

Chocolate Peppermint Dippers *When firm and set, dip half of each peppermint cream into melted plain chocolate. Leave to set on lightly oiled foil or waxed paper.*

COFFEE CREAMS

makes about 40

1 pound icing sugar
2 ounces margarine
2 tablespoons milk
1 tablespoon instant coffee granules

Sift icing sugar into bowl. Put all remaining ingredients into pan. Leave over low heat until margarine melts. Leave until lukewarm. Gradually stir into sugar. Mix well. Turn out on to work surface dusted with sifted icing sugar. Knead until smooth. Break off 40 pieces of mixture. Roll into balls. Flatten slightly. Leave in cold place until firm.

Vanilla Creams *Make exactly as Coffee Creams but omit coffee. Instead, add 2 teaspoons vanilla essence and $\frac{1}{2}$–1 teaspoon red food colouring to melted margarine and milk.*

Lemon or Orange Creams *Make exactly as Coffee Creams but omit coffee. Instead, add finely grated peel of 1 medium lemon or orange and $\frac{1}{2}$–1 teaspoon lemon or orange food colouring to melted margarine and milk.*

If mixture is too soft *Fork in little extra sifted icing sugar.*

NO-COOK CHOCOLATE FUDGE

makes about 40 pieces

1 pound icing sugar
4 ounces plain chocolate
2 ounces margarine
4 tablespoons evaporated milk
2 tablespoons vanilla essence

Sift icing sugar into bowl. Break up chocolate. Put into basin over pan of hot water. Add margarine. Leave until both have melted. Remove from heat. Stir in milk and essence. Gradually work in icing sugar. When smooth and evenly combined, transfer to greased tin. Leave in cool place until firm and set. Cut into squares. Store in air-tight tin.

No-cook Mocha Fudge *Make exactly as No-cook Chocolate Fudge, but add 1 rounded tablespoon instant coffee granules or powder to chocolate and margarine while they are melting.*

No-cook Nut Fudge *Make exactly as No-cook Chocolate Fudge but add 2 ounces finely chopped nuts, such as unsalted peanuts, to icing sugar before adding liquid ingredients.*

TRADITIONAL FUDGE

makes about 40 pieces

1 small can evaporated milk
2 tablespoons water
1 pound granulated suger
1 level tablespoon golden syrup
2 ounces margarine
2 teaspoons vanilla essence

Put all ingredients, except vanilla, into large, heavy saucepan. Stir over low heat until sugar dissolves. Slowly bring to boil, stirring. Cover. Boil gently 3 minutes. Uncover. Continue to cook about 15 minutes or until a little of the mixture, when dropped into cup of cold water, forms soft ball when rolled gently between finger and thumb. Stir often while Fudge is cooking to prevent burning and sticking. Remove from heat. Cool for 15 minutes. Add vanilla. Beat hard until Fudge becomes thick and creamy. Spread into greased, shallow pan. Leave until firm and set. Cut into squares. Store in air-tight tin when cold.

Chocolate Fudge *Make exactly as Traditional Fudge but add 2 level tablespoons cocoa powder with all other ingredients.*

Fruit and Nut Fudge *Make up either of the two Fudges above. Add 2 ounces each, chopped raisins and unsalted peanuts with vanilla.*

CARAMELS

makes about $\frac{3}{4}$–1 pound

4 ounces margarine
2 level tablespoons golden syrup
8 ounces granulated sugar
1 large can sweetened condensed milk

Put all ingredients into large, heavy pan. Stir over low heat until sugar dissolves. Bring slowly to boil, stirring. Cover. Boil gently 2 minutes. Uncover. Continue to boil, stirring often, about 12–15 minutes or until little of the mixture, when dropped into cup of cold water, forms hard ball when rolled gently between finger and thumb. Pour into well-greased shallow tin. When half-set, mark into squares with sharp knife. When completely set—another 3 hours— turn out of tin and cut into squares by sawing through with knife. Wrap each caramel in small square of waxed paper or foil.

To vary *Stir in 2 teaspoons vanilla essence after removing mixture from heat.*

Nut Caramels *Add 1–2 ounces chopped, unsalted peanuts or walnuts after removing mixture from heat.*

131

TOFFEE

makes ¾–1 pound

5 tablespoons water
2 tablespoons golden syrup
2 teaspoons vinegar
1 pound granulated sugar
2 ounces margarine

Put all ingredients into large, heavy pan. Stir over low heat until sugar dissolves. Bring to boil, stirring. Cover. Boil gently 2 minutes. Uncover. Boil, without stirring, about 15 minutes or until a little of the mixture, when dropped into cup of cold water, separates into hard, brittle threads. Pour into greased tin. Leave until set. Break up with small hammer.

Chocolate Toffee *Make exactly as Toffee, adding 2 level tablespoons cocoa powder with all other ingredients.*

Nut Toffee *4 ounces chopped nuts (any variety to taste) may be stirred into toffee before it is poured into tin.*

TREACLE TOFFEE

makes ¾–1 pound

10 ounces granulated sugar
2 tablespoons milk
3 tablespoons black treacle
2 ounces margarine
2 tablespoons vinegar

Put all ingredients into pan then proceed exactly as directed in recipe for Toffee.

Living Alone

Young or old, this is something many of us experience at some stage in our lives and the tendency is to exist on 'pickings' rather than go to the trouble of planning a balanced diet. I wouldn't even pretend that cooking for oneself is fun or an inspiring occupation and I know only too well that the temptation is to grab a newspaper or book in one hand, an indifferent cheese sandwich in the other and wash it all down with a cup of stale tea or coffee ! Knowing too, that old habits die hard, all I can do is give a few dishes which are trouble-free to make, economical, fairly easy to digest and pleasant. Perhaps the loners in our midst will co-operate and give them a try ! All portions are for one.

MILK SOUP

This may sound peculiar but is quite delicious for supper on a cold winter's night. Put thick slice of currant, or other fruit, bread into soup plate. Sprinkle with soft brown sugar. Heat ¼–½ pint milk in saucepan. Pour over bread in plate. Eat while hot. Follow with fresh fruit, such as an apple, pear or banana.

To vary *Trickle about 1 level tablespoon clear honey or golden syrup over bread instead of sugar.*

FRIED SANDWICH FRITTERS

Make a cheese or ham sandwich in usual way. Cut into 2 triangles. Dip in 1 small egg beaten with 2 tablespoons cold milk. Fry in hot margarine or dripping until golden on both sides. Eat straight away. Follow with glass of fruit juice (including tomato) or piece of fresh fruit.

FRENCH FRIED FINGERS

Beat 1 small egg with 2 tablespoons milk. Cut two slices de-crusted bread into fingers. Dip in egg and milk mixture. Fry in little hot margarine or dripping until crisp and golden on both sides. Eat with a piece of mild cheese and a whole tomato.

QUICKIE SUPPER MINCE

Heat 1 small can mince with same size can spaghetti in tomato sauce. Pile on to slice of freshly made toast. Follow with glass of fruit juice or piece of fresh fruit.

CAULIFLOWER IN YOGURT SAUCE

Cook ½ medium cauliflower (or little less, depending on appetite) in boiling salted water until tender. Drain. Keep hot. Heat 3 tablespoons natural yogurt in small pan with 1 egg yolk, 1 ounce grated cheese and seasoning to taste. Cook over low heat, stirring often, until sauce has thickened. Put cauliflower into greased dish. Coat with yogurt sauce. Sprinkle with little extra grated cheese. Brown under hot grill.

STEAMED FISH AND VEGETABLES

2–3 medium potatoes
1 medium carrot
knob margarine
2 small plaice fillets
2 tablespoons milk
1 medium tomato (optional)
salt and pepper to taste

An uncomplicated one, because everything cooks together.

Peel, wash and quarter potatoes. Peel, wash and slice carrots. Put into pan of boiling salted water. Cover. Cook 10 minutes. Meanwhile, brush enamel plate (which should fit comfortably on top of pan) with margarine. Add plaice fillets. Pour in milk. Slice tomato. Arrange on top of fish. Sprinkle with salt and pepper. Stand plate on top of pan. Cover. Continue to cook vegetables, and steam fish at same time, for further 15–20 minutes. Drain vegetables. Serve with fish and any liquor left in enamel plate.

To vary *Include a peeled and quartered onion with other vegetables.*

Parcel Meals

These are simply a collection of ingredients, cooked together in foil. No nursing the foods while cooking; no washing-up afterwards; completely unproblematic!

FISH FILLET IN FOIL

Brush largish piece of foil with margarine. Stand 4-ounce piece fish fillet in centre. Sprinkle with salt and pepper. Top with 1 or 2 cold cooked potatoes, sliced first. Dot with flakes of margarine. If liked, sprinkle with fresh or dried parsley. Fold foil over fish and other ingredients to form parcel. Seal edges and joins well together. Stand on baking tray. Cook in centre of moderately hot oven, 375°F or Gas 5 (190°C) 30 minutes. Transfer to plate and eat straight away.

To vary *If preferred, one cleaned and boned herring may be used instead of the fish fillet.*

CHICKEN IN FOIL

Brush largish piece of foil with margarine. Stand medium joint roasting chicken in centre. Sprinkle with salt and pepper. Top with 1 or 2 mushrooms, 1 thinly sliced cooked potato and 2 or 3 canned carrots. To improve flavour, a sliced raw onion may be added as well. Dot with margarine. Fold foil over chicken, etc., to form parcel, then continue as given in recipe for Fish Fillet in Foil above, cooking chicken 45–60 minutes depending on size and thickness.

LAMB IN FOIL

Make as Chicken in Foil (p. 133), but instead of chicken use 1 lamb chop or 2 chump ends. If liked, sprinkle lightly with mixed herbs and use onion salt instead of ordinary salt. Cook between 30–40 minutes only.

DEVILLED PORK IN FOIL

Especially for those who like spicy foods!

Brush largish piece of foil with margarine. Stand pork chop on top. Sprinkle with Worcester sauce, curry powder, paprika, garlic salt and scattering of mixed herbs. Peel and slice 1 small apple. Stand on top of chop. Now proceed exactly as given in recipe for Chicken in Foil (p. 133), but cook 30–40 minutes only.

SMOKED HADDOCK PUFF OMELET

**1 small fillet smoked haddock
1 large egg, separated
pepper to taste
knob margarine**

An appetizing light lunch or supper dish.

Cook haddock in milk or water until fish flakes easily with fork. Remove from pan. Flake fish with 2 forks. Mash finely. Stir in egg yolk. Season with pepper. Beat egg white to stiff snow. Gently fold into yolk mixture. Heat margarine in smallish frying pan. Spoon egg and fish mixture into it. Cook until underside is golden. To brown top, stand pan under hot grill. Eat straight away with bread and butter. Follow with fresh orange or glass of tomato juice.

134

SAUSAGEMEAT NEST

**4 ounces pork or beef sausagemeat
pinch mixed herbs
1 egg
salt and pepper**

Line small baking tray with piece of foil. Brush with melted fat. Mix together sausagemeat and herbs. Shape into 3-inch round cake. Stand on foil. Make dent in centre, building up sides to form nest. Bake in centre of moderate oven, 350°F or Gas 4 (180°C) 20 minutes. Remove from oven. Break egg into centre. Return to oven 10 minutes or until egg is set. Accompany with vegetables to taste. Follow with canned or stewed fruit.

CHEESE AND TOMATO TOAST

**1 large slice white bread
margarine
1 large tomato, sliced
salt and pepper to taste
1 slice processed cheese**

Toast bread on one side only. Spread untoasted side with margarine. Cover with sliced tomato. Sprinkle with salt and pepper. Top with cheese. Cook under hot grill until cheese begins to melt. Serve straight away.

EASY CREAMED CHICKEN

**1 small can
condensed cream of chicken soup
1 tablespoon milk
4 ounces cooked chicken, diced
3–4 tablespoons cooked rice**

Put soup and milk into pan. Heat until hot, stirring. Add chicken. Heat through gently 15 minutes. Add rice. Simmer further 10 minutes. Serve with crisp toast. Follow with fresh fruit.

QUICKIE EGG BROTH

Make up omelet with 1 egg. Remove from pan. Cut into strips. Dissolve 2 teaspoons Bovril in ½ pint hot water. Pour into soup plate. Add egg strips. Eat straight away with bread and butter. Follow with fresh fruit.

SEMOLINA CHEESE

½ pint milk
1 ounce semolina
knob margarine
2 ounces dry cheese, finely grated
1 egg, separated
salt and pepper to taste

Put milk and semolina into pan. Cook, stirring, until mixture comes to boil and thickens. Add margarine, 1½ ounces cheese, egg yolk and salt and pepper to taste. Stir over low heat until cheese melts. Beat egg white to stiff snow. Gently fold into semolina mixture. Transfer to small greased pie dish. Sprinkle rest of cheese on top. Brown under hot grill. Serve straight away with grilled tomatoes. Follow with canned or stewed fruit or glass of fruit juice.

MOCK APPLE CHARLOTTE

1 cooking apple
2 ounces margarine
3 small slices white bread
2 level tablespoons granulated sugar
½ level teaspoon cinnamon

Peel, core and slice apple. Cut into rings. Heat 1 ounce margarine in pan. Add apple rings. Fry slowly on both sides about 5 minutes, turning twice. Move to one side of pan. Add rest of margarine. When hot, add the bread, cut into ½-inch cubes. Fry about 3 minutes or until crisp. Combine apples and fried bread in pan. Add sugar. Stir well to mix. Turn out on to plate. Dust with cinnamon. Serve straight away.

BANANA DESSERT

Slice 1 or 2 mini jam-filled Swiss rolls into dish. Top with 1 sliced banana and 4–5 tablespoons freshly made or canned custard. Add a blob of jam. Eat straight away.

BANANA RICE CARAMEL

Heat ½ large can rice pudding. Put into greased heatproof dish. Top with 1 sliced banana. Sprinkle with little brown sugar. Dot with flakes of margarine. If liked, dust with cinnamon or mixed spice. Stand under hot grill until sugar is golden and caramelized.

YOGURT SWEET

Flavour 1 carton natural yogurt with 1–2 level dessertspoons jam, honey or chunky marmalade.

LUNCH-IN-A-FLASH

Make an unusual 'milk shake' by blending ½ carton of fruit yogurt (flavour to taste) with 1 glass chilled milk. Accompany with brown roll and butter or margarine. Follow with crisp apple.

Low-cost Entertainment

A difficult task these days, especially if large numbers are involved. One always wants to put on a good show for one's guests with exciting dishes and decorative touches yet, over the years, I have discovered that it is the straightforward foods which are the most appreciated and, if they can be served in a straightforward manner as well, so much the better. Fortunately this makes for economy. Thus, in this section, I have included a selection of random and reasonably-priced recipes and ideas which are mainly informal and suitable for all age groups.

For those occasions when formality is important—such as dinner parties—there are four assorted menus at the end of the section; all are three-course and each serves 8 people.

Cheese and Cider Party

Although people have been saying, for a very long time, that the Cheese and Wine Party has had its day, they seem to be completely wrong for it pops up everywhere and is always greeted with enthusiasm and pleasure. Although wine is cheaper than it has ever been, 20 bottles or so can prove an expensive outlay and for reasons of economy, cider, both sweet and dry, makes an admirable substitute as does beer, light and dark. For non-drinkers, tomato and other bottled or canned fruit juices should be provided, as should a selection of mineral waters.

The simplest way to present the food is to arrange everything on a long table around which people can circulate freely. Diagonally sliced French bread, wedges of wholemeal bread, rolls and biscuits (including crispbreads for slimmers) should be put in baskets or dishes; butter on plates or table margarines left in their tubs; cheese—a selection of about 8 English and continental varieties plus cottage for dieters—on boards; fresh celery in tall containers; whole tomatoes left in bowls; jars of pickled onions and cucumbers alongside. Plenty of knives for cutting and spreading should be around. So should paper serviettes, plates and bottle openers. Fruit is always a popular attraction at this sort of party and apples and pears team particularly well with cheese and cider.

To prevent bread from drying out *If the party is to be a long one, keep bread and rolls (but not biscuits) covered with gaily coloured dampened cloth table napkins. Also keep some uncut bread in reserve.*

Soup'n'Hot Breads

For entertaining hungry groups on cold days, steaming bowls of chunky soups with accompanying hot breads couldn't be better. There are recipes for all sorts of soups throughout the book. You can, if preferred, use canned or packet soups instead of home-made. You may even like to try your hand at a few chowders—such as the ones given below. These are warming and filling soup meals with origins in the United States. Serve them with some of the hot breads suggested later.

GOLDEN WHOLEMEAL SLICES

Beat 3 ounces margarine with 1 egg yolk, 1 level teaspoon onion salt and 2–3 level teaspoons poppy or sesame seeds. Spread liberally over thickish slices of wholemeal bread. Brown under hot grill. If preferred, half butter and half margarine may be used.

CORN AND BACON CHOWDER

serves 12

3 ounces margarine
3 medium onions, chopped
12 ounces streaky bacon, chopped
3 ounces flour
2 pints milk
1 pint water
3 pounds cold cooked potatoes, diced
12 ounces sweetcorn, frozen or canned
salt and pepper to taste
chopped parsley

Heat margarine in large pan. Add onions and bacon. Cover. Fry gently 10 minutes, shaking pan frequently. Stir in flour. Cook 2 minutes without browning. Gradually blend in milk (skimmed or diluted evaporated if liked) and water. Bring slowly to boil, stirring. Add remaining ingredients except parsley. Cover. Simmer 20 minutes. Serve each portion topped heavily with chopped parsley.

Corn and Haddock Chowder *Make exactly as Corn and Bacon Chowder but omit bacon. Ten minutes before soup is ready, add 1 pound smoked haddock or cod fillet, cut into cubes. (Make sure haddock or cod is skinned first.)*

Mixed Vegetable Chowder *Make exactly as Corn and Bacon Chowder but add 1 pound diced cooked potatoes, ¾ pound diced cooked carrots, ¾ pound cooked peas and ½ pound cooked and sliced frozen or canned green beans.*

Curried Chowders *If liked, any of the above chowders may be flavoured with curry powder. Simply add from between 1–3 tablespoons with the flour.*

HOT ONION BREAD

serves 4

Cut 1 medium French loaf into 1-inch diagonal slices but *do not cut through to base*. Beat 4 ounces softened table margarine with onion salt to taste (1–2 level teaspoons). Spread on to French bread in between cuts, so that both sides of each slice are covered. Sprinkle loaf lightly with salt. Wrap in foil. Heat through near top of moderately hot oven, 400°F or Gas 6 (200°C) 10–15 minutes. Remove from oven. Unwrap. Allow people to break off slices of oven-fresh hot bread. For 12 servings, allow approximately 3 loaves.

Hot Garlic Bread *Make exactly as Onion Bread, but beat softened table margarine with garlic salt or 2 or 3 crushed garlic cloves to taste.*

Mustard Bread *Make exactly as Onion Bread, but beat softened table margarine with 1 level tablespoon prepared mild or continental mustard and ½ level teaspoon onion salt.*

Hot Herb Bread *Make exactly as Onion Bread, but beat softened table margarine with 2–3 level teaspoons mixed dried herbs.*

Cheese Bread *Make exactly as Onion Bread, but beat softened table margarine with equal quantity of finely grated dry Cheddar cheese. Beat in also ½–1 level teaspoon prepared English mustard.*

For novelty touch *After spreading slices of bread with flavoured margarine, slide thin slices of onion or tomato in between slits. Wrap and bake as given for other hot breads.*

SPEEDY CORN AND TUNA CHOWDER

serves 12

3 10-ounce cans
condensed cream of chicken soup
3 7-ounce cans tuna, drained and flaked
3 10-ounce cans creamed corn
1½ pints water
3 tablespoons Worcester sauce
1 level dessertspoon *mild* mustard
salt and pepper to taste

Put all ingredients, except salt and pepper, into pan. Slowly bring to boil, stirring. Lower heat. Simmer 7 minutes. Season and serve.

To vary *Use condensed mushroom or celery soup instead of chicken.*

Chinese-Style Buffet

An easy one to prepare and enjoyable for guests because they can serve themselves. Make a large bowl of Sweet-sour Sauce (recipe below) and stand it on a table hotplate. Serve with freshly cooked chipolata sausages, fried or roasted chicken drumsticks and meat balls. Accompany with dishes of plain boiled rice, crispy fried noodles and large coleslaw salad. Fresh fruit makes a good dessert.

SWEET-SOUR SAUCE

enough for 12

$\frac{1}{4}$ pint plus 4 tablespoons vinegar
8 ounces soft brown sugar
3 level tablespoons tomato concentrate
6 tablespoons soy sauce
$\frac{3}{4}$ pint canned pineapple juice
1$\frac{1}{2}$ pints water
3 medium onions, chopped
2 large green peppers,
de-seeded and chopped
3 level tablespoons cornflour
salt and pepper to taste

Put vinegar, sugar, tomato concentrate, soy sauce, pineapple juice and 1 pint water into pan. Add onions and green peppers. Bring to boil. Cover. Lower heat. Simmer 15 minutes. Blend cornflour to smooth paste with rest of water. Add to pan. Cook, stirring, until sauce comes to boil and thickens; it should also clear at the same time. Simmer 1 minute. Season.

To vary *For chunkier sauce, 1 can pineapple titbits may be added with onion and green*

pepper. If pineapple is used, reduce pineapple juice by $\frac{1}{4}$ pint.

Sweet-sour Orange Sauce *Make exactly as previous recipe but use canned orange juice instead of pineapple. For decorative touch, 1 can mandarin oranges may be added at the end and heated through for few minutes with the sauce.*

CRISPY FRIED NOODLES

Allow about 2–3 ounces flat ribbon noodles per person. Cook as directed on packet. Drain *thoroughly*. Heat some salad oil in frying pan. Add noodles. Fry slowly until crisp and golden on both sides. Serve straight away.

Baked Potato Party

This goes down well with all age groups and can be fun both indoors and as an outside barbecue. Surprisingly enough, jacket potatoes vanish faster than hot cakes and at a party I went to recently, people were getting through as many as four large ones each. Therefore be generous in your calculations!

BAKING POTATOES

Choose large ones and preferably those which have a regular shape. Wash, scrub and wipe dry. Prick with fork to prevent skins from bursting. Stand on oiled baking tray. Brush potatoes themselves lightly with oil. Bake near top of moderately hot oven, 400°F or Gas 6 (200°C) for about 1$\frac{1}{2}$–2 hours or until potatoes feel soft when gently pressed. Cut a deep cross on top of each then stand in tea-towel. Squeeze base of potato between hands until the cross-cut opens out. Top with a large knob of butter or table margarine. Hand salt and pepper round separately.

To vary *Top each potato with one or two heaped teaspoons soured cream and sprinkle liberally with scissor-snipped chives.*

Accompaniments *For a complete meal, serve potatoes with: freshly fried, grilled or baked sausages, rolls of freshly grilled bacon, cubes of Cheddar cheese, grated cheese (for those who want to sprinkle some over their potatoes), freshly fried or grilled beefburgers, meat balls and cubes of extra butter or margarine and soured cream with chives. Have at hand salt and pepper, curry powder, chili powder and paprika.*

To save washing-up *Wrap each pricked potato in square of oiled foil. Bake on tin as directed, but allow extra 15–25 minutes. Peel back foil, make cross-cut on each and continue as directed in recipe for baking potatoes. Serve potatoes in their foil instead of on plates.*

STUFFED POTATOES

If preferred, halve each baked potato, hollow out middles and mash with any filling you fancy, such as grated Cheddar cheese, chopped ham, cottage cheese, flaked canned fish, etc. Beat with margarine and milk until creamy. Season well. Return mixture to potato halves. Reheat near top of moderately hot oven, 400°F or Gas 6 (200°C) 15–20 minutes. Allow minimum of four halves per person.

Rice Dishes

Long grain rice combines happily with most other ingredients and acts as a nourishing and inexpensive filler in savoury dishes. Below are a few examples of budget-type recipes which are admirable for parties.

JAMBALAYA

serves 12

4 ounces margarine or dripping
1½ pounds onions, thinly sliced
1 pound long grain rice
2 level tablespoons
dried red and green pepper flakes
2 pints chicken stock
1 tablespoon Worcester sauce
2 level teaspoons curry powder
salt and pepper to taste
1½ pounds cooked frozen or
canned mixed vegetables
1¼–2 pounds luncheon meat, cubed
4 hard-boiled eggs, sliced
4 heaped tablespoons
finely chopped parsley

Soak pepper flakes in hot water for 15 minutes Heat margarine or dripping in large pan. Add onion. Fry *gently* until pale gold. Add rice. Fry further 2 minutes, stirring. Drain pepper flakes. Add to pan with stock, Worcester sauce, curry powder and salt and pepper to taste. Bring to boil. Stir once or twice with fork. Lower heat. Cover. Simmer 15 minutes. Add rest of ingredients, except eggs and parsley. Heat through further 10 minutes or until rice grains are tender and have absorbed moisture. Pile into warm bowl. Garnish with egg slices. Sprinkle with parsley. Serve with large mixed salad.

Jambalaya with Chicken *Instead of luncheon meat, add the coarsely diced meat from 2 medium-sized roasted chickens.*

Jambalaya with Sausages *Instead of luncheon meat, add 2–2½ pounds cooked pork sausages, sliced.*

CHINESE FRIED EGG RICE

serves 12

¼ pint salad oil
1 pound onions, chopped
3 pounds cooked long grain rice
(about 1½ pounds raw)
1½ pounds cold roast pork,
cut into strips
½–¾ pound cooked peas
8 eggs, beaten
3 tablespoons soy sauce
salt and pepper to taste
1 breakfast cup finely chopped parsley

Heat oil in large pan. Add onions. Fry gently until pale gold. Add rice and pork. Fry slowly 15 minutes, stirring frequently with fork. Add peas. Heat through further 5 minutes. Stir in eggs and soy sauce. Cook until eggs are lightly scrambled and cling to rice and the other ingredients. Stir frequently with fork to prevent sticking. Pile into warm dish. Sprinkle with parsley. Serve with large mixed salad.

To vary *The same amount of luncheon meat, also cut into strips, may be used instead of pork.*

KEDGEREE

serves 12

1½ pounds cooked
smoked cod or haddock fillet
1 pound cooked
cod or coley fillet (unsmoked)
½ pound table margarine
2½ pounds cooked long grain rice
(about 1¼ pounds raw)
6 hard-boiled eggs, chopped
¼ pint undiluted evaporated milk or
rich milk such as Channel Island
salt and pepper to taste
about 1 breakfast cup
finely chopped parsley

A good old British standby and another appetizing rice dish which may be varied to suit individual taste.

Flake fish with two forks, discarding skin and bones. Heat margarine in large pan. Add all ingredients except parsley. Stand over low heat until very hot. Stir often with fork. Pile into warm dish. Sprinkle heavily with parsley. Accompany with hot toast and large mixed salad.

Kipper Kedgeree *Make exactly as above, substituting 1½ pounds cooked kipper fillets for smoked cod or haddock fillets.*

Prawn or Mussel Kedgeree *For luxury touch, garnish kedgeree with 4 ounces peeled prawns. Alternatively, use bottled and well-drained mussels.*

CREOLE-STYLE RICE

serves 12

4 level tablespoons
red and green pepper flakes
4 ounces margarine
1 pound onions, chopped
2–4 garlic cloves,
finely chopped or crushed
3 pints chicken stock
1½ pounds long grain rice
4 level tablespoons tomato concentrate
1 pound tomatoes, skinned and chopped
1 pound streaky bacon,
coarsely chopped
about 1 breakfast cup
finely chopped parsley

Soak the pepper flakes in water for 15 minutes. Heat margarine in large pan. Add onions, well-drained pepper flakes and garlic. Fry gently until soft and pale gold. Pour in stock. Bring to boil. Add rice, tomato concentrate and tomatoes. Stir once or twice with fork. Lower heat. Cover. Simmer 15–20 minutes or until rice grains are tender and have absorbed moisture. Meanwhile, fry bacon in its own fat until crisp. Stir into rice just before serving. Pile into warm dish. Sprinkle with parsley. Accompany with large green salad.

To vary *Use ½ bacon and ½ diced liver. Fry bacon until fat runs. Add liver. Fry until cooked through, stirring frequently.*

RICE TUMBLE

serves 12

2½ pounds boiled long grain rice
(about 1¼ pounds raw weight)
½ pint French dressing with herbs
(see below)
1 level tablespoon paprika
8 ounces raw mushrooms, thinly sliced
4 ounces salted peanuts,
coarsely chopped
8 medium celery stalks, chopped
1 breakfast cup
chopped watercress or parsley
leaves of 1 medium lettuce
4 large carrots, finely grated
about 2 tablespoons seedless raisins
lemon juice

A delicious and decorative rice salad which goes excellently with sliced ham and tongue, halved hard-boiled eggs, cold sausages and cold poultry.

Put cold rice into large bowl. Moisten with dressing, adding little extra if rice is on dry side. Add paprika, mushrooms, nuts, celery and watercress or parsley. Toss well. Arrange lettuce on large platter. Pile rice on top. Garnish with mounds of carrot. Top each with a few raisins. Sprinkle carrot with lemon juice.

FRENCH DRESSING WITH HERBS

Beat ½ pint salad oil with 2 tablespoons Worcester sauce, 2 level teaspoons mild mustard, 1 crushed garlic clove (optional), 2 level teaspoons mixed herbs, 1 teaspoon sugar and salt and pepper to taste. Gradually beat in 4 tablespoons vinegar and 4 tablespoons lemon juice.

Left-over dressing *Transfer to plastic container with lid. Store in cool place; shake before using.*

FANCY RICE CHEESE

serves 12

12 ounces long grain rice
1½ pints boiling water
1½ level teaspoons salt
3 ounces margarine
1 large onion, chopped
2 large celery stalks, chopped
12 ounces streaky bacon, chopped
3 ounces flour
1½ pints milk (skimmed or
diluted evaporated if liked)
1–2 level teaspoons prepared mustard
12 ounces strong Cheddar cheese, grated
salt and pepper to taste
4 large tomatoes, sliced
4 level tablespoons breadcrumbs

Put rice, boiling water and salt into pan. Return to boil. Stir twice with fork. Lower heat. Cover. Simmer 15 minutes or until rice grains are tender and have absorbed all the moisture. Meanwhile, heat margarine in large pan. Add onion, celery and bacon. Fry gently until soft and just beginning to turn golden. Stir in flour. Cook slowly 2 minutes. Gradually blend in milk. Cook, stirring, until sauce comes to boil and thickens. Simmer 3 minutes. Add mustard and 8 ounces cheese. Season. Stir in cooked rice. Mix thoroughly. Transfer to 2 or 3 greased heatproof dishes. Arrange tomato slices, in a line, along centre of each. Sprinkle with rest of cheese and breadcrumbs. Bake towards top of hot oven, 425°F or Gas 7 (220°C) about 15 minutes or until golden brown. Serve with mixed salad.

TOMATO AND ORANGE SALAD

serves 12

Skin and slice 2–3 pounds tomatoes. Peel oranges as close to flesh as possible. Slice. Arrange alternate rows of tomatoes and oranges on long flat dishes. Moisten with French dressing. Sprinkle with chopped chives or parsley.

BARBECUE BEEF AND RICE

serves 12

½ pint home-made or canned
tomato sauce (not ketchup)
4 tablespoons Worcester sauce
4 tablespoons vinegar
½ pint beef stock
2 level teaspoons chili powder
1 level teaspoon paprika
4 12-ounce cans corned beef
2 pints boiling water
1 pound long grain rice
1–2 level teaspoons salt
1 long strip lemon peel
1 medium green pepper
1 medium onion for garnish

Put tomato and Worcester sauce, vinegar, stock, chili powder and paprika into saucepan. Slowly bring to boil. Mash corned beef. Add to pan. Mix thoroughly with sauce. Lower heat. Cover. Simmer gently 15 minutes. Pour boiling water into clean pan. Add rice, salt and lemon peel. Stir twice with fork while boiling. Lower heat. Cover. Simmer 15 minutes or until rice grains are tender and have absorbed moisture. Remove lemon peel. Stand rice in border round edge of large plates or shallow dishes. Fill centres with beef mixture. Garnish with strips of green pepper and onion rings. Serve with large green salad.

RICE AND SALAME SALAD

serves 12

12 ounces Danish salame, cut into strips
1 pound cooked sweetcorn
2½ pounds cooked long grain rice
(about 1¼ pounds raw weight)
4 ounces currants
2 large pickled cucumbers,
coarsely chopped
1 small can red pimiento caps,
cut into small dice
Blue-cheese Dressing (see below)

Put salame into large bowl with corn, rice, currants, cucumber and ¾ of the pimiento dice.
142

Add dressing. Toss thoroughly. Garnish attractively with remaining pimientos.

BLUE-CHEESE DRESSING

2 ounces Danish blue cheese
¼ pint and 2 tablespoons salad oil
1 level teaspoon paprika
½ level teaspoon dry mustard
5–6 tablespoons malt vinegar
pepper to taste

Put cheese into bowl. Mash finely. Gradually blend in oil, paprika and mustard. Beat in vinegar. When dressing is evenly combined, season to taste with pepper. Add to salad as directed.

Other dressing *If preferred, toss salad with an ordinary French dressing made from ⅔ oil and ⅓ vinegar, plus seasonings to taste.*

RICE JUMBLE

serves 12

4 ounces margarine
1 pound onions, chopped
12 ounces streaky bacon, chopped
1½ pounds long grain rice
3 pints chicken stock
(use cubes and water)
3 cans (each about 7 ounces) tuna,
drained and flaked
12 ounces sweetcorn, cooked
4 ounces salted peanuts
3 medium bananas, sliced
salt and pepper to taste
4 slightly rounded tablespoons
desiccated coconut

This is something I often make when I know I am going to be confronted with a large group of young people. It's gimmicky enough to be interesting but at the same time basic enough not to be regarded with suspicion!

Heat margarine in large pan. Add onions and bacon. Fry gently until both are pale gold. Stir in rice. Fry 1 minute, shaking pan frequently. Pour stock into pan. Bring to boil. Stir twice with fork. Lower heat. Cover. Simmer 10 minutes. Add tuna, corn, peanuts and bananas. Season. Heat through further 10 minutes, stirring often with fork. Meanwhile, toast coconut under grill until pale gold. Pile hot rice mixture into warm bowl. Sprinkle heavily with toasted coconut. Accompany with Tomato and Orange Salad (page 141).

Children's Parties

Whereas at one time children happily accepted dainty sandwiches scattered with cress, sponge fingers, jellies, trifles, blancmanges and the inevitable iced birthday cake at their own and other people's parties, these days they appear to have much more sophisticated tastes and seem to prefer—if my own son and his horde of friends are anything to go by—much more down-to-earth foods with crisps, hot sausages, cheese and savoury biscuits heading the list. Thus, below, is a random selection of recipes which should appeal to our discriminating youngsters. Note that I have avoided the traditional decorated birthday cake altogether because children rarely, if ever, eat it. My most successful cake to date was a plain chocolate one adorned only with candles. It vanished, I am happy to say, in a flash. The reason, apparently, was because it was plain, simple and easy to eat!

HOME-MADE LEMONADE

makes about 40 glasses

**1 large lemon
2 pints water
1½ pounds granulated sugar
1 ounce citric acid
(available from chemists)**

Lemonade is vastly cheaper to make than to buy. The recipe below, when diluted with water, gives about 10 pints.

Wash and dry lemon. Grate off peel with fine side of grater. Put into saucepan with water. Squeeze lemon. Strain juice. Add juice to pan. Bring to boil. Stir in sugar and citric acid. Reduce heat. Stir until sugar dissolves. Remove from heat. When completely cold, strain and bottle. Dilute 1 part lemon with 3 parts cold water.

Lemon and Orangeade *If liked, include finely grated peel of two washed and dried medium oranges as well.*

To grate peel in blender *If you have a blender, peel fruit very thinly, cutting away as much white pith as possible. Break peel into smallish pieces. Put into blender with ½ pint water (taken from the 2 pints). Run machine at high speed about 1 minute or until peel is very finely chopped.*

CHEESE SCONES

makes about 10

**8 ounces self-raising flour
½ level teaspoon baking powder
½ level teaspoon salt
½ level teaspoon dry mustard
1½ ounces margarine
2 ounces dry Cheddar cheese,
finely grated
¼ pint milk**

Preheat oven to very hot, 450°F or Gas 8 (230°C). Sift dry ingredients into bowl. Rub in margarine finely. Add cheese. Mix to soft, but not sticky, dough with milk, adding it to dry ingredients all at once. Turn out on to floured surface. Knead lightly until smooth. Roll out to ½ inch in thickness. Cut into rounds with 2½-inch cutter, re-kneading, rolling and cutting trimmings to make total of about 10 scones. Put on to lightly greased baking tray. Bake near top of oven 8–10 minutes or until well-risen and golden. Cool on wire rack. Split apart with fingers when cold. Spread scone halves with butter or margarine and thin coating of Marmite.

To enrich scones *Beat 1 egg in measuring jug. Make up to ¼ pint with cold milk.*

Alternative spreads *Try peanut butter; fish or meat paste; cheese spread.*

Alternative toppings and garnishes *Scone halves, after being spread with butter or margarine, may be topped with ham, luncheon meat, corned beef, mashed canned salmon, slices of processed cheese or slices of hard-boiled egg. The most suitable garnish for children is simply a slice of tomato on top of each.*

Crunchy Cheese and Peanut Scones *Because children are addicted to salted peanuts, one or two ounces chopped ones may be added to scone mixture with cheese.*

Plain Scones *These are a useful base for some of the sweet toppings many children enjoy, such as jam, honey, golden syrup, lemon curd and chocolate spread.*
Follow recipe for Cheese Scones but omit mustard and cheese. Sift dry ingredients with 1 level tablespoon caster sugar.

BASIC CHEESE BISCUITS

sufficient for about 12

8 ounces self-raising flour
1 level teaspoon salt
½ level teaspoon dry mustard
4 ounces margarine
2 ounces Cheddar cheese,
finely grated
cold water to mix

Preheat oven to hot, 425°F or Gas 7 (200°C). Sift dry ingredients into bowl. Rub in margarine finely. Add cheese. Toss ingredients lightly together. Using knife, mix to *stiff* dough with cold water, sprinkling about 8–12 teaspoons over rubbed-in mixture. Draw together with finger tips. Knead lightly until smooth. Roll out evenly on floured surface. Cut into rounds with 2-inch cutter. Transfer to greased tray. Prick lightly all over with fork. Bake near top of oven 7–10 minutes or until golden-brown. Cool on wire rack. Store in air-tight tin when cold.

Novelty-shaped Cheese Biscuits *If preferred, cut dough into shapes with assorted cutters, such as animals, stars, gingerbread men, etc.*

Comic Faces *The plain round biscuits can have comic faces put on them, using cottage or grated cheese for hair, raisins for eyes, strips of tomato for lips and triangles of cucumber skin for noses. In order to make the trimmings stick, spread biscuits first with a thin layer of margarine or butter.*

Cheese Twists *These always appeal to children and are quite easy to do. Make up Basic Cheese Biscuit mixture as directed above. Roll out thinly. Cut into ½-inch wide strips. Twist each. Stand on greased baking tray. Bake as given for Cheese Biscuits.*

SAUSAGE ROLLS

makes about 12

2 level teaspoons sugar
½ pint warm water
2 level teaspoons dried yeast granules
8 ounces wholemeal flour
8 ounces plain flour
1 level teaspoon salt
12 ounces pork or beef sausagemeat
little milk
2 ounces dry Cheddar cheese,
finely grated
beaten egg for brushing

Another favourite with children. This recipe for sausage rolls is an especially nourishing version because the dough is a yeasted wholemeal one and the rolls themselves contain cheese as well as sausagemeat. If the thought of tackling a yeast dough puts you off, please have a go at this one as it is quicker to make than most other yeast mixtures, requires no kneading and has a delicious flavour.

Dissolve 1 teaspoon sugar in ½ the warm water. Stir in yeast. Leave about 15 minutes in warm place until frothy. Sift rest of sugar into bowl with flours and salt. Make a well in centre. Add frothed-up yeast liquid and remaining warm water. Using finger tips, work ingredients to soft, scone-like dough adding little extra white flour if dough is very sticky.

Put into greased basin. Cover with cloth or greased polythene bag. Leave to rise until double in size; 30 minutes in warm place (such as sink half-filled with hottish water) or 1–1½ hours at kitchen temperature. Turn dough out on to floured surface. Roll into 12 by 10-inch rectangle. Cut in half to give two strips, each measuring 12 by 5-inches. Divide sausagemeat in two. Shape each piece into 12-inch long roll. Brush each piece of pastry with milk. Sprinkle with cheese. Stand length of sausage on each. Fold dough over, completely enclosing sausagemeat. Press edges well together to seal. Cut each roll into six individual sausage rolls. Stand on greased baking tray. Cover with greased polythene. Leave to rise until double in size. Brush with beaten egg. Bake near top of very hot oven, 450°F or Gas 8 (230°C) 20 minutes. Cool on wire rack.

To vary *Spread each piece of dough very thinly with Marmite instead of sprinkling with cheese. Brushing dough with milk will therefore be unnecessary.*

SIMPLE CHOCOLATE CAKE

sufficient for 10–12

6 ounces plain flour
2 ounces cocoa powder
5 ounces caster or soft brown sugar
1 level teaspoon baking powder
1 level teaspoon bicarbonate of soda
½ level teaspoon salt
3 ounces easy creaming margarine
¼ pint milk
2 eggs
1 level teaspoon black treacle

Preheat oven to cool, 300°F or Gas 2 (150°C). Brush 7-inch round cake tin or 2-pound loaf tin with melted fat. Line base and sides with greaseproof paper. Brush with more fat. Sift dry ingredients into bowl. Add margarine, milk, eggs and treacle. Stir gently to combine. Beat briskly 3–4 minutes or until mixture is smooth and ingredients well-combined. Pour into prepared tin. Bake in centre of oven 1 hour or until wooden cocktail stick, inserted into centre, comes out clean. Leave in tin about 10 minutes. Turn out on to wire cooling rack.

Peel away paper. Store in air-tight tin when cold. A simple finish is to dust top with sifted icing sugar and then insert as many candles, in holders, as are required.

To vary *Split cake in half, fill and cover top with Chocolate Spread (see below) or butter cream.*

HOME-MADE CHOCOLATE SPREAD

2 ounces butter or
table margarine, softened
1 level tablespoon black treacle
2 level tablespoons
sweetened condensed milk
4 level tablespoons sifted cocoa powder
2 level teaspoons fine semolina
1 teaspoon vanilla essence
1 tablespoon boiling water

Beat butter or margarine to a cream with treacle and milk. Stir in rest of ingredients. Beat well again. Transfer to jar with screw-top. Store up to 1 month in cold place such as refrigerator.

To vary *If chocolate/coffee combination is liked, 2–3 teaspoons instant coffee granules may be dissolved in the tablespoon of boiling water.*

LIVER SAUSAGE SQUARES

makes about 20 squares

Make up double quantity of Basic Cheese Biscuit mixture. Divide in half. Roll each out into about 12-inch square. Stand 1 piece on greased baking tray. Spread completely with soft liver sausage. Cover with remaining square of pastry. Prick all over. Brush with little beaten egg or milk. Bake near top of hot oven, 400°F or Gas 6 (200°C) about 20 minutes or until well-risen and golden. Remove from oven. Leave until lukewarm. Cut into squares. Cool on wire rack. If possible, make and eat on same day.

Dips and Dunks

Another popular form of party food is an assortment of dips, in bowls, surrounded by dunks of carrot sticks, 2-inch lengths of celery, cucumber slices, radishes, savoury biscuits, potato crisps, cocktail sausages and small meat balls. The following dips are worth a try because they go a long way and are extremely tasty.

SPICED TOMATO DIP

serves 12–16

1 packet tomato soup
2 cartons soured cream
2 teaspoons Worcester sauce
shake of Tabasco or pinch Cayenne pepper
2 level teaspoons horseradish sauce
finely grated peel of 1 small orange

Combine all ingredients well together. Cover. Refrigerate overnight. Transfer to serving bowl. Sprinkle with finely chopped parsley. Surround with suggested dunks.

ONION DIP

serves 12–16

1 packet onion soup
2 cartons (each ¼ pint) soured cream
pinch ground nutmeg
paprika

Combine onion soup with soured cream and nutmeg. Cover. Refrigerate overnight. Transfer to serving bowl. Sprinkle lightly with paprika. Surround with suggested dunks.

Celery, Leek or Asparagus Dip *Make exactly as Onion Dip, substituting celery, leek or asparagus soup for the onion.*
To vary *Use ¼ pint double cream and ¼ pint natural yogurt instead of soured cream.*

146

Crunchy Dips *Make up any of the above dips but include 2 ounces chopped salted peanuts.*

Cheesy Dips *Make any of the above dips but include 1–2 ounces grated Parmesan cheese.*

Alternative garnishes *Instead of paprika, sprinkle tops of dips with sifted hard-boiled egg yolk, chopped nuts, chopped parsley or curry powder.*

Menus

Menu 1

Potted Beef

Somerset-style
Stuffed Mackerel or Herrings
Baked Tomatoes
Parsley Potatoes

Plum Sponge Crumble

POTTED BEEF

serves 8

1 pound beef shin
2 bay leaves
2 cloves
pinch ground nutmeg
1 medium onion
2 tablespoons water
salt and pepper
2 ounces table margarine
1 ounce butter, melted

Preheat oven to cool, 300°F or Gas 2 (150°C). Cut meat into *small* cubes, discarding fat and gristle. Put into heatproof dish. Add bay leaves, cloves, nutmeg, whole onion and water. Sprinkle with salt and pepper. Cover closely with greased foil. Cook in centre of oven about 3–4 hours or until meat is very tender. Remove meat from dish. Mince finely. Beat with margarine and enough left-over meat juices to give smooth, thickish consistency. Adjust seasoning to taste. Transfer to small dish. Pour melted butter over top. Refrigerate overnight. To serve, spoon potted meat out of dish and accompany with freshly made hot toast.

For really fine beef *Pass meat twice, or even three times, through mincer.*

Fuel economy *As the beef takes such a long time to cook in the oven, it makes good sense to bake a rice pudding with it at the same time. The pudding can be eaten cold on another occasion or even be used in place of the Plum Sponge Crumble recommended in the menu.*

SOMERSET STUFFED MACKEREL OR HERRINGS

serves 8

**8 large mackerel or herrings, heads removed, skinned and boned
2 ounces margarine
2 medium onions
2 medium celery stalks
2 large cooking apples
8 ounces fresh white breadcrumbs
4 level tablespoons finely chopped parsley
2 eggs, beaten
salt and pepper
½ pint dry cider**

Sauce

**1 level tablespoon cornflour
½ pint dry cider
2 tablespoons lemon juice
salt and pepper
4 tablespoons undiluted
evaporated milk or single cream**

Wash mackerel or herrings. Wipe dry with paper towels. Preheat oven to moderate, 325°F or Gas 3 (170°C). Heat margarine in pan. Add grated onion and finely chopped celery. Fry gently 5 minutes. Peel, core and finely chop the apples and add. Fry further 5 minutes. Stir occasionally. Remove from heat. Stir in

crumbs, parsley, eggs and salt and pepper to taste. Mix thoroughly. Spread equal amounts along insides of fish; the effect will be fish 'sandwiches'. Transfer to well-greased baking dish. Coat with ½ pint cider. Cover closely with lid or foil. Cook in centre of oven 35–40 minutes. Strain liquor from dish and reserve. Return fish to oven and keep hot while making sauce.

Mix cornflour to smooth cream with cider and lemon juice. Add reserved liquor. Pour into saucepan. Season with salt and pepper. Cook, stirring, until sauce comes to boil and thickens. Simmer 1 minute. Stir in milk or cream. Reheat without boiling. Stand fish on individual warm plates. Coat with sauce. Accompany with halved baked tomatoes and boiled potatoes, which have been tossed in margarine and sprinkled with parsley.

To vary *Apple juice may be used in place of cider.*

PLUM SPONGE CRUMBLE

serves 8

**2 large (1¼ pound) cans plums
8 ounces self-raising flour
2 level teaspoons baking powder
6 ounces margarine (easy cream)
6 ounces caster sugar
1 teaspoon vanilla essence
3 standard eggs
3 tablespoons cold milk**

Crumble Topping

**4 ounces plain flour
2 level teaspoons
mixed spice or cinnamon
2 ounces margarine
4 ounces soft brown sugar
about 1 tablespoon melted golden syrup**

Drain off and reserve the plum syrup. Preheat oven to moderately hot, 375°F or Gas 5 (190°C). Place drained plums in 3½–4-pint well-greased heatproof dish which is shallow rather than deep. Sift flour and baking powder into bowl. Add margarine, sugar, essence, eggs and milk. Stir gently to combine. Beat for 2–3 minutes or until smooth. Spread over plums. Bake in centre of oven 35–40 minutes or until sponge topping is well-risen and golden. Meanwhile, make crumble. Sift flour and spice into bowl. Rub in margarine. Add sugar. Toss ingredients lightly together to mix. Leave on one side. Remove pudding from oven. Spread top gently with syrup. Sprinkle with crumble. Return to oven. Bake further 10–15 minutes or until topping is golden. Accompany with reserved plum syrup, heated through until hot.

Using fresh plums *When plums are in season, halve and stone about 2–2½ pounds and put into dish with 4–6 ounces granulated sugar and 4 tablespoons water. Cover with sponge mixture then continue as directed in previous recipe. Accompany with custard.*

Menu 2

Easy Liver Pâté

Grapefruit Braised Chicken
Buttered Pimiento and Nut Rice
Peas

Ice Cream with Chocolate Raisin Sauce

EASY LIVER PATE

serves 8

1 pound ox liver (or chicken livers)
2 ounces margarine or bacon dripping
2 small slices brown bread
2 ounces flour
¼ pint plus 2 tablespoons milk
salt and pepper to taste

Cube liver. Fry in margarine or dripping 5 minutes. Remove from pan. Mince finely with bread. Stir flour into remaining fat in pan. Gradually blend in milk. Cook, stirring, until mixture comes to boil and forms thick sauce. Combine with liver. Season to taste with salt and pepper. Transfer to small bowl. Leave until cold. To serve, spoon out of bowl. Accompany with fingers of hot toast.

To increase flavour *Mince 1 small onion or 2–3 rashers fried and chopped bacon with liver and bread; add crushed garlic clove to minced liver; stir 1 tablespoon Worcester sauce into liver mixture.*

GRAPEFRUIT BRAISED CHICKEN

serves 8

4 tablespoons melted
bacon dripping or margarine
2 large onions, chopped
2 large celery stalks, chopped
8 medium size joints roasting chicken
flour
2 large grapefruit
¾ pint chicken stock
4 level tablespoons tomato concentrate
½ level teaspoon rosemary
1 small bay leaf
2 level teaspoons salt
pepper to taste

Heat dripping or margarine in large pan, shallow rather than tall. Add onion and celery. Fry gently until pale gold. Meanwhile, coat chicken joints fairly heavily with flour. Add to pan, two at a time. Fry until crisp and golden on both sides. Remove to plates. Peel grapefruit. Divide into segments by cutting out fruit with sharp knife in between membranes. Do this over saucepan so that no juice is lost. Add segments and all remaining ingredients to pan. Bring to boil. Replace chicken. Cover. Lower heat. Simmer gently about ¾ hour or until chicken is tender. Stir occasionally.

BUTTERED PIMIENTO AND NUT RICE

Cook 1 pound of long grain rice as directed on the packet. Using a fork, stir in 1 ounce of butter or margarine, two canned and chopped pimiento caps and 2 ounces chopped, salted peanuts.

ICE CREAM WITH CHOCOLATE RAISIN SAUCE

serves 8

2 ounces seedless raisins
1 tablespoon boiling water
4 ounces plain cooking chocolate
1 ounce margarine
2 tablespoons black treacle
2 tablespoons milk
1 teaspoon vanilla essence
vanilla or coffee ice cream
to serve eight

Cover raisins with boiling water. Break up chocolate. Put into basin with margarine. Stand over pan of hot water. Leave until melted, stirring occasionally. Gently beat in treacle, milk and essence. Drain raisins. Add to chocolate sauce. Divide ice cream equally between eight sundae glasses. Top with equal amounts of hot sauce. Serve straight away.

Menu 3

Mock Smoked Salmon

Meat-stuffed Marrow Rings
Creamed Potatoes
Broad Beans

Hot Creamed Fruit Fluff

MOCK SMOKED SALMON

8 kipper fillets
1 large lemon
horseradish sauce
thinly sliced brown bread and butter

Slice each kipper very thinly with sharp knife. Arrange equal amounts on eight individual plates. Add wedge of lemon to each. Pass horseradish sauce and bread and butter separately.

MEAT-STUFFED MARROW RINGS

8 marrow slices, each 2 inches thick
8 ounces raw minced beef
8 ounces pork or beef sausagemeat
1 medium onion, finely grated
2 medium carrots, grated
4 ounces fresh white breadcrumbs
½ level teaspoon mixed herbs
salt and pepper to taste
1 egg, beaten
milk to bind
¼ pint chicken stock
1 ounce table margarine, melted

Peel marrow slices. Remove inside fibres and seeds. Put rings into large pan. Cover with boiling water. Simmer 5 minutes. Drain. Put into large greased baking tin. Combine beef with sausagemeat, onion, carrots, crumbs and herbs. Season. Bind to stiffish mixture with egg and milk. Put equal amounts into centre of marrow rings. Pour stock into dish. Brush marrow rings and stuffing with melted margarine. Cover dish with foil. Cook in centre of moderate oven, 350°F or Gas 4 (180°C) 15 minutes. Uncover. Continue to cook further 10–15 minutes or until marrow is tender and stuffing cooked through. Accompany with creamed potatoes and freshly cooked fresh or frozen broad beans.

SIMPLE MARROW SAUCE

If liked, drain liquor from baking dish. Pour into pan. Mix about 3 level teaspoons cornflour with 2 tablespoons cold water. Add to liquor in pan. Crumble in gravy cube. Cook, stirring, until sauce comes to boil and thickens. Simmer 1 minute. Serve with marrow.

HOT CREAMED FRUIT FLUFF

3 pounds sweetened and
freshly cooked stewed fruit
1½ pints milk
2¼ ounces semolina
3 ounces caster sugar
3 eggs, separated
1 teaspoon vanilla essence
2 level tablespoons crushed biscuits
(such as Nice, Marie or digestive)

Preheat oven to moderately hot, 375°F or Gas 5 (190°C). Put stewed fruit (apples, rhubarb, plums, greengages, damsons, etc.) into fairly large, greased heatproof dish. Pour milk into pan. Add semolina and sugar. Bring to boil, stirring continuously. Simmer 5 minutes. Beat in egg yolks and essence. Cook 1 minute. Remove from heat. Whisk egg whites to stiff snow. Fold into semolina mixture. Pile on top of fruit. Sprinkle with crumbs. Brown near top of oven 10–15 minutes.

To prevent sogginess *Drain fruit first before putting into dish. Pour drained syrup into pan. Heat gently until hot. Serve as sauce with pudding.*

Menu 4

Corn, Egg and Cucumber Cocktail

Baked Stuffed Lambs' Hearts
Creamed Potatoes
Buttered Carrots
Redcurrant Jelly or Cranberry Sauce

Crunchy Apricot Crumble

CORN, EGG AND CUCUMBER COCKTAIL

serves 8

10 ounces frozen sweetcorn
1 small lettuce
4 hard-boiled eggs, chopped
½ medium cucumber
4 tablespoons salad oil
salt and pepper to taste
1 tablespoon Worcester sauce
½ level teaspoon prepared mustard
pinch caster sugar
2 tablespoons vinegar

Cook the sweetcorn and leave until cold. Wash lettuce. Thoroughly dry leaves. Shred. Put equal amounts into eight wine glasses. Combine corn with eggs. Peel the cucumber, and cut into small dice. Add to corn and eggs. Beat remaining dressing ingredients very well together. Add to corn mixture. Toss gently. Spoon equal amounts into glasses on top of lettuce. If liked, garnish each with wedge of tomato.

BAKED STUFFED LAMBS' HEARTS

serves 8

8 lambs' hearts
1 medium onion, grated
10 long rashers streaky bacon
2 ounces porridge oats
1½ level teaspoons mixed herbs
salt and pepper to taste
1 egg
cold milk
1 ounce margarine, melted
2 tablespoons water

Soak hearts in cold water 30 minutes. Drain. Remove tubes. Cut through membranes in each heart so that there is one cavity in each. Wipe each heart dry with paper towels. Put onion into bowl. Finely chop 2 bacon rashers. Add to onion with oats and herbs. Season. Bind with egg and a little milk. Put equal amounts into hearts. Remove the rinds and wrap a rasher of bacon round each heart. Hold in place with cocktail sticks. Put into greased roasting tin or large heatproof dish. Brush with melted margarine. Pour water into dish. Cover. Cook in centre of moderate oven, 350°F or Gas 4 (180°C) 1½–2 hours or until hearts are tender. Remove cocktail sticks before serving. Accompany with creamed potatoes, freshly cooked or canned carrots tossed with knob of butter, and the jelly or sauce.

CRUNCHY APRICOT CRUMBLE

serves 8

2 cans apricot pie filling
almond essence
8 ounces plain flour
½ level teaspoon salt
1 level teaspoon cinnamon
3 ounces table margarine
3 ounces soft brown sugar
1 ounce finely chopped walnuts

Put apricot filling into fairly large, greased heat-proof dish. Sprinkle lightly with almond essence. Sift plain flour, salt and cinnamon into bowl. Rub in margarine. Add sugar and walnuts. Sprinkle mixture thickly over fruit filling. Cook in centre of moderate oven, 350°F or Gas 4 (180°C) about 30–40 minutes or until crumble is pale gold. Serve with cream, dessert topping, custard or ice cream.

To vary *If preferred, use any other fruit filling to taste but keep crumble topping as it is.*

Student Fare

Remembering my own student days and how I struggled with primitive cooking equipment and limited finances, my heart goes out to students everywhere because, from what I hear, the same problems still exist. Apart from the famous 'fry-ups', the repertoire of student meals remains limited and although I am unable to offer a magic remedy, here are a few recipes, which, hopefully, are a bit more imaginative, varied and nutritious than the usual run.

SAVOURY BREAD AND BUTTER PUDDING

serves 4

6 slices white bread
butter or margarine
4 ounces dry Cheddar cheese, grated
3 standard eggs
1 pint milk (skimmed if liked)
salt, pepper and mustard

Cut crusts off bread. Spread bread slices with butter or margarine. Cut into fingers or squares. Put half into greased 2-pint heatproof dish. Sprinkle with 3 ounces cheese. Top with rest of bread. Beat eggs and milk well together. Season to taste with salt, pepper and mustard. Pour gently into dish over bread, etc. Leave to stand 30 minutes. Sprinkle rest of cheese on top. Bake in centre of moderate oven, 325°F or Gas 3 (170°C) ¾–1 hour or until pudding is golden-brown and firm. Choice of vegetables must be left to individual taste, but some grated raw carrots team well with the pudding and an orange per person to follow makes the whole thing a fairly well-balanced meal.

Savoury Bread and Butter Pudding with Bacon *Use 3 large rashers coarsely chopped bacon in centre of pudding instead of cheese.*

For brown top, 1 ounce grated cheese should still be sprinkled over topping before baking.

MACARONI AND BEAN CASSEROLE

serves 4

6 ounces macaroni
1 level tablespoon
dried red and green pepper flakes
1 level tablespoon dried onion flakes
boiling water
1 ounce margarine
1 garlic clove, chopped
1 large can (about 1 pound) baked beans
4 ounces dry Cheddar cheese, grated

Cook macaroni as directed on packet. Meanwhile, cover pepper and onion flakes with boiling water. Leave 5 minutes. Drain thoroughly. In clean saucepan or large frying pan, heat margarine until hot. Add vegetable flakes and garlic. Fry gently until pale gold; about 5 minutes. Drain macaroni, reserving about 8 tablespoons water. Add both to pan of vegetables with baked beans and cheese. Heat thoroughly until piping hot, stirring with fork all the time. Pile on to four warm plates and serve straight away. Follow with some fresh fruit.

If only one pan is available *Cook macaroni. Drain, reserving 8 tablespoons water. Keep macaroni warm. Wash and dry pan then continue as above.*

To vary *Provided cooking smells are tolerated by landladies and/or fellow students, fry 1 small chopped onion in margarine before adding egg mixture. It makes the whole dish much tastier.*

EGGS ON CURRY TOAST

serves 4

2 ounces margarine, softened
3 level teaspoons semolina
1 teaspoon peanut butter
2 level tablespoons curry powder
1 level teaspoon Marmite
pinch of sugar
1 dessertspoon vinegar or lemon juice
4 slices hot toast or
freshly fried bread
4 freshly poached or fried eggs

Mix margarine with semolina, peanut butter, curry powder, Marmite, sugar and vinegar or lemon juice. Spread over toast or fried bread. Top each with an egg. Serve straight away.

Left-over spread *Transfer to jar with screw-top lid. Leave in cold place up to 1 month.*

PORK AND APPLE CAKES

serves 4

2 large slices white bread
1 pound pork sausagemeat
1 small onion, grated
1 medium cooking apple,
peeled and grated
½ level teaspoon mixed herbs (optional)
1 egg, beaten
lard, dripping or margarine for frying

Cover bread with hot water. Leave 5 minutes. Squeeze dry. Combine with sausagemeat, onion, apple, herbs and egg. Mix thoroughly. Shape into eight flattish cakes. Fry in hot fat about 5–7 minutes, turning once. Serve hot with canned spaghetti in tomato sauce and canned or frozen peas. Follow with an orange per person.

CORN AND CHEESE SCRAMBLE

serves 4

6 large eggs
4–6 tablespoons milk
2–3 ounces dry Cheddar cheese, grated
½ can (about 6 ounces) sweetcorn
salt and pepper to taste
½ ounce margarine
4 slices freshly made
toast or fried bread

Beat eggs and milk well together. Stir in cheese and corn. Season. Melt margarine in pan. Add egg mixture. Scramble over low heat until set. Pile on top of toast (which may be first spread with butter or margarine if liked), or on fried bread. Eat with whole tomatoes. Follow with fresh fruit such as apples or pears.

CHEESE AND EGG PIE

6 ounces mild Cheddar cheese
4 eggs
salt and pepper to taste
½ ounce margarine

An easy-to-make, rich in protein dish which is delicious accompanied with crisp rolls and a drink of cider, apple juice or beer. To get a reasonable balance, follow it with either an orange or sugared half-grapefruit per person.

Slice ¾ of the cheese thinly. Arrange over base of shallow, greased heatproof dish. Break eggs on top. Season with salt and pepper. Grate rest of cheese. Sprinkle over eggs. Dot with flakes of margarine. Bake in centre of moderately hot oven, 375°F or Gas 5 (190°C) about 10–15 minutes or until eggs are just set.

SOUP POT

serves 4–5

1 thick slice white bread
¾ pound raw minced beef
1 small onion, finely chopped or grated
1 egg, beaten
salt and pepper to taste
2 beef or chicken stock cubes
2 pints water
1 large can (about 1 pound) baked beans

This is a kind of soup meal which goes down well with hunks of French or brown bread.

Cover bread with hot water. Leave 5 minutes. Squeeze dry. Combine with beef, onion and egg. Season. Roll into smallish balls. Crumble stock cubes into water. Bring to boil. Add meat balls. Lower heat. Cover. Simmer slowly 20 minutes. Add beans. Cover. Continue to cook further 10 minutes. Serve very hot.

Instead of onion *Omit ordinary salt, and season beef mixture with onion salt instead.*

BACON STEW WITH LENTILS

serves 4–5

1½ pounds collar of bacon (medium cured)
2 ounces dripping
6 small onions
2 large carrots, sliced
1 pound lentils, soaked overnight
1 garlic clove, crushed (optional)
pepper to taste
cold water

Put bacon into large pan. Cover with cold water. Bring to boil. Drain. (This reduces excessive saltiness.) Wash pan and wipe dry. Add dripping. Heat until hot. Add onions and carrots. Fry gently about 7 minutes or until pale gold. Move to one side of pan. Add bacon. Fry all over until joint is golden. Add lentils, garlic (if used) and pepper to taste. Just cover with cold water. Bring slowly to boil. Lower heat. Cover. Simmer gently 1½–2 hours or until

bacon is tender. To serve, slice meat and accompany with lentil mixture. Follow with fresh fruit or fruit yogurt. If preferred, start off meal with glass of tomato juice and omit dessert.

CURRIED CAULIFLOWER WITH SAUSAGES

serves 4

1 medium-large cauliflower
boiling water
2 ounces margarine
2 tomatoes, roughly chopped
1 small green pepper,
de-seeded and chopped
1 large onion, chopped

Sauce

1 level dessertspoon curry powder
1 level dessertspoon tomato concentrate
1 level tablespoon tomato chutney
¼ pint water
salt and pepper
1 pound pork sausages

Break cauliflower into florets. Put into bowl. Cover with boiling water. Leave 5 minutes. Drain thoroughly. Melt margarine in large frying pan. Add cauliflower. Move about until pieces are well-coated with margarine. Add tomatoes, green pepper and onion. Cover. Cook over low heat 5 minutes. Meanwhile, combine curry powder, tomato concentrate and chutney in small basin. Gradually blend in water. Pour into pan over cauliflower. Season. Cover pan. Simmer 10–15 minutes or until cauliflower is tender but still slightly crisp. Serve with freshly fried, baked or grilled sausages.

MINUTE-STEAK FRIED SANDWICHES

serves 2

2 minute or flash-fry steaks
2 ounces dripping or margarine
4 large slices white or brown bread
prepared mustard

Since 'minute' or 'flash-fry' steaks are far less expensive than other cuts of tender beef, they are a good buy for the occasional treat.

Fry steaks in hot dripping or margarine until browned on both sides and either well done or still pink in middle according to taste. Stand each steak on slice of bread. Spread thinly with mustard. Top with second slice of bread. Fry the two sandwiches in remaining dripping until golden brown on both sides. Remove from pan. Serve straight away. Accompany with fresh tomatoes or Coleslaw salad. Follow with fresh fruit.

To vary *If preferred, spread steaks thinly with horseradish sauce instead of mustard.*

FRIED CHEESE AND CHUTNEY SANDWICHES

serves 2

Spread 4 slices bread with butter or margarine. Sandwich together, in pairs, with slivers of Cheddar cheese and chutney. Press well down to prevent them falling apart. Fry in hot dripping or margarine until golden-brown on both sides. Serve straight away. Munch small raw carrots with sandwiches. Follow with fresh fruit.

LUNCHEON MEAT AND CORN TOASTIES

serves 4

1 6-ounce packet frozen sweetcorn
about 2 ounces dripping or margarine
4 large slices of white or brown bread
1 7-ounce can luncheon meat
1 medium onion, chopped
1 dessertspoon Worcester sauce
salt and pepper to taste
½ bunch watercress
or
4 small gherkins

Cook sweetcorn as directed. Drain. Heat dripping or margarine in pan. Add bread. Fry fairly briskly on both sides until golden. Pile one on top of the other and keep hot. Cut the luncheon meat into ¼-inch cubes and add,

with the onion, to remaining dripping in pan. Fry gently 5 minutes. Stir in sweetcorn and Worcester sauce. Season. Arrange bread on four individual plates. Top with equal amounts of hot corn mixture. Garnish with watercress or gherkins.

LAMB AND TOMATO STEWPOT

serves 4

2 pounds scrag end neck of lamb
1 pound carrots
1 small turnip
1 large onion
1 tube tomato concentrate
1¼ pints hot water
1 level teaspoon sugar
salt and pepper to taste
8 ounces long grain rice
½ small cauliflower

Cut lamb into neat pieces, trimming away and discarding as much surplus fat as possible. Put meat into pan. Slice carrots thinly. Dice turnip. Coarsely chop onion. Add to pan. Dissolve tomato concentrate in hot water. Add sugar. Pour into pan. Bring to boil and remove scum. Lower heat and season. Cover. Simmer 45–60 minutes or until meat is just tender. Add rice and cauliflower. Cover. Simmer further 20 minutes when rice grains and cauliflower should both be tender. To make eating easier, serve in soup plates and give everyone spoons and forks.

BAKED STUFFED BAP ROLLS

serves 2–3

Beat together 2 ounces table margarine, 2 teaspoons horseradish sauce, 1 small finely grated onion, 1 ounce finely grated dry Cheddar cheese and salt and pepper to taste. Split 3 bap rolls. Spread both sides of each with margarine mixture. Sandwich together with slices of boiled bacon. Stand on small baking tray. Bake in moderate oven 350°F or Gas 4 (180°C) about 15 minutes. Serve hot with any salad or pickles to taste.

CHEESE AND BACON BAP RAREBIT

serves 2

Beat 1 ounce margarine with 3 ounces grated Cheddar cheese, 2 teaspoons milk and ½ level teaspoon prepared mustard. Split 2 bap rolls in half. Spread with cheese mixture. Stand under hot grill until cheese just begins to melt. Stand half rasher (or 1 small rasher) bacon on top of each. Continue to grill until cheese around bacon is golden and bubbly, and bacon itself is crisp. Top each with slices cut from small peeled onion. Follow with fresh fruit.

SAVOURY GRIDDLE CAKES

makes 12–15

4 ounces self-raising flour
½ level teaspoon *each*
dry mustard and salt
1 standard egg
¼ pint milk (skimmed if liked)
2 teaspoons cooking oil
about 1 ounce
lard or cooking fat, melted

Easy to make in a heavy frying pan, freshly cooked griddle cakes are admirable with hamburgers, all types of sausages and cooked chicken or fried fish bought from the local 'take away' shop. Certainly they make a much needed change from the inevitable chips!

Sift flour, mustard and salt into bowl. With wooden spoon or fork, mix to smooth, creamy batter with egg and half the milk. Beat until bubbles rise to surface. Gently stir in rest of milk and oil. Brush base of heavy frying pan with melted fat. Heat until hot. Pour tablespoon of batter mixture into pan (about four at a time) leaving space round each. Cook until base is set and golden, and bubbles rise to surface of each cake and burst. Flip over. Fry second sides until golden. Stack in tea-towel to keep warm. Spread with butter or margarine (or leave plain). Serve straight away.

EASY BRAISED PIQUANT CHICKEN

serves 4

4 joints roasting chicken
2 medium onions, chopped
3 level tablespoons pearl barley
1 can condensed tomato soup
1 soup can water
1 dessertspoon Worcester sauce
½ level teaspoon mixed herbs
salt and pepper

Put chicken joints into large saucepan. Add onions, barley, tomato soup, water, Worcester sauce, herbs and salt and pepper. Bring to boil, stirring. Lower heat. Cover. Simmer 45 minutes or until chicken is tender. Serve with canned peas or beans.

To tenderize barley more quickly *Put required amount into small bowl. Cover with boiling water. Leave to soak 3 hours. Drain.*

PARTY FISH CAKES WITH ASPARAGUS SAUCE

serves 6

Frozen fish cakes are excellent and extremely useful if a crowd of you get together and want a reasonable meal at a reasonable price.

Fry 1 dozen frozen fish cakes as directed. While they are cooking, make sauce by heating 1 can condensed asparagus soup with 2–3 tablespoons milk. Toast 12 small slices of bread. Top each with a fish cake. Coat with hot sauce. Sprinkle lightly with paprika. Allow two per person. Follow with fresh fruit or fruit salad.

BEAN AND MUSHROOM CURRY

serves 4

**8 ounces dried haricot beans,
soaked overnight
3 tablespoons salad oil
2 large onions, sliced
12 ounces mushrooms
1–2 level tablespoons curry powder
1 level tablespoon flour
½ tube tomato concentrate
1 teaspoon Worcester sauce
½ pint water**

A meatless but filling dish which is tasty and comparatively economical.

Drain beans. Cook in boiling salted water until tender. Strain. Leave on one side. Heat oil in large pan. Add onions. Fry gently for about 7 minutes until pale gold. Add mushrooms. Toss about in margarine and onion mixture about 5 minutes. Add all remaining ingredients. Slowly bring to boil, stirring. Lower heat. Cover. Simmer 15 minutes. Add beans. Continue to cook further 10 minutes. Serve very hot. Accompany with freshly boiled rice and chutney.

For speed   *1 large can (about 1 pound) baked beans may be used instead of the dried ones.*

Index

Alcohol 82
Almond Paste 114, 115, 116
Angelica 126
Austrian Dishes 40-5

Bacon 123
  with Barley and Beans 61
  and Barley with Curly Kale 21
  and Bean Stew Pot 22
  and Cheese Bap Rarebit 156
  and Chicory in Cheese Sauce 8
  and Corn Chowder 137
  and Curd Cheese Pasties 62
  and Fried Onion Stuffing 121
  Glazed Collar 124
  Knuckles 12
  Loaf 124
  Mousse, Danish 50
  and Mushroom Curry 157
  and Onion with Jacket Potatoes 73
  Soufflé 30
  Stew with Lentils 154
Beef
  Balls 102
  Boeuf Bourguignonne 101
  Boeuf en Daube 26
  Carbonades Flamandes 7
  and Liver Loaf 67
  Potted 146
  Poulet Sans Têtes 9
  and Rice Barbecue 142
  Sauerbraten 23
Beefburgers 66
Belgian Dishes 7-10
Biscuits 82, 128, 144-5
Blanching 90-1
Bread
  with Bacon, Savoury 152
  Brussels Cramique 10
  Cheese 137
  Decorated Plaits 53
  French Fried Fingers 133
  Fruited Cider 128
  Fruity Plaits 53
  glazing 127
  Golden Wholemeal Slices 136
  Hot 137
  Irish Tea Loaf 127
  Limpa 54
  Malt 127
  Poppy Seed 44
  Spicy Coffee 52
  Stuffing 120
  Syrup 57
  Vienna 44
  Vienna Rolls 45
  Yeasted Spice 52
Breadcrumbs 41
Buffet, Chinese 138
Buns, Cinnamon Ring 54
158

Cabbage 8, 58, 61, 93
Cake
  Apple 23
  Apple Purée Fruit 128
  Apple, with Raisins 23
  Baby Layer 7
  Banana Nut 126
  Belgian Layer 7
  Birthday 116
  board 116
  Brussels Cramique 10
  Cellophane wrapped 116
  Chilled Cheese 82
  Chocolate 117, 145
  Chocolate Brownies 127
  Christening 116
  Christmas 114, 116
  Date and Orange Loaf 125
  Devil's Food 118
  Fruit, No-bake 117
  Plum 54
  Scalloped 54
  sizes, different 116
  testing consistency 116
  Upside-down Spiced 111
Cassoulet 31
Cheese 82
  and Biscuits 82
  Biscuits 82, 144
  Cauliflower 77
  and Chutney Sandwiches, Fried 155
  Crab-Apple 93
  Fancy Rice 141
  Ginger Apple 93
  Hot Squares 11
  and Mushroom Coccotes 70
  Onion 77
  and Onion Puff Flan 102
  Quince 93
  Semolina 135
Chicken
  Baked Curried 69
  and Barley Hot-pot 67
  Braised Piquant 156
  Cacciatore 15
  Cold, with Sweet-sour Sauce 69
  Creamed 134
  Devilled, Marinaded 68
  in Foil 133
  Fricassée 30
  Goulash 42
  Grapefruit Braised 148
  Grilled 68
  Hot-pot 67
  with Jambalaya 139
  à la King 104
  Livers with Macaroni 13
  Marengo 16
  Mock Paella 55
  and Mushroom Casserole 100
  and Mushroom Pancakes 107
  Neapolitan 68
  Noodle Snack 65

Normandy 29, 30
Paprika 42
Piquant Roast 68
Poulet au Riz 29
Poultry Rissoto 14
  Stock 63
  Waterzooi de Volaille 8
Chili Con Carne, Quick 95
Chili powder 95
Chocolate Spread 145
Chowder 137
Chutney 94, 155
Cinnamon Ring Buns 54
Cinnamon Sugar 44
Coccotes 70
Cocktail Starter, Citrus 81
Coleslaw, All-in-one 76
Corned Beef 99
Cream 35-6
Custard 81

Date Fingers, Crunchy 125
Desserts and Puddings
  Apple Charlotte 135
  Apple Cheese, Spiced 93
  Apples and Custard 81, 109
  Apples, Spiced 81
  Apricot Cream Whip 119
  Apricot Crumble 151
  Apricot Shortbread Crunch 110
  Banana Butterscotch Sundae 110
  Banana Dessert 135
  Banana Rice 57
  Banana Rice Caramel 135
  Bread and Butter Pudding 152
  Butterscotch Sponge Sundae 110
  Cheese Cake, Chilled 82
  Chocolate Roll Trifle 108
  Christmas 117, 119
  Coral Reef Sundae 80
  Cream Cheese and Fruit 109
  Cream Nut and Apple Trifle 119
  Crème Caramel 34
  Crêpes Suzette 34
  Fruit Fool 109
  Fruit Layer Pudding 108
  Fruit Meringue Flan 108
  Fruit Trifle 108
  Golden Crumb Orange Pie 109
  Gozette 9
  Grapefruit Sorbet 81
  Hot Creamed Fruit Fluff 150
  Jamaican Sundae 79
  Knickerbocker Glories 79
  Lemon Apples 81
  Mandarin Jelly Flip 111
  Mandarin Sundae 110
  Melba Style Sundae 79
  Mincemeat Tart 113

  Mincemeat Upside-down Pudding 113
  Mousse 32, 110
  Orange Milk Pudding 57
  Orange Sorbet with Yogurt 81
  Orange Whip 79
  Oranges, Carmelized 17
  Peasant Girl with Veil 52
  Plum Sponge Crumble 147
  Rhubarb Custard 81
  Riz à l'Imperatrice 33
  Rødgrød med Fløde 52
  Rote Greutze 24
  Semolina Pudding with Jam Sauce 47
  Slimmers Fools 80
  Spanish Pudding 57
  Spongy Yule Pudding 118
  Tarte au Riz 10
  Yogurt Fools 80
  Yogurt Sweet 135
  Zabaione 16
Devil's Food Cake 118
Dips 66, 146
Dressings 74, 75, 141, 142
Dumplings 21, 40
Dutch Dishes 45-8

Egg
  Anchovy and Onion Pancakes 107
  in Celery Cheese Sauce 101
  and Cheese Pie 153
  Corn and Cucumber Cocktail 150
  Corn and Cheese Scramble 153
  on Curry Toast 153
  Fish Stuffed 70, 75
  Florentine 99
  glaze 35
  Herb-stuffed 75
  Mayonnaise 35
  Piperade 28
  to shell hardboiled 75
  sieving yolks 75
  Yolk Scramble 35
  yolks, spare 35
  Wiener Schnitzel Holstein 41

Fish
  Baked Spanish 56
  Balls with Piquant Sauce 49
  Braise 71
  Cakes 156
  Casserole, Crispy 106, 134
  in Foil 71, 133
  Haddock 61, 104, 107, 134, 137
  Herrings 18, 50, 147
  Kedgeree 140
  Layered Hot-pot 46
  Mackerel 50, 71, 72, 147

and Potato Casserole 106
Salmon 149
Soufflé 30
Stuffed Eggs 75
Stuffed Tomatoes and Egg 70
with Tomato and Orange 71
Tuna 104, 137
Waterzooi 8
White, with Paprika 62
Fondue 37-8
Freezing 53, 91
French Dishes 24-36
Frikadeller with Sauce 50
Fritters, Salzburger 44
Fruit
  bottling 92-3
  Cheeses 93
  to freeze 92
  Rote Greutze 25
  Shortcakes 111

Gazpacho 55, 64
German Dishes 17-24
Giblets, Turkey 120
Gingerbread 126
Glacé Icing 53
Glaze 53, 127
Gnocchi 16
Goose, Imitation Sage and
  Onion 124
Gravy 122
Greek Dishes 58-61
Greek Dolmathes 58
Green Peppers, Stuffed 41
Griddle Cakes, Savoury 156

Hamburgers, 20, 102, 103
Hash 49
Heart, Bavarian Ox 18
Heaven and Earth 20
Hot-pot, Finnish 48

Ice Cream 78
Ice Cream with Chocolate
  Raisin Sauce 149
Icing
  the cake 115
  on Date and Orange Loaf
    126
  Royal 115
  Sugar, home-made 53
  using glycerine in 115
Irish Stew 104
Italian Dishes 11-17

Jam 84-9
  Apricot 88
  Apricot and Almond 88
  Apricot and Orange 88
  Black Cherry 87
  Blackberry 87
  Blackberry and Apple 87
  Blackcurrant 84
  Cherry and Gooseberry 87
  Cherry and Redcurrant 88
  Currant, Mixed 84
  Damson 84
  Fruit, Mixed 88
  Gooseberry 86

Gooseberry and Straw-
  berry 86
Greengage 84
hints 83
Loganberry 86
Marrow and Ginger 89
Mulberry and Apple 88
Mulberry and Rhubarb 88
Plum 84
Quince 88
Raspberry 86
Raspberry and Apple 86
Raspberry and Blackcur-
  rant 85
Raspberry and Goose-
  berry 86
Raspberry and Redcurrant
  85
Rhubarb and Apple 84
Rhubarb and Blackberry
  85
Rhubarb and Strawberry
  84
Sauce 47
Strawberry 86
Strawberry and Redcur-
  rant 87
Jambalaya 139
Jellies
  Apple 89
  Apple and Blackberry 89
  Apple and Elderberry 89
  Apple and Ginger 89
  Apple, Minted 89
  Apple and Orange 89
  Apple, Spicy 89
  Blackcurrant 89
  Bramble (Blackberry) 89
  Crab-Apple 89
  Gooseberry 89
  Mandarin, Flip 111
  Redcurrant 89

Kale with Bacon and Barley
  21
Kedgeree 140

Lamb
  Breasts, Stuffed 59
  in Foil 134
  Mediterranean 101
  Navarin of 26
  Pilaff 60
  Shoulder, Stuffed 31
  and Tomato Stewpot 155
Lambs' Hearts, Baked
  Stuffed 150
Lasagne 13, 108
Leeks with Rice 61
Lemonade 143
Liver
  Pâté, Easy 148
  Pâté Maison 30
  Pilaff 60
  Sandwiches 99
  Sausage Squares 145
  Sweet-sour 42
Lunch-in-a-Flash 135
Luncheon Meat 47, 155

Macaroni
  and Bean Casserole 152

Cheese 73, 105
  Mushroom Cheese 105
  Tomato Cheese 105
  with Tomato Sauce 74
Mackerel 59, 71, 72, 147
Marmalade 90
Mayonnaise 38, 39
Meat
  Ball Casserole 67
  Ball Fondue 38
  Balls, Danish 48
  Balls, Koenigsberg 19
  Beefburgers 66
  Cakes, Spanish 68
  Hash, Mixed 49
  Loaf 65, 102, 103
  Minute-steak Fried Sand-
    wiches 154
  Nasi Goreng 47
  Paprika 42
  reheating 103
  Risotto 14
  Stuffed Marrow Rings 149
  Stuffed Tomatoes 70
  and Vegetable Pie 96, 97
  White Cabbage with 61
  see also Beef, Lamb,
    Liver, Mince, Pie,
    Pork, Steak, Veal
Menus 146, 148, 149, 150
Meringues 34, 35
Milk Shakes 77
Mince
  Pies 113
  Quickie Supper 133
  to tenderize 66
Mincemeat 112, 113
Moussaka 60
Mousse 32, 110
Museli 36-7
Mushroom and Bean Curry
  157
Mushroom and Cheese
  Coccotes 70

Noodles, Crispy Fried 138
Nut and Pimiento Rice,
  Buttered 148

Omelet
  Potato 56
  Smoked Haddock Puff
    134
  Spanish 56
Onion
  Cheese 77
  and Cheese Puff Flan 102
  Pickled 94
Orange Twists 51
Orangeade 143
Ox Heart, Bavarian 18

Pancakes 18, 46, 106, 107
Paprika 62, 75
Parcel Meals 133
Parties 136, 138, 143
Pasta 73
  cooking 12
  Lasagne 13
  Shell Salad 74
Pasties 62
Pâté 26, 30, 98, 148

Peel, to grate 143
Peppers, Green Stuffed 41
Pickles 93-4
Pies
  All-in-One Cobbler 97
  Cheese and Egg 153
  Cheese-topped 96
  Cottage 67
  Crispy-topped Steak 96
  Crumble Steak 97
  Meat and Vegetable 96
  Meat and Vegetable with
    Pastry 97
  Mince 113
  Savoury Supper 103
  Shepherd's, Easy 96
  Speedy-topped Steak 97
  Steak Cobbler 97
  Steak, Corn and Potato 96
  Steak and Kidney 105
  Supper, with Bacon 103
  Turkey 122
Pilaff 60-1
Pimiento 62, 148
Piperade 28
Pizza 14, 15
Pork
  and Apple Cakes 153
  Ball Fondue 38
  Balls in Clear Soup 45
  and Broccoli, Chinese 104
  and Carrot Stew 20
  Casserole, Marinaded 19
  Chops, Baked with Orange
    57
  in Foil, Devilled 134
  Mock Sweet-sour 98
  and Onion Balls in Clear
    Soup 46
  Sausagemeat Stuffing 121
Potatoes
  Baked 138-9
  Duchesse 35
  Dumplings 20, 21
  Jacket 72, 73
  Omelet 56
  Paprika 42
  Roesti 40
  and Sausage Braise 21
Potted Beef 146

Quiche Lorraine 28

Ratatouille 27
Ravioli 13
Rice
  Basic Pilaff 60
  Buttered Pimiento and Nut
    148
  Cheese Fancy 141
  Chinese Fried Egg 140
  Creole-style 140
  Dishes 139
  Jumble 142
  Kedgeree 140
  with Leeks 61
  with Minestrone 12
  Mock Paella 55
  Nasi Goreng 47
  Poulet au Riz 29
  reheating 29
  Tumble 141

159

Risotto 14
Roasting 121
Rolls, Vienna 45

Saffron 55
Salad Cream 74-5
Salads
  Egg and Mushroom 76
  Mackerel 72
  Moulded Tomato 76
  Nicoise 28
  Pasta Shell 74
  Potato with Tuna 11
  Rice and Salami 142
  Tomato and Orange 141
  Toss-up 76
Sandwiches
  Cheese and Chutney Fried 155
  Fritters, Fried 132
  Liver 99
  Minute-steak Fried 154
  Open 50-1
Sauces
  Asparagus, with Fish Cakes 156
  Bolognaise, Mock 95
  Bread 22, 122
  Butterscotch 110
  Cheese 8, 77
  Chocolate Raisin 149
  Curry Yogurt Fondue 38
  Egg Fondue 38
  freezing left-over 103
  Hollandaise, Mock 35
  Horseradish Fondue 38
  Italian 95
  to keep left-over 111
  Marrow, Simple 149
  Mustard Fondue 38
  Orange, Sweet-sour 138
  Raisin 149
  Rum 114
  Sherry 123
  Spring Green Fondue 38
  Sweet-sour 69, 138
  Tomato 38
  Vanilla 114
  Yogurt 133
Sauerkraut 24
Sausages
  in Beer 19
  with Curried Cauliflower 154
  in Curry Sauce, Baked 100
  with Goulash Soup 40
  with Jambalaya 139
  and Potato Braise 21
  with Sauerkraut 24
Scandinavian Dishes 48-54
Scone-based Pizza 15
Scones
  Cheese 143

Crunchy Cheese and Peanut 144
  to enrich 144
  Plain 144
Semolina
  Cheese 135
  Dumplings, in Clear Soup 40
  Gnocchi 16
  Pudding with Jam Sauce 47
Shallots, Pickled 94
Shortbread 48, 135
Shortcakes 111
Silverside with Mock Robert Sauce 103
Sundaes 79-80, 110
Soufflé 30
Soups
  Avgolemono 58, 59
  Bacon and Pea 17
  Bean 22
  Bread 25
  Brodo Misto 11
  Cabbage with Pork 26
  Canned and Packet 65
  Carrot and Onion 64
  Cauliflower and Onion 63
  Chicken Broth 70
  Chicken Purée 69
  Clear, with Pork Balls 45
  Clear, with Pork and Onion Balls 46
  Clear, with Semolina Dumplings 40
  Consommé 63, 65
  French Cabbage 25
  French Onion 24
  Egg Broth 135
  Garlic 56
  Goulash 40
  and Hot Breads 136
  Leek 64
  Milk 132
  Minestrone 12
  Onion 24, 63, 64
  Pea 17, 45
  Pot 154
  Potato 11, 17
  Snacks 12, 65
  Tomato, Cauliflower and Onion 63
  Tomato and Orange 64
  Vegetarian Bread 25
  Vegetarian Onion 24
  Vichysoisse, Economical 25
  Westphalian Bean 22
  Zuppa Pavese 11
Spaghetti
  Bolognese 12
  alla Carbonara 13
  cooking 12

Spanish Dishes 55-7
Spreads
  Home-made Chocolate 145
  Tangy Mackerel 72
Steak
  Creole-style 97
  Dutch Spiced 47
  Minute, Fried Sandwiches 154
  see also Pies
Sterilizing Fruit 92
Stew, Irish 104
Stracciatella 12
Strudel 43
Stuffed
  Eggs 75
  Green Peppers 41
  Lamb 31, 59
  Potato Dumplings 21
Stuffing
  Bacon and Fried Onion 121
  Bacon, Pineapple and Rice 121
  Bread, Basic 120
  Breadcrumbs 41
  Mexican Rice 121
  Orange and Raisin 120
  Pork Sausagemeat 121
  Rice 121
  Tomato and Peanut 120
  Turkey 120
  using egg or milk in 120
Sugar
  Cinnamon 44
  Icing, home-made 53
  and Spice Slice 109
  Vanilla 43
Summer Casserole 22
Summer Frikadeller 48
Sundaes 79, 80, 110
Sweetcorn, Scalloped Tuna and 104
Sweets
  Caramel Potatoes 48
  Caramels 131
  Chocolate Fudge 131
  Chocolate Peppermint Dippers 130
  Chocolate Potatoes 129
  Cocoa Truffles 129
  Coconut Ice 130
  Coffee Creams 130
  Coffee Truffles 129
  Fruit and Nut Fudge 131
  Fudge, Traditional 131
  Honeycomb 129
  Lemon Creams 130
  No-cook Fudge 131
  Orange Creams 130
  Rum Truffles 129
  Toffee 132

Truffles 129
Vanilla Creams 130
Swiss Dishes 36-40
Syrup, for bottling fruit 92

Taramosalata 58
Tarragon Flavoured Salad Cream 75
Tartlets 33
Tarts
  Cheese 39
  Mincemeat 113
  Mincemeat Crumble 113
  Tarte au Riz 10
Tomato
  Burgers 66
  and Cheese Toast 134
  to skin 55
  Stuffed 70, 71
Tongue 123
  with Sherry Sauce 123
Toss Up 76
Tripe-Caen Style 27
Tumeric 55
Tuna 11, 98, 104, 137
Turkey
  choosing the 120
  Crispy Fried 123
  Curried 123
  au Gratin 122
  Left-over 122
  Pie 122
  in Sauce 122
  Stuffing 120
  thawing frozen 120

Vanilla Sugar 43
Veal
  Cutlets Holstein, Mock 66
  L'Osso Buco 16
  Wiener Schnitzel 41
Vegetables
  blanching 90
  Chowder 137
  Pilaff 61
  Ratatouille 27
Vegetarian
  Bread Soup 25
  Mincemeat 112
  Onion Soup 25
Vinegar, Spiced 94

Waffles 10
Waterzooi de Volaille 8
Welsh Rarebit 35
Wheat Germ, Museli with 37
Wiener Schnitzel 41
Wine in Sauerkraut 24

Yogurt Sweet 135
Yolk Scramble 35
Yugoslavian Dishes 61-2